How To
Look Things Up and
Find Things Out

How To Look Things Up and Find Things Out

Bruce L. Felknor

QUILL   WILLIAM MORROW

New York

027
F

Library of Congress Cataloging-in-Publication Data

Felknor, Bruce L.
How to look things up and find things out.
Includes index.
1. Libraries—Handbooks, manuals, etc. 2. Reference books—Handbooks, manuals, etc. 3. Research—Method-ology—Handbooks, manuals, etc. I. Title.
Z710.F44   1988   027   87-22096
ISBN 0-688-06166-4 (pbk.)
0-688-07850-8

Printed in the United States of America

2 3 4 5 6 7 8 9 10

BOOK DESIGN BY KATHY PARISE

58831

For Terry Miller, P.L.

FOREWORD

This is a book of secrets: the secrets of making reference publications work for you.

As soon as any bit of knowledge or information is written down somewhere, it is effectively hidden there and—except by accident—can be found again only by someone who knows exactly where to look. The person who recorded it, we may hope, was following a plan or organizing principle. In the world of reference works, there are abundant clues to the plan of each particular work. It's a simple matter to follow these clues and find out the plan.

It takes a few minutes to do this with each reference book you encounter for the first time, but taking that few minutes can save you much more than the time you spend. Indeed, it can save you heartburn, high blood pressure, and, conceivably, hives.

So much for what this book is, or is intended to be. A word now about what it is not. It is not a list of reference works in all the categories it deals with. It has some recommendations and cites a lot of examples, but it is not a bibliography *per se*. There are, of course, book lists and bibliographies in every corner of the reference world (as discussed in Chapter 21). But the purpose of this book is to help you find the easiest possible access to the reference sources you need and the easiest way to extract the information hidden there.

Many home libraries are built around an encyclopedia and a dictionary, and will include a current encyclopedia yearbook or a general almanac, perhaps both. But with the exception, perhaps, of a thesaurus and a foreign language dictionary or two, few home libraries will contain any of the relatively specialized reference works discussed throughout this volume. For that reason, lookers-up and finders-out who have occasion to search beyond their own collections may profit from a word about libraries—and librarians.

A person who has not done sustained research in a good large or medium-sized public library may not have any idea how substantial its reference section and services really are. If you fit into that category and find yourself needing to use its resources, an interesting first step might be to walk your way around the library slowly, browsing. See which encyclopedias are there, where the general reference section is, look over the periodicals section. Find out where new books are displayed. Seek out sections housing books on subjects you are curious about or interested in. And make the acquaintance of a person who knows where all the bodies are buried: the reference librarian. You will hear that over and over in these pages, and if you follow the suggestion, you will be glad you did.

It is obvious that this book is not directed at scholars or professional researchers; they don't need what's here, and any who come this way are either misguided or slumming, which is worse. This is for good-hearted people who are intelligent, literate, and curious; people who enjoy reading and looking things up but who really hate being sent away empty-handed from a search they have conducted in good faith. If you've ever gone into an encyclopedia, or for that matter a library, looking for a particular subject and come away irritated and frustrated because it was hidden too well, read on. There is hope.

This book is written out of the experience of a lifetime of looking things up, often professionally, but very often indeed purely for fun, and sometimes just for the hell of it. It is written with grateful acknowledgment of the courteous and friendly help I have gotten from librarians who have unlocked their precious resources for me in many places: the New York Public Library, perhaps the greatest private library in the world and one of the nation's cultural jewels; the Library of Congress, its temple of learning; those magnificent private libraries the Morgan in New York City and the Newberry in Chicago.

I also acknowledge the friendly and courteous assistance of librarians toiling under slum conditions in the wretched warehouse quarters of the Chicago Public Library. I owe much gratitude to the excellent and imaginative Deerfield Public Library in suburban Chicago and its reference librarian Jack Hicks. Most of all I am grateful to the editorial library of *Encyclopaedia Britannica* and its head librarian, Terry Miller.

Lake Bluff, Illinois
April 2, 1987

CONTENTS

CONTENTS

CHAPTER 1

FINDING DEVICES

Your odds are better in a dice game than in a reference book that lacks adequate finding devices. And they are equally against you if you don't know how to use the ones that are there. Fortunately, it is fairly easy to figure out what they are, where they are, and how to use them. The best way to start is with some understanding of what the editor has in mind for finding devices, what he or she intends them to accomplish for you, the reader.

Three things determine how useful such devices really are. One is the competence and common sense of the author-editor combination that creates them. The other two are under the control of the reader or looker-up: taking the time necessary to understand the system of finding devices in the book at hand; and then actually using them.

Perhaps it is best to start by taking a general look around, as you would on entering a strange library. There you would scan the place to see whether and where there is a special reference section, whether the general reader may have access to the stacks where the main collection is kept, whether there is a reference librarian in the main reading room, etc. In a book, a minute or two spent scanning the title page and the various finding devices in the volume will pay dividends in time you don't have to waste later.

There are five kinds of finding devices. Most books intended for reference service have at least three of them: a table of contents, an index, and a system of cross-references. Most scholarly books have a fourth: footnotes identifying the sources of quotations, statistics, and other information taken from the work of another writer or compiler. The fifth kind is a list of illustrations, maps, charts, diagrams, etc., in whatever combination they may appear in the work.

THE TABLE OF CONTENTS

The function of the table of contents is to show the reader the general plan of the work and how it is divided in parts and chapters, and usually the page on which each part or chapter begins. Chapter titles are the backbone of a table of contents, and they owe it to the reader to be straightforward and communicative. This is not always the case; if they are too cute or obscure, like a newspaper headline whose clarity has been sacrificed to preserve a pun, a table of contents may fail to help the reader. In practical terms, there is nothing you can do if you find yourself so victimized, but you should realize that the deficiency is not yours but built into the book.

There are several additional elements that may be part of a table of contents, and authors and editors use them in various combinations. They include: the page number where a part or chapter begins; a capsule description of the content of each chapter or part; and a breakdown of each chapter into its major sections. If the reader is reasonably lucky, the author and editor will have supplied as much or as little detail as they think the audience will find helpful. A work of scholarship addressed to an audience of scholars in the same field as the author will need a completely different table of contents from a primer on the subject addressed to lay readers who know little or nothing about the topic.

Here, for illustration, are a few of the various ways in which a history of the United States might treat a hypothetical chapter on the U.S. Constitution:

CHAPTER III. THE U.S. CONSTITUTION
............................page 116

CHAPTER III. THE U.S. CONSTITUTION: Its
Origins and Provisions...................116

CHAPTER III. THE U.S. CONSTITUTION
....116
Failure of the Articles of Confederation.
Maryland-Virginia Dispute. The Annapolis

Convention. Convention of 1787. Ratification.
Summary of the Constitution. Ratifying Con-
ventions. The Amending Process. The Bill of
Rights.

Occasionally a table of organization is shown without locating
any of its elements by page. One example is the 1985 revision of the
Encyclopaedia Britannica, which removed volume and page numbers
from its one-volume *Propaedia* after reorganizing that book-length
table of contents to make it simpler to look things up by alphabet.
And page numbers do not even apply to computer programs and
audiovisual materials of various sorts, many of which come
equipped with a table of contents in the form of a user's or
teacher's manual or study guide. Such a manual, even though it
serves as a table of contents to the work it accompanies and
explains, may not have a page-numbered table of contents to
itself.

THE INDEX

Generally speaking, it is a waste of time to look to a table of
contents to locate specific information. If you want to find out, for
instance, the date on which the Constitutional Convention ad-
journed for the last time (September 17, 1787), turn to the index,
for it is there that the locations of the particulars should be
shown.

"Locations" is meant precisely here, for it is the locations and not
the particulars that the index undertakes to present. The index is
not substantive information; it points out where information may
be found. And "should be shown" is a necessary qualification,
because, unfortunately, indexes frequently err or omit. Probably,
as the history of computer use in indexing lengthens, such errors
will become less frequent, but don't bet on it yet. Wherever people
work—including writing and editing—mistakes are made. How-

ever, there is an easy and usually effective antidote to the failure of an index.

This antidote can't work if you know nothing at all about the setting of the incident or fact you are looking up. Indeed, you must have at least some modest acquaintance with the subject you are looking up to find it in a nearly perfect index.

Before looking up a word in the index, it is important to know how it is actually spelled. Ordinarily this is simple enough, but if the term is unfamiliar, or if you aren't an especially good speller (some editors believe no one under age fifty can spell), it will pay you to take pains. In addition, if you are looking up a word you heard by telephone or on the radio or television, be sure you are spelling it conventionally, not phonetically (fonix? phonicks? phonics? fawnex?). And if you are dealing with a British or British-oriented work, you need to be prepared for its British spellings. *Encyclopaedia Britannica,* even after a century of U.S. ownership, still affects what its editors call mid-Atlantic English, following British rules on -or and -er word endings (colour for color, centre for center, etc.).

You also need to understand the basic rules of indexing, and imparting such an understanding is one of the reasons for this book. First of all, look for the key word, the substantive term, the basic substance of the fact or event. If you want the closing date of the Constitutional Convention, looking up "closing date" in its alphabetical position in the index will be a waste of time. Even if you turn to "Constitutional Convention," where a list of subordinate entries will appear, you probably won't find "closing date" among them. But common sense will associate the idea of closing date in your mind with a number of other terms, one of which is likely to appear: final agreement, conclusion, signing, adjournment, and so on. That is the other key, common sense.

Substantive word and common sense: Of these, the more important is common sense. This is the basic key to every aspect of looking things up, and nowhere is it more essential than in using an index. You need it to figure out what the indexer really meant. You also need it to understand the rules and conventions followed by the indexer. Only rarely does an index begin with a statement of those rules, but to make it work you've got to understand and follow them. You may play the game all night by your own rules, but if you ignore those followed by the people who put the thing together, you are sure to lose.

Almost all indexes use a good many abbreviations, and for help in deciphering them see the section on abbreviations in this chapter. Frequently in indexes as well as other finding devices differences in typeface convey differences in meaning. An example is using boldface type to refer to a page containing an illustration. When you consult an index with a distinction in typefaces that you don't understand, take the few seconds necessary to look up the mystifying page reference and you will soon discover what the difference in type means.

More often than not, indexes are shot through with Latin phrases and their abbreviations. You may not find the reason why very satisfying: That's just the way it is done. It is an ancient tradition, nearly as old as Western scholarship. These conventions became fixed in the days when only that rarity, the highly educated person, could read at all. In our present time of widespread concern because only 90-odd percent of our population is literate, it is perhaps hard to realize that the vast majority of medieval Europe's population was wholly uneducated and completely illiterate.

In any case, the conventions reached Gutenberg and movable type via the scholarly monasteries of the church in the dawn of the Middle Ages, when the universal language of those who were literate was Latin. When books began to be typeset in German, then French and English and other languages, the footnotes and other references remained in Latin, and this practice (but not including the text of footnotes) has continued right down to the age of typesetting computers.

But Latin is no longer universal. Not infrequently, basic refer-ences are given in English these days, but even when this is the case certain fundamental abbreviations still appear in Latin. The obvi-ous reason for the use of English is that some of the Latin forms are just too arcane for readers outside the academic community. The reason the Latin initials survive is that they are just too compact and convenient to do without.

For the convenience of lookers-up everywhere, following is a list of terms and abbreviations used in indexing, footnotes, and bibliographies, and also in internal references within text. These terms are arranged here in alphabetical order in three ways: by abbreviation, by the original Latin where applicable, and by English words and meanings. (A few widely used abbreviations from other languages are included, with original language noted.)

Abbreviation	Original	English
ab init.	*ab initio*	from the beginning
abr.		abridgment
ad init.	*ad initium*	in the beginning
ad loc.	*ad locum*	at the place
anon.		anonymous (from Greek)
app.	*appendix*	appendix
art.		article
b.		born, sometimes brother
bibl.	*bibliotheca*	library
bibliog.		bibliography
biog.		biography
bk.		block, or book
c., ca.	*circa*	about, around
c.		century; in legal citations, chapter
©		copyright
cf.	*confer*	compare
chap.		chapter
col.	*columna*	column
colloq.		colloquial
comp. (pl., *comps.*)		compiled by; comparison, comparative
con.	*contra*	against
cont.		continued
contr.		contraction
copr.		copyright
cp.		compare
d.		died, daughter
def.		definition, definite
dept.		department
deriv.		derivative

Abbreviation	Original	English
dial.		dialect
dict.		dictionary
dim.		diminutive (*i.e.*, nickname)
dist.		district
div.		division, divorced
do.		ditto
dram. pers.	*dramatis personae*	persons in the play
ed. (pl., *eds.*)		editor; edited by, edition
e.g.	*exempli gratia*	for example
enc. or *encyc.*		encyclopedia
esp.		especially
et al.	*et alii*	and others
etc.	*et cetera*	and so forth
et seq.	*et sequentes*	and the following
ex. (pl., *exx.*)		example
f. or *fem.*		feminine, female
fig.		figure, figuratively
fl.	*floruit*	flourished
fol.	*folio*	page number or page size
fr.		from
gen.		genitive; genus
geog.		geography, -er, -ical
geom.		geometry, -ical
hdqrs., or *HQ*		headquarters
hist.		history, -ical, -ian
ibid.	*ibidem*	in the same place
id.	*idem*	the same
i.e.	*id est*	that is
incl.		including, inclusive
inf.	*infra*	below
in pr.	*in principio*	in the beginning

Abbreviation	Original	English
inst.	*instant*	this month; also institute, -ion
lit.		literally
loc.	*locus*	place; also locative
loc. cit.	*loco citato*	in the place cited
loq.	*loquitur*	he or she speaks
m.		married, male, meter, mile
m.m.	*mutatis mutandis*	with necessary changes being made
med.		median, medical, medieval
ms. (pl., *mss.*)	*manuscriptum*	manuscript
mus.		museum, music, -al
n. (pl., *nn.*)	*natus*	born; note, noun; footnote
nat.		national, natural
N.B.	*nota bene*	note well
no.	*numerus*	number
non obs.	*non obstante*	notwithstanding
non seq.	*non sequitur*	it does not follow
N.S.		New Style (calendar)
ob.	*obiit*	died
obs.		obsolete, obsolescent
op. cit.	*opere citato*	in the work cited
O.S.		Old Style (calendar)
p. (pl., *pp.*)		page
par.		paragraph
pass.	*passim*	here and there throughout; passive
path.		pathology, -ist, -ical
perh.		perhaps
pers.		person, -al
pl.		plural
P.S.	*post scriptum*	postscript
pt.		part
pub.		publication, publisher, published by

Abbreviation	Original	English
Q.E.D.	*quod erat demon-strandum*	which was to be demonstrated
q.v.	*quod vide*	which see
r.	*recto*	right-hand page; also reigned
repr.		reprint, -ed
rev.		review, revised, revision
sg., sing.		singular
subj.		subject, subjective
subst.		substantive
sup.	*supra*	above
supp., suppl.		supplement
syn.		synonym, -ous
theol.		theology, -ian, -ical
trans.		transitive; translated, -or
ult.	*ultimo*	last month
univ.		university
u.s.w. (Ger.)	*und so weiter*	and so forth
ut sup.	*ut supra*	as above
v.	*verso; vide*	left-hand page; see
v., vs.	*versus*	versus
viz.	*videlicet*	namely
vol.		volume
y., yr.		year, your

"Index" is simply a Latin word meaning "one who points out," thus a discloser, discoverer, or informer. The idea of an index is older than the name; in fact, it is many centuries older than printing. Indexes of the topics covered in individual manuscript books appeared in the first millennium A.D., and indexes—*i.e.*, lists—of books were in use at least as early as the second century.

The most famous, or notorious, such index may have been the Roman Catholic Church's *Index Librorum Prohibitorum* or *Index of*

Forbidden Books, which existed in one form or another from 170 to 1966, when it was suppressed. That index listed heretical works and other books that could, if read, endanger the faith or morals of Catholics. Although the list originated in the second century, it did not acquire the title of index until 1559, when it was so named under the imprimatur of the Sacred Congregation for the Roman Inquisition. The term quickly spread to embrace the individual indexes, or lists of topics, of particular books of a secular as well as religious nature. Early indexes were arranged in topical order, thus resembling contemporary tables of contents more than present-day indexes. This began to change in the seventeenth century. Some indexes were organized in numerical order, others alphabetically, by color, and by other schemes. Gradually alphabetical order came to predominate.

So a contemporary index is any list of items that points out where things may be found. Indexes of topics treated in magazines are almost as old as magazines, and as publishing proliferated so did such lists of books and indexes in books. Most of the publications discussed in this book are themselves indexes of one sort or another. Here, however, our concern is for the index of an individual work.

Users as well as makers of alphabetical indexes need to know and remember some basic rules. One of the most basic is that the key word, the one that is alphabetized in an index entry, is the first substantive word in the term being indexed. For example, usually you will find the American Articles of Confederation alphabetized as "Confederation, Articles of." This practice of rearranging the actual name or title to put the first substantive word "in front" is known as inversion. However, be warned that opinions differ among both editors and indexers, and you may encounter such terms alphabetized without inversion in some books. Maddeningly enough, occasionally you will encounter a mix of alphabetizing practices in the same book.

Other rules deal with the names of persons. First of all, general indexes are usually intended to list only the names of persons about whom some fairly substantial information appears at the place recorded. If a name is only mentioned, perhaps in a string of names as a "for instance" or an illustration, that mention should not be indexed.

For example: "Among the popular fiction writers of the 1950s were X, Y, and Z, but the real giants of the period were A and B.

A reached the zenith of his fame in 1954 with publication of. . . . B appeared a few years later with the great novel. . . ." In this case, X, Y, and Z should not be indexed, but A and B, with substantial passages about their work, should be.

The reason for this rule is to spare the reader the disappointment of turning to the cited page hoping to find some substantial information about X when there is nothing of real substance there. What results in this case is frustration. Nevertheless, it often happens just that way. For the most part this is clear evidence of sloppy indexing. There is an exception: In some works—of history, for example—there are separate name indexes listing every person named in the book, and these are placed separately from the general index.

To make the names in an index findable—look-uppable—personal names are inverted to place the family name first and alphabetize it. Thus Charles Dickens becomes Dickens, Charles. Most names from English-speaking countries create few problems for the reader of English: Einstein, Albert; Stevenson, Robert Louis. But for that English-reader, foreign names often are a Pandora's box.

The key question is, in languages other than English, where does the proper indexing point—the family name—appear in a person's full name as it is usually written? There's the rub: Ordinarily last in English, it comes first in Chinese and often in Japanese, and in many other languages it comes somewhere else. For a full discussion of this problem, see Chapter 5 (How to Look Up People), beginning at page 90.

In most languages, titles of royalty or nobility cause their share of difficulties. What, for instance, do you do with Robert Cavelier, Sieur de la Salle? A case could be made for alphabetizing him under C, D, L, or S. Usually L wins, and he is found as La Salle, Robert Cavelier, Sieur de. This requires double inversion, a practice that gives scrupulous indexers fits, but with such an array of names and titles, something has to give. The British demand equal time: What are we to make of a man christened Robert Cecil who became the First Earl of Salisbury? Following the same logic, we come up with Salisbury, Robert Cecil, First Earl of.

Indexers, however, are little less fallible than the rest of us, so you may not find either of these names where you might expect them. In that event, the looker-up simply has to ring the changes on the names, seeking one element after another until the man turns up. Similar juggling is necessary with titles in other languages.

Inversion can be carried to extremes in other ways, perhaps especially in nonpersonal names. One standard of indexing is that titles of works of art are alphabetized at their first substantive word. Thus Mozart's opera should be listed as *Marriage of Figaro, The,* and not inverted further to *Figaro, The Marriage of* or *Figaro, Marriage of, The.* Above all, it should not appear in the index under *The.*

Phrases identifying fields of activity, school subjects, and academic disciplines, for example, are treated like works of art, with the first substantive word alphabetized. Therefore it is political science and not science, political; so also political parties. Some encyclopedia editors, by the way, are fixated on singular-article titles, with the result that the title may be "political party" and some convoluted language following it makes clear that the topic really is plural.

Subordinate categories and synonyms are often troublesome to lookers-up. If you can't find "sales tax" in the index—a perfectly reasonable expectation, by the way, as long as the work you're in deals with such subjects—look under "tax." It may even be necessary to go to "taxation." Under either, the subordinate category of "sales tax" should appear. As to synonyms, if you can't find "motion pictures" look under "cinema" or "film," and so on down the line.

Synonyms figure in another kind of look-up trouble, the euphemism, and its cousin, the excessively scientific or technical term. If you can't find "guerrilla" or "terrorist," try "freedom fighter." The hyperscientific title will be a problem only when you are dealing in scientific or technical terms, and if you can't find the topic you are looking for, consulting a dictionary for synonyms is a good next step. And as government and industrial bureaucracies churn out their endless sea of publications internal and external, the resourceful looker-up will not lose sight of bureaucratese as a last alternative. If you can't find it under "period" or "era," try "time-frame"; for "opportunity," see "window." Academese is no better. Consult the dictionary (unabridged if available): "learning" may be lurking at "cognition," or "physique" at "somatotype."

All this places a heavy load on the imagination of the reader, but it may develop your character. And quite apart from the outrageous synonyms cited above, perfectly common and acceptable synonyms also introduce uncertainty into the indexer's game. Avocation, hobby, sport, pastime, recreation—all of them are plausibly interchangeable in many a situation. In general, the rule is: If you don't find it where you think it should be, list the synonyms and try them one by one.

Finally, remember that indexing in alphabetical order offers two opportunities for organization: indexing by word and indexing by letter. In letter indexing, alphabetical order is followed regardless of separation between words. In word indexing, all phrases beginning with the word (*e.g.,* air base) are treated before moving to the first compound form of the word (airboat). Examples of letter and word alphabetization follow.

Letter Alphabetization	Word Alphabetization
air base	air base
air bladder	air bladder
airboat	air brake
airborne	air chief marshal
air brake	air coach
airbrush	air commodore
airburst	air force
airbus	air gun
air chief marshal	air hole
air coach	air lane
air commodore	air letter
air-condition	air lock
air-cool	air marshal
aircraft	air mass
aircraft carrier	air mattress
aircrew	Air Medal
air-cushion vehicle	air mile
airdate	air piracy
airdrome	air plant
airdrop	air pocket
airdry	air police
Airedale terrier	air power

Letter Alphabetization	Word Alphabetization
airer	air pump
Air Express	air raid
airfare	air rifle
airfield	air right
airflow	air sac
air force	air vice-marshal
airframe	airboat
airfreight	airborne
airglow	airbrush
air gun	airburst
airhead	air-condition
air hole	air-cool
airing	aircraft
air lane	aircraft carrier
air letter	aircrew
airlift	air-cushion vehicle
airline	airdate
airliner	airdrome
air lock	airdrop
airmail	airdry
airman	airer
airmanship	airfare
air marshal	airfield
air mass	airflow
air mattress	airframe
Air Medal	airfreight
air mile	airglow
air-minded	airhead
airmobile	airing
airpark	airline

From these examples it is evident that the principle used—word indexing or letter indexing—can be discovered immediately. Take the necessary moment to find out first instead of wading through the lines and pages, perhaps looking for "air mattress" somewhere after "airmail" while it is actually tucked away well before airboat— or vice versa. It is also worth remembering that not only dictionaries but also other works, such as concise encyclopedias, directories, and anthologies of various kinds (including some hymnals and other songbooks) are organized in strict alphabetical order. Being thus "self-indexed," they contain no separate index.

CROSS-REFERENCES

Wherever an index uses a term that has several synonyms, it ought to provide a cross-reference for each one. The purpose of the cross-reference is to convey a message like this: "It was perfectly logical to look for your topic here. However, in this book it is located under ———. Please see that reference." Suppose you are looking up, in a good general encyclopedia or an encyclopedia of the visual arts, ukiyo-e, the genre of Japanese wood-block print exemplified by the work of Hokusai and Hiroshige. If you don't find it under that heading, you have every right to expect a cross-reference telling you where to look: *e.g.*, "ukiyo-e: *see* Japanese wood-block prints," or "*see* visual arts, Japanese: wood-block printing," or some such. The same thing is true in reverse: If the page number is at ukiyo-e, the index owes you a cross-reference at wood-block print.

There is another symbol used in indexes to tell you something about the way you will find your subject when you get to the pages cited. It is *passim*, literally "spread" or "scattered about." It tells you that in the pages listed you will find your topic in several places— here and there. It should appear something like this:

> Morris, Gouverneur, role in convention 306–15 *passim*

In that span of pages Morris might be treated at length at the start and then mentioned a dozen times in his interactions with other Founding Fathers, without another sustained passage about him alone. This situation would merit two kinds of reference, *viz.*,

> Morris, Gouverneur, role in convention 306–7 and 308–15 *passim*

It is possible, in a badly executed index, that you will find the abbreviation *f.*, or its plural, *ff.*, where *passim* should appear. The notation "308 *ff.*" means "in the pages following 308," but it is a bibliographic term and should not appear in an index. A related term, also taboo in good indexes, is *et seq.* (*et sequentes*), "and the following." It, too, sometimes appears where *passim* belongs, and if you encounter *et seq.* in an index you are entitled to a slight sneer while you mutter to yourself, "that idiot!"

The obligation of the reference work to help you find what you are seeking makes cross-reference important far beyond the relatively narrow category of the index. Well-executed dictionaries will always send you to the subject from any plausible synonym— always, that is, to the extent of their perfection. They fail on occasion, but they always try.

Cross-references appear in a number of guises. One of the most visible is sometimes called a title cross-reference because it appears in its alphabetical position among other entries, and its type has the same face and weight as that of other titles. This kind of cross-reference is also called an external or exterior cross-reference.

Suppose, for instance, that you are looking up "bobcat." You may find the reference right there, between "bobbin" and "bobolink." Instead of the reference, however, there may be a title cross-reference:

> bobcat: *see* wildcat

or perhaps

> bobcat, also called wildcat or bay lynx. *See* lynx

If the latter, there should be a comparable title cross-reference at wildcat, because any one of those three titles is a fair place to look.

The other major variety of cross-reference is found within the text, and it is called an internal, interior, or embedded cross-reference. One of the most common of these alerts you to another article, *which see* for additional light on the subject. Another invites you to *see also* one or several other articles bearing on related subjects that may amplify your understanding of the article you're reading. Still another suggests that you *compare* this article with another whose subject is related to but significantly different from or perhaps diametrically opposite to the one at hand.

Most of the time when these indications appear in text they are set in italics, and more often than not the first and third are given as Latin abbreviations. (*See* the fuller list of abbreviations above.) Thus *which see* is usually rendered as *q.v.* (*quod vide*), and *compare* as *cf.* (*confer*, Latin for "compare"). *See also,* curiously enough, is usually presented in English.

To illustrate the appearance of these finding devices and their use in text, here is an abridged entry from a hypothetical concise encyclopedia about the bobcat we encountered earlier.

> bobcat, *Felis rufa,* also called bay lynx or wildcat, a short-tailed (hence its name) cat of the family *Felidae* found across North America from Canada to northern Mexico. It is closely related to the Canada lynx (*q.v.; Felis canadensis*). The bobcat's habits are largely nocturnal and its . . . *Cf.* caracal, pardel. *See also* lynx.

As noted previously, these signals have certain duties to the reader, but they do not always deliver. The *q.v.* in the preceding example should say to you, "You will get a better picture of where the bobcat fits into the North American wildcats by looking up 'Canada lynx' in addition to the present article." Incidentally, its location indicates that you should look up "Canada lynx" and not *Felis canadensis*. (If the reverse were true the reference should read "*Felis canadensis, q.v.*)." The *See also* in this example signifies that if you want information about other cats outside the Canada lynx family you may find it at "lynx."

It doesn't take long to find out whether the editor has been marching to a different drummer. Look up two or three *q.v.*s and you will begin to see. The editor's temptation is to misuse the *q.v.* to advertise the presence of other articles that for your purposes may not be worth finding. The *cf.* also should shed additional light, by, in this case, showing you the differences between the bobcat and the caracal and pardel. If those articles do not make clear both the relations and the differences among these creatures, the *cf.* is misplaced. The *See also* is a more general signal than the others; it lets you know about other related articles that might interest you. In this case it suggests that the lynx article might contain enough information about lynxes generally to be worth your turning to it, but it doesn't urge you to look it up as the *q.v.* does.

FOOTNOTES

Footnotes and bibliographic notes or citations are the remaining kinds of finding devices commonly used in reference works. Unlike the others we have considered, however, they direct you out of the book at hand. Footnotes indicate the source of the quotation or information bearing the footnote, usually some other work of scholarship, or perhaps a letter in the author's (or someone else's) possession. Ordinarily they are numbered in sequence chapter by chapter, with the number appearing in small superscript beside the quotation in the text, and the same number identifies the note where it appears. It usually does not appear at the foot of the page (whence its name), as in the following illustration, but at the back of the book in a section devoted to footnotes chapter by chapter, or sometimes in a special section at the end of each chapter.

Occasionally a footnote will appear at the bottom of the page; when this appears it is usually to convey some bit of additional knowledge or information about the subject—an interesting sidelight but far enough away from the immediate subject so that including it in the original sentence would have been awkward (not that interrupting the reader to send his eye to the bottom of the page is anything but awkward). See the bottom of this page for an example.[1] Notes of this kind are usually marked by an asterisk; where more than one appears on a page the second is marked by a dagger (†) and the third by a double dagger (‡). Once in a while the insatiable researcher will come across a work with footnotes at the bottom of each page, and in some older historical works, for instance, numbered footnotes may be interspersed with others carrying asterisks, daggers, and double daggers, the whole thing looking like an untended garden. If that kind of exposure proves bad for your blood pressure, see if the librarian can steer you to a popular treatment.

BIBLIOGRAPHIES

Bibliographic notes appear at the back of the book, in a special section commonly located between the footnotes and the index. They list, in abbreviated form, books (*biblia* in Greek) on a

---

[1] The information in this type of footnote would be here.

particular subject or by a particular author treated in the book you are reading. A proper bibliography identifies each book it cites by author, title, and place (sometimes) and date of publication. Where appropriate, the bibliographic reference will include notes that describe its general quality or identify the portions pertinent to the subject of the book in hand. This makes it an annotated bibliography.

The term *bibliography,* by the way, is used for much more than books, embracing musical works and their composers, ballets and their choreographers, paintings and their painters, etc. *Discography* has become popular for lists of sound recordings and the artists who made them, but the generic *bibliography* still applies.

Abbreviations are rife in bibliographies. All the standard ones can be found in the abbreviation table on pages 18–21. The most frequent and important of them are identified here. *Ibid.* (*ibidem*—in the same place) avoids repeating author or title of the last book named. When *op. cit.* (*opere citato*—the cited work) follows the name of an author, it refers to his or her previously mentioned book, and it is the only one by that author so listed.

LIBRARIES

Essentially, the organization of a library and that of a reference work are similar, except that every good library contains much more than a single source for each topic and subtopic. Whereas an encyclopedia will likely have only a single article (or major sub-article) on, for example, U.S. history in the Civil War era, a well-equipped library may number books on the subject in dozens or even hundreds. The encyclopedia probably will locate the article alphabetically—but where? Perhaps under Civil War, U.S.; or U.S. History, Civil War; or History, U.S., Civil War.

But if this kind of ambiguity existed among libraries, with their dozens or hundreds of "entries" on every important topic, scholars, students, and just plain browsers and readers would always be off balance. Clearly the alphabet, an awkward organizing scheme even in a encyclopedia, is out of its depth when it comes to the library. What is needed is some device to combine the functions of table of contents and index but capable of working on a massive scale. How to do it?

In the 1870s an acting librarian at Amherst College named Melvil Dewey solved this problem by inventing a numerical classification system that enabled libraries to organize books by subject instead of in alphabetical order by title or author. Civil War histories, for example, could be bunched together so that only within the Civil War section would the tyranny of the alphabet prevail.

Dewey's scheme is called the Dewey Decimal System for its use of ten digits to identify categories of books. He began by breaking down the fields of knowledge and scholarship and the regions of the world (and hence the fields addressed by books) into manageable proportions, and he assigned to each field a three-digit number beginning, naturally, with a numeral from 0 to 9. Although other systems have been devised that made significant improvements on the Dewey Decimal System, it is still used in most libraries in the United States, and to be at home in a library the reader needs to know something about it.

Something, but not very much. There is no reason to carry around in your head the significance of the ten primary digits the system uses to subdivide classes of books, but you should know enough about it to understand how it works. This will enable you to read a library catalog card without calling for help. If you understand how the classification system works you know what to look for in the library stacks, which is to say shelves.

Here are the numbers marking the basic Dewey divisions:

000	general works
100	philosophy and aesthetics
200	religion
300	social sciences and sociology
400	linguistics and languages
500	mathematics and the natural sciences
600	applied sciences (medicine, engineering, etc.) and technology
700	the arts and recreation
800	literature
900	history (including geography and biography)

The second and third digits in the Dewey Decimal System provide geographic and topical breakdowns. For example, in division 900, history:

900	history (the subject itself)
910	geography
920	biography
930	ancient world history
940	European history
950	Asian history
960	African history
970	North American history
980	South American history
990	Oceanian history

The third digit cuts things finer still; North American history (970), for instance, is subdivided by the third digit, where 2 stands for Canada and 3 for the United States. Thus 972 represents Canadian history and 973 that of the United States. For further subdividing, the Dewey Decimal System uses a decimal point and still more digits, to wit:

973	American (U.S.) history
973.1	American discovery and exploration
973.2	the Colonial period
973.3	the American Revolution
973.4	the Constitutional period (from 1787)
973.5	early nineteenth century, and so on to the twentieth century

France is represented by 44 in the second and third digits, so 944 is French history, 444 a French dictionary.

Numbers to the right of the decimal point carry on the scheme as necessary; since 910 is geography and France is 44, French geography becomes 914.4; U.S. (73) geography is 917.3.

That's enough to illustrate how the Dewey Decimal System works.

It is obvious that the alphabet, with its twenty-six digits, offers a great many more categories than do the ten numerical digits for the precise classification of knowledge and hence of books. That recognition is applied in the Library of Congress system, which uses letters for its first two digits, and numbers beyond them. The primary LC class numbers, as they are known, have the following significance:

A	general works (encyclopedias, etc.)
B	philosophy and religion
C	auxiliary sciences of history
D	general and Old World history
E	general U.S. history
F	local history in the United States, and Canadian and Latin American history
G	geography and anthropology
H	the social sciences
I	omitted to avoid confusion with the numeral 1
J	political science
K	law
L	education
M	music
N	fine arts (in this usage meaning the visual arts)
O	omitted to avoid confusion with the numeral 0
P	language and literature
Q	the natural sciences
R	medicine
S	agriculture
T	technology
U	military science
V	naval science
W, X, and Y	omitted because enough is enough
Z	bibliography and library science

There are other classification systems, based on either the Dewey or the LC, that are sometimes found in university or specialized libraries, but the main thing for the reader is to be able to figure out quickly and easily how to use any system.

Until the late 1970s, the card catalog was the universal library finding device; increasingly the old card catalog is giving way to microform catalogs manipulated by the library patron using manually operated knobs or motor controls or a combination of both. Computerized catalogs are also appearing. But be it card, microfilm, microfiche, or computer, the catalog tells the reader where to find the book, and it provides the invaluable further help of telling you what you will find there.

This where-to-find information is a book's call number, a combination of the basic Dewey or LC (or other) classification number followed, usually on the next line down, by a letter or two and a number. The letters are the initial, often followed by the second letter, of the author's family name (remember, it's the last name in English, but Deng Xiaoping's family name is Deng, Mario Vargas Llosa's family name is Vargas, and that is how they are—or should be—alphabetized).

The information about contents is contained on the card itself, or its filmed counterpart. The catalog is organized by subject, title, and author. Each card lists those elements, number of volumes and pages, and the place and year of publication. When appropriate, the card goes into more detail, such as number of illustrations and maps, and sometimes a brief description describing the work. Examples of the three kinds of card follow.

001.2
ADL   Adler, Mortimer Jerome, 1902–
        A guidebook to learning: for a lifelong
        pursuit of wisdom/Mortimer J. Adler.—
        New York: Macmillan, c. 1986.
        163 pp.; 22 cm.
        ISBN 0-02-500340-2

        1. Learning and scholarship.
      I. Title

IDf   09 APR 86   12969579   JFAAsc   85-23778

The foregoing is an author, or name, card generated by computer for a city library that is part of a consortium of municipal and college libraries. The call letter (Dewey Decimal System) is at the upper left. The author card is headed by the author's full name and birth year.

Next lines: title; subtitle; author's name as it appears in the book; city of publication; publisher; copyright year.

Next line: number of pages; height of book in centimeters.

Next line: International Standard Book Number (ISBN). At the bottom of the card are "added entries," or other parts of the catalog where you can look the book up, *i.e.*, (1) by the subject and (I) by its title.

The last line has (from left) a code identifying the library; the date of order; code sequences of numbers and letters assigned to the book by the consortium; and the book's serial number in the Library of Congress.

Many libraries use printed cards from the Library of Congress catalog, as here:

JOURNALISM—U.S.

071.3   **Mott, Frank Luther,** 1886–
M858   American journalism; a history, 1690–1960. 3d ed. New York, Macmillan [1962]
     901 p. illus. 25 cm.

     1. Journalism—U.S. 2. American newspapers. 3. Press—U.S.
     I. Title.

PN4855.M63   1962   071.3   62—7157‡

Library of Congress   [62f5]

On the line above the Dewey class number, the subject category reveals that this is a subject card. Next come the author's name in full and birth year, followed by the title, publication information, and the size of the book. Added entries show that the book has three subject cards: (1) the one shown above, (2) American newspapers, (3) Press—U.S., and (I) it also can be looked up under its title.

The bottom of this card, which comes from another library, is a bit different. It shows the LC catalog number at the left, the year, then the Dewey number, and the LC serial number at the right.

The way this card starts out (after the Dewey class number) indicates that it is a title card:

R291.03 **Abingdon dictionary of living reli-**
Ab58   **gions**/Keith Crim, general editor; Roger
    A. Bullard, Larry D. Shinn, associate
    editors.—Nashville, Tenn.: Abingdon, c.
    1981.
      xviii, 830 pp., [8] leaves of plates: ill.
    (some col.); 26 cm.
      Includes bibliographies.
      ISBN 0-687-00409-8

      1. Religions—Dictionaries. I. Crim,
    Keith R. II. Bullard, Roger Aubrey.
    III. Shinn, Larry D., 1942– . IV. Title:
    Dictionary of living religions.

BL31.A24   291'.03'21—dc19   81-1465
                        AACR 2   MARC
Library of Congress

Here the editors are identified instead of hundreds of authors of individual articles. The sixth and seventh lines tell us that "front matter" occupies xviii pages, text 830 pages, that there are eight leaves of plates, that there are illustrations, some of which are in color, and that it's twenty-six centimeters (a little over ten inches) high. We also learn that it has bibliographies. There is one subject card and there are three "author" cards. The fact that this book is commonly called the *Abingdon Dictionary of Living Religions* but that it is also known as the *Dictionary of Living Religions* makes necessary another point of entry (IV) into the catalog at a second title card.

The line following the added entries gives the LC catalog number at the left, followed by an extended version of the Dewey number, which the Library of Congress sometimes does. The "—dc19" tacked on to it means it is derived from the Dewey Code, nineteenth edition. Then comes the LC's own serial number for the book. AACR 2 signifies that the card is compiled according to the Anglo-American Cataloging Rules, second edition. MARC is the acronym for the LC's computer-access system in which this information is entered.

As the foregoing samples make apparent, a glance at a book's call number, on either its spine or the upper left-hand corner of the catalog card, reveals instantly whether the system is Dewey (first digit a numeral, as in the examples above) or LC (first digit a letter). When you go to the stacks, it is only necessary to find the section displaying the first two or three digits of the call number you are seeking. Not all libraries have signs on the ends of the stacks listing the range of call numbers housed there, but no matter: The spine of the nearest book will reveal where you are.

If you reach the spot where your sought-for book should be and find it missing (borrowed, or stolen, alas), try the "next to" school of research. The book next to the missing one is quite apt to address your subject, and it may fit your needs nicely. If so, score one for knowing how to use call numbers. And in any case, if time is not of the essence, the situation offers opportunities for a nice, quiet browse.

Of course, the ultimate finding device in any library is a librarian. Many public libraries feature a desk in the reading or card catalog room, conspicuously not behind a counter, occupied by a reference librarian whose job is answering questions. The desk may even have a sign saying something like "interrupt me."

Every librarian expects to be asked for help by clients who are not familiar with the ins and outs of organization and the kinds and uses of inanimate finding devices addressed in this chapter. Most of them are patient with beginners and with sensible questions. However, as a class librarians don't suffer fools more gladly than the rest of us, and one of the keys to the enjoyment of any library is: Use your head; think first and ask later. You also will derive a lot of pleasure from improving your own library skills and from the sense of freedom that will bring you.

A final word about libraries: You are not restricted to just the books you see in its stacks. If you poke around long enough in the world of books, sooner or later you will come across a title you want to consult that your own library does not have. Here is where the interlibrary loan system comes to the rescue. Virtually every public library participates in at least one such system, and the user's only cost in getting access to a book from some other collection is a slight lapse of time—two or three weeks, perhaps. Many variations on the basic system exist, including regional networks and local-area consortiums set up at the initiative of particular libraries and imaginative librarians. If you haven't given this system a try, do so at the first opportunity. You will be astonished at what it can do for you.

CHAPTER 2

HOW TO USE GENERAL REFERENCE WORKS

For the literate human being with an adequately developed curiosity, general reference works—dictionaries and encyclopedias—can be the greatest tools on earth. They hold the seeds to learning a great deal about almost any word in the language or subject on Earth. But they also hold the seeds of madness, which you, the user, can bring to instant maturity by not using them in the way they were designed to be used. In the case of dictionaries the commonest source of reader frustration is expecting the book to deliver something it cannot—that is, to be something a dictionary is not.

DICTIONARIES

Perhaps it is useful to clarify the distinctions among three words that often are used interchangeably and sometimes incorrectly: dictionary, lexicon, and glossary. Today we may expect a dictionary to list and define the words in a language; to inform us about their origins and special meanings; to show us how to spell and pronounce them, how to hyphenate them, and how to use them; to present synonyms, and where appropriate, antonyms for them; and to acquaint us with their social connotations. The word comes to us from the Latin *dictio,* "speaking."

A lexicon is a word list pure and simple. It merely lists and defines the words of a language or a special field of interest. The term derives from the Greek *lexis,* "word." The idea is ancient; a small and primitive list of words in the Akkadian language and dating to seventh-century B.C. Mesopotamia has been found by archaeologists in Iraq.

"Glossary" also comes to us from the Greek: *glossa,* "tongue" or "language." A glossary is a list, with meanings, of special, foreign, or difficult words in a work of literature or scholarship, and the glossary is contained in the same volume. By the early sixteenth century a glossary of words from Scripture appeared in English when Tyndale made it part of his English-language Pentateuch, the first five books of the Old Testament.

In classical times the dictionary flourished under both the Greeks and the Romans, and as Western culture grew out of those times Latin became its dominant language, and the *dictionarium* listed and defined the words scholars employed.

At the dawn of the 17th century a short dictionary of the English language appeared, and in 1702 John Kersey (the Younger) published a much larger work clearing away thickets of doubtful and fantastic words that had found their way into earlier and less rigorously edited dictionaries. in 1721 a schoolmaster in one of London's Tower Hamlets, Nathan Bailey, produced *An universal etymological English Dictionary,* which, especially with its 1727 supplement, which introduced marks indicating word pronunciation, was popular and influential for the rest of the century. His emphasis on etymology and pronunciation really defined the trend for future dictionaries, and Bailey's larger and later *Dictionarium Britannicum* was used by Samuel Johnson in his production of his own *A Dictionary of the English Language.* This monumental work appeared in 1755 and it, with its 43,500 words that Johnson concluded were the basic word-stock of the language, became the new standard of linguistic scholarship.

In America lexicography was aggressively pursued from 1828 well into midcentury by two rival scholars whose work was pushed even more aggressively, and competitively, by their publishers. The two were Noah Webster and Joseph Emerson Worcester. When Webster died in 1843 his son-in-law carried on for the publishing house of G. & C. Merriam Company. Other important dictionary-makers emerged in nineteenth-century America, among them William Dwight Whitney (*The Century Dictionary*) and Isaac Kauff-man Funk (*A Standard Dictionary of the English Language*). The descendants of those famous works had great influence down to the mid-twentieth century and beyond.

From the time of Bailey in the early eighteenth century, it has been agreed that dictionaries should show the right spelling of words (literally, orthography), supply their etymological background, and define their meanings. Ambiguity has existed about the degree to which (if at all) new words and vulgar words should be included. Johnson, like his contemporaries, wished the language could be stabilized, to end the flow of neologisms that made dictionary revision an unending task. But he realized that "permanence and stability cannot be derived" from the works of man, and this recognition came to be adopted generally, although slowly.

One of the first American dictionaries, the *Columbian Dictionary of the English Language,* by Caleb Alexander, raised a furor when it appeared in 1800 containing "many new words, peculiar to the United States." Even a scant two decades after the Revolution, in the better circles proper English words were preferred to rough Yankee coinages. Make war, not words, the attitude seemed to be. This position yielded gradually, and new words that actually worked their way into the language came to be adopted by lexicographers as well as the folk who used them in everyday discourse.

Resistance to the inclusion of the coarse language of the streets (and bedroom and outhouse) was another matter. Long after all American dictionaries, and their severest critics, willingly accepted Americanisms and other new coinages, the partisans of propriety remained vigilant against the language of the street—and sea, waterfront, the military, bistro, bordello, and, of course, cloakroom and playground. Many critics were scandalized when in 1961 *Webster's Third New International Dictionary,* published by G. & C. Merriam Company, came out with a full panoply of four-letter words, enabling any schoolchild to learn not only the meaning but also the etymology of graffiti found on rest-room walls and subway cars.

"That dictionary," as scholars called it, some angrily and others sardonically, epitomized the view that dictionaries should describe the language as it is used and not prescribe what it ought to be. It told the reader the meaning and correct spelling of words, including slang, neologisms, and four-letter words.

It is not the only dictionary on its side of the fence, but it is the largest and most influential. Perhaps as much criticism was aimed at *Webster's Third* for not attaching pejorative status labels to vulgar words as for including the words themselves. In subsequent printings the use of such labels ("usu. vulgar," for instance) was significantly increased. And for a few years a three-volume version of the dictionary sold with the *Encyclopaedia Britannica* was bowdlerized to remove the more hair-raising of the explicit Anglo-Saxon words for sexual union and various body parts.

Incidentally, for many years both parties to the debate over propriety have been in general agreement that borrowings from foreign languages should be included once they are well established, and this is as true of British as of American dictionaries. The English language has long been extremely free about accepting foreign words and phrases when they are apt and concise, as witness *polka* (Czech), *kimono* (Japanese), *spiel* (German), *skoal* (*skål*, Swedish), *libretto* (Italian), and *sabotage* (French). Many other languages are also quite accepting of loan words, among them German, Russian, and Japanese (notably), but certainly excluding French (from which we borrowed *chauvinism*). The actual language French people use borrows abundantly from English (*le* drug store, *le* hot dog, *le* parking), but the French government—regardless of the political party in power—is at considerable pains and expense to stamp out *franglais*, which, urged on by the country's cultural guardians, it despises as sabotage of the French language.

For American users of English-language dictionaries there are several bases for comparison among the number of excellent works on the market and in the library. For practical purposes there are three kinds of dictionary. The great classic of the genre occupies a class entirely by itself. That, of course, is *OED*, the *Oxford English Dictionary*. The other varieties are, simply put, abridged and unabridged.

The *OED*

In London in 1857, the Philological Society, taking note of scholarly concerns about certain inadequacies in English dictionaries, initiated a program to produce a completely new work on an unprecedented scale. Its objective was to define and provide historical background—etymology—for every word in the English language from the year 1160. This included every word in all five dialects of Middle English that were in use through the end of the sixteenth century. Moreover, the shifts in meaning over the eight centuries of its scope were to be recorded and explained in every case.

Understandably, this was no rush job. In 1879 its third and most famous editor, a Scottish grammar-school teacher and philologist named James Murray, took over. His impact on the lengthy project was such that it was widely called "Murray's Dictionary" when it was finally complete in 1928, thirteen years after Murray's death.

The work was published, at Oxford, in sections, the first of which (A–Ant) appeared in 1884. The completed work, originally titled *A New English Dictionary on Historical Principles,* consisted of 12 volumes with 15,500 royal quarto pages of three columns each. To demonstrate usages of its 414,825 words it uses 1,827,306 quotations from a collection of nearly six million sent in by Englishmen and -women after Murray issued a call for such illustrative citations. Within five years after the set was complete it was reissued with a supplementary volume, and this time it appeared under its present name, the *Oxford English Dictionary.* (It is sometimes cited under either name or either set of initials, *i.e., OED* or *NED.*)

In 1986 a massive four-volume supplement was completed. Begun in 1957, the supplement began to see daylight with Volume 1 in 1972. The second and third appeared in 1976 and 1982, respectively. It includes much slang, abundant Americanisms, and a fairly copious roster of four-letter words, which raised the eyebrows of the fastidious as soon as Volume 1 came out. As a part of that revision process, the entire text of the monumental work has been "captured" by computer at long last, enormously facilitating future revisions and abridgments, which because of the monumental cost of such a venture will be a long time coming.

The *OED* succeeded brilliantly in carrying out one of its original intentions, supplying extensive etymological background, tracing its words to their origins with variations of spelling and meaning at every step of the way. It also fully treats variations in usage, and it supplies the year of the first recorded use of each meaning of its words.

Unabridged Dictionaries

A conventional unabridged dictionary undertakes to cover virtually all the words in its language and to supply for them full etymological detail, all variant spellings, variations in meaning, and all their various usages, with illustrative quotations. It does not attempt to supply the whole wealth of historical detail provided by the *OED.* In practice, the few unabridged dictionaries still being published in America vary rather widely in several of these connections.

Before turning to them, however, a word about words. For the lexicographer, and linguists generally, "word" is far too informal a term. What to us is a word is more precisely a lexeme (an item in a language's vocabulary), and it may consist of several phonemes (the smallest unit of speech—*e.g.*, the *h* in heads). These phonemes may be bound forms (always occurring with another phoneme, as *s* in heads) and others free forms (capable of bearing meaning alone, as *head* in heads). A word may have several morphemes (the smallest meaningful unit of a language, as *red* and *head* in redheads). But no matter how you slice it, our word will be a lexical unit, and perhaps on that we and the linguists can agree.

Not all lexical units will find their way into any dictionary. For instance, there are some two million named insects on Earth, and hundreds of thousands of brand and trade names, and place and personal names are almost as numerous. Not more than a relative handful of these can be found in any ordinary dictionary, unabridged or not.

Only two unabridged dictionaries are still published in the United States, but a third work of high quality was last issued in 1963 and is held widely in libraries across the country, so it is discussed here. That is the *Funk & Wagnalls New Standard Dictionary*. It has about 450,000 words, some sixty-five thousand of which are proper nouns—biographical and geographical entries. Its definitions begin with the current meaning of the word, and not all obsolescent and obsolete meanings appear. An appendix includes a list of foreign words and phrases and an inevitably outdated list of places and populations.

The *Random House Dictionary of the English Language* (second edition), or *Random House Unabridged II,* covers some 315,000 words, including proper nouns, and has an atlas among other "back of the book" features. It is rich in new words and current and recent usage. Definitions start with the most widespread meaning. First published in 1963, it was enlarged and substantially revised in 1987.

Webster's Third New International Dictionary, "that dictionary," has a list of about 450,000 words excluding names of persons and places, and its definitions are organized with the oldest meanings first, the current definition appearing last.

All three of these works indicate the derivation of words, use quotations to show usage and shifts in meaning, defining idiomatic phrases where necessary for clarity. *Funk & Wagnalls* and *Random House* are on the prescriptive side of the propriety debate, although no dictionary today can wholly avoid vulgar words. In these two, a few four-letter words do appear, but "screw" and "crap" are about as racy as it gets. *Webster's Third*, as the saying has it, goes all the way.

Abridged Dictionaries

The editor of *Encyclopaedia Britannica*'s first edition (1768) began his article on abridgment with a definition that is still serviceable: "a term signifying the reduction of a book into smaller compass." The most obvious step in abridgment is the elimination of obsolescent and arcane words. Although some lexicographers distinguish between unabridged and desk or college dictionaries, for practical purposes an abridged dictionary may be defined as having fewer than two hundred thousand words and more than twenty thousand. An abridged dictionary supplies the same kind of information on origins, meanings, usages, status, etc., as its unabridged forebear, but in "smaller compass." (The smallest dictionaries, mostly in paperback, are not considered here, since their functions are usually limited to spelling, a bare-bones definition, and hyphenation.)

The highly regarded *American Heritage Dictionary of the English Language* is a rare example of the desk dictionary that was not reduced from an existing unabridged work owned by the same publishing house. In such a case, as a starting point a large word list must be compiled, then pruned to fit the intended scope. Definitions are shorter in any abridged version and etymological notes are fewer, as are examples of usage and special meanings.

There are four major abridged dictionaries in print in the United States today. They are the *American Heritage Dictionary of the English Language*, the *Funk & Wagnalls Standard College Dictionary*, the *Random House Dictionary of the English Language: College Edition*, and *Webster's Ninth New Collegiate Dictionary*. A fifth, no longer in print but still in numerous libraries across the country, is the *Thorndike-Barnhart Comprehensive Desk Dictionary*.

The *American Heritage Dictionary*, first published in 1969 under the editorship of William Morris, reflects a high standard of English, strong emphasis on demonstrating usage, and an antipathy for the "permissiveness" of the Merriam-Webster dictionaries in not attaching adequate status labels to obscenities, etc., and was designed in part to capitalize on the strong reaction against the vulgarities in *Webster's Third* after its appearance in 1961. The *American Heritage Dictionary*'s 155,000 entries include many geographical names and other proper nouns. Its entries present the major current meaning first, accompanied by illustrative quotations and followed by older meanings and etymological notes.

The *Funk & Wagnalls Standard College Dictionary* was created in 1963 by abridging the publisher's *New Standard Dictionary*. Annual reprinting and revision keep it essentially up-to-date, and it reflects the approach of the publisher's *New Standard Dictionary* in its order of definitions, illustrations of usage, and reluctance to define four-letter words. It contains useful aids to the reader, among them a guide to punctuation, a list of symbols, and other fringe benefits.

The *Thorndike-Barnhart Comprehensive Desk Dictionary* was derived from a series of school dictionaries compiled in the 1930s by Edward Lee Thorndike and brought up to college level a decade later by Clarence L. Barnhart. Out of print since 1975, it is still, apart from its slowly increasing datedness, one of the most popular and useful of the college or desk dictionaries. It is distinguished by its numerous illustrations of usage and its attention to the construction of an adequate vocabulary.

Webster's Ninth New Collegiate Dictionary is abridged from the *Webster's Third New International Dictionary* and presents in "smaller compass" the strengths and "sins" of the larger work, frankly defining the language as it is used and presenting etymology first, oldest definitions next, and current meanings last. It is revised and reprinted annually, with more massive revisions appearing at intervals of several years. (In 1983 the *Ninth* replaced the unnumbered eighth *New Collegiate*, which replaced the *Seventh* in 1973.)

All the foregoing dictionaries are illustrated with drawings as well as quotations, and all are useful to the reader, their utility varying with the needs and expectations of the user. The following tables highlight and compare some of their particular features:

UNABRIDGED

Dictionary	No. of Entries	Includes Proper Nouns	Language Four-Letter	Included Slang	Usage Labels	Illustrations Quotes	Illustrations Drawings
F&W New Std.	450,000	yes	no	yes	yes	yes	yes
OED	415,000	no	all	yes	yes	yes	no
Random House	315,000	yes	all	yes	yes	yes	yes
Webster's Third	450,000	no	all	yes	yes	yes	yes

Pronunciation Key	Synonyms	Antonyms	Table of Abbreviations	Biography Section	Geographic Names	Section
every pg.	yes	yes	yes	no	yes	no
front	no	no	yes	no	yes	no
every pg.	yes	no	yes	yes	yes	yes
front of bk.	no	yes	yes	yes	yes	yes

ABRIDGED

Dictionary	No. of Entries	Includes Proper Nouns	Language Four-Letter	Included Slang	Usage Labels	Illustrations Quotes	Illustrations Drawings
Am. Her.	155,000	yes	all	yes	yes	yes	yes
F&W Coll.	150,000	yes	none	yes	yes	yes	yes
Random House Coll.	155,000	yes	some	yes	yes	yes	yes
Webster's Coll.	160,000	no	all	yes	yes	yes	yes

Pronunciation Key	Synonyms	Antonyms	Table of Abbreviations	Biography Section	Geographic Names	Section
alt pgs.	yes	yes	no	no	no	no
alt. pgs.	yes	no	no	yes	yes	no
every pg.	yes	yes	no	no	no	no
alt. pgs.	yes	yes	yes	no	no	yes

ENCYCLOPEDIAS

So far as we know, the earliest encyclopedias originated, apparently quite independently, within about 600 years of each other in Greece and China. One of Plato's nephews, Speusippus, recorded the philosopher's teachings in a whole range of subjects in the mid-fourth century B.C. In China, around the end of the Han dynasty in A.D. 220, the emperor ordered an encyclopedia to be compiled. The two works reflected different approaches to encyclopedia-making that persist to this day. The Western version was a collection of discourses of varying lengths describing and explaining a great variety of subjects. The Asian approach was a collection of existing books on a similarly wide range of subjects (or at least we may so infer from Chinese successors to the original, which is known only from references to it by other writers).

The word "encyclopedia" is from the Greek *en kyklios paideia* (roughly "the circle of learning," or the full cycle of knowledge), and it found its way into English via Latin, hence the "... paedia" spelling in the older forms, which indeed prevailed far into the twentieth century until the urge to simplify caught up with it in the United States.

Plato and Aristotle are generally counted the fathers of the encyclopedia in its Western guise, for they taught in their lectures and dialogs a full course or cycle of knowledge. The encyclopedias that recorded their thoughts were essentially written records of their oral teachings. The Romans introduced written knowledge, as distinct from written-down oral discourses, into the encyclopedia. By far the most influential of these works, though by no means the first, was the massive *Historia naturalis* (*Natural History*) of Pliny the Elder. Its thirty-seven books, completed just two years before his death in A.D. 79, systematically attempted to embrace the whole of human knowledge, or in his words, "the nature of things, that is, life." Pliny, unlike his predecessors and many of his successors, listed his sources scrupulously.

Some of his translations from Greek authors were careless, and thus and otherwise a good many errors found their way into the work, but its vast scope and size, its general authority, and perhaps also its simplicity of style made it the premier work of the age. Its influence on other encyclopedists persisted for a millennium and a half, throughout the Middle Ages. And in scholarship *per se*, over the centuries *Historia naturalis* came to substitute for the Greek works themselves from which much of it was drawn as, gradually, they disappeared into antiquity.

Pliny's encyclopedia was organized by topic. Following Book I, a summary and list of books and authors cited, Book II treated astronomy and cosmology, III–VI geography, VII–XI zoology (including man), and so on to Books XXXIII–XXXVII, minerals and metals. Latin remained the language of encyclopedists, as it was of scholarship, until the late thirteenth century, when Brunetto Latini produced one in French to reach the educated laity in Italy.

The original topical or systematic arrangement of articles prevailed until 1674, when Louis Moréri brought out his *Grand Dictionnaire historique,* which was organized alphabetically. Its ease of use made it popular and effectively cast the die for alphabetical order.

The first English encyclopedia not a translation from the French appeared in 1704 from the hand of John Harris, and a modern reader would see in it the whole apparatus of a contemporary work down to the illustrations and a bibliography. In 1728 Ephraim Chambers introduced his *Cyclopaedia,* a most influential work that went through repeated revisions. Indeed, the great but strongly opinionated French *Encyclopédie* had its origins in an undertaking by Denis Diderot to translate Chambers's *Cyclopaedia* into French.

But Diderot, abetted by his coeditor Jean Le Rond d'Alembert, sidetracked the original project in favor of a greatly enlarged work that became a major polemical and revolutionary voice of the Enlightenment and rationalism, espousing materialist atheism and winning the enmity of church (notably the Jesuits) and state alike. He was jailed briefly but persisted, and the work, begun in 1751 and completed in 1772, became popular because of its controversial radical bias as much as for its intellectual content. Its twenty-eight volumes included eleven devoted to plates of extremely high quality.

Near the end of that project a "society of gentlemen"—a printer, an engraver, and an editor they hired—came together in Edinburgh, Britain's capital of the Enlightenment and "the Athens of the North," to create a new encyclopedia, in part to correct the shortcomings of the radical Frenchman. Diderot had dropped duller articles from his plan where necessary to accommodate titles from which his ideological and political polemics could pour. The Scotsmen creating *Encyclopaedia Britannica* undertook to eschew passion for objectivity, and they set about enlisting subscribers to buy the fairly steady flow of fascicles, or pamphlets, from 1768 to 1771, when the work was complete and could be bound by any cobbler into three fat tomes.

Encyclopedia-making flourished throughout the nineteenth century, and the French encyclopedia of Pierre Larousse and the German *Konversations-lexikons* of Arnold Brockhaus and then Joseph Meyer made their own contributions to encyclopedic style (respectively, readability and conciseness). The *Britannica*, meanwhile, continued through edition after edition under a succession of owners until toward the end of the 1880s—several years after the first appearance of its classic ninth edition—the ownership of its plates passed to a pair of American entrepreneurs, one of whom, Horace Hooper, moved the enterprise from London to New York and then to Chicago, where it continued to thrive, and sustained the stature it had long since been accorded as the reference standard of the English-speaking world.

The famous eleventh edition of the *Britannica* (1910–11) was prepared under American ownership though jointly edited in London and New York with numerous contributors from each country—and from many others. After a couple of supplements numbered as editions, the *Britannica* came out in 1929 with a completely new fourteenth edition, which it revised annually from 1938 to 1973.

Finally, in 1974 a wholly reorganized fifteenth edition supplanted the much-patched fourteenth. The new edition introduced a short-entry section (*Micropaedia*) of some fourteen million words and combined with it (in ten volumes) the function of index, an arrangement hugely unpopular with librarians. Major articles, from a thousand words to book length (100,000 words or more) were in a nineteen-volume *Macropaedia*. A separate *Propaedia* volume displayed the organizing scheme and provided a topical table of contents. A major revision rearranged the set further beginning in 1985, with a two-volume separate index (placating the librarians), an enlarged *Micropaedia*, and a *Macropaedia* reorganized so that, for example, all the major articles on various forms of transportation—ancient and modern; land, sea, and air—were incorporated into a single superarticle, "Transportation." Moreover, a serious effort was made to remove statistical tables from the text volumes and present them in a *World Data Annual*.

The fourteenth, during its long "run," found its way into virtually every library of any size in the United States, and many thousands of mostly late printings of the edition can still be consulted there, often alongside the fifteenth.

Encyclopaedia Britannica as a publishing enterprise was preceded to North America by *Encyclopedia Americana,* first published in 1903, although its roots can be traced, via an earlier *Americana* (1833–c. 1860), to a translation from the German of the seventh edition of *Konversations-lexikon.* The twentieth-century *Americana* was created under the direction of Frederick C. Beach, who had been editor of *Scientific American.* It was revised partially from time to time until 1918–20, when a complete revision was carried out, and the encyclopedia has been maintained in a generally current condition since then by reprinting annually to accommodate necessary updating and revisions. Mandated by the same accumulation of great events that moved the *Britannica* to its fifteenth edition, the *Americana* completed a major overhaul in 1967 and continues its annual revision. One of its strengths is its coverage of U.S. cities and towns.

Funk & Wagnalls bought a 1930 casualty of the Great Depression, the outstanding *New International Encyclopaedia,* which stayed out of print for decades. Eventually it was revised, and in 1971 a major revision and updating program was launched and sustained with a heavy annual revision effort. The combined effort reinstated the *New International* to the ranks of modern general encyclopedias (and about the least costly of the lot).

The *Lincoln Library of Essential Information* is a respected single-volume encyclopedia first published in 1924. (It has appeared at various times in two volumes.) The *Lincoln Library* is organized topically instead of alphabetically, and it has the excellent alphabetical index that such organization demands.

Another outstanding single-volume work is the *Columbia Encyclopedia,* which first appeared in 1935 under the auspices of Columbia University Press. Its relatively compact entries number some fifty thousand in the fourth edition, published in 1975 with more than three thousand pages.

Three new general encyclopedias have been introduced in the United States since midcentury. The first of these was *Collier's Encyclopedia,* built on the pattern of the *Britannica*'s fourteenth edition. *Collier's* articles are clearly written in popular style but less detailed and comprehensive than in either the *Britannica* or the *Americana. Collier's* first edition was complete in 1951, and it began both continuous revision and annual updating volumes at the start. It is published by Macmillan Educational Corporation.

Random House produced an encyclopedia of its own in 1977, a bulky one-volume work of 2,856 pages aimed at a general and family audience. It adapted the dichotomy between long general articles and concise ones on narrower topics reflected in the *Britannica* fifteenth. It also adapted, like *Britannica*, the "pedia" terminology, styling its color-illustrated large-article section the "Colorpedia" and the concise-articles portion the "Alphapedia"; *Britannica* uses *Macropaedia* for its seventeen volumes of large articles (some book-length) and *Micropaedia* for the twelve-volume section of concise entries.

A new multivolume English-language set was brought out in the United States in 1980 by Aretê, a Dutch publishing group, and was later acquired by Grolier, the publisher of the *Americana*. Called the *Academic American Encyclopedia*, its twenty-one volumes and copious color illustrations are aimed at an audience less demanding than the *Britannica*'s and more demanding than that of the juvenile encyclopedias (described later). The articles are relatively concise, and they reflect a high degree of accuracy. It is revised annually.

Chambers's Encyclopaedia, not to be confused with the eighteenth-century *Cyclopaedia* of Ephraim Chambers, is a popular, multivolume English work that first appeared in 1850–68. It is listed here because it is found in many U.S. libraries. It has been partially revised from time to time, and substantially so in 1950. A modest revision was completed in 1973.

Juvenile Encyclopedias

This term is used by the American Library Association in its evaluation and description of reference works to distinguish encyclopedias intended for a younger audience from those clearly intended for older students and adults. This characterization is fair enough but ironically it segregates what is probably the most widely sold encyclopedia in the world from most of its competition, the adult encyclopedias named earlier.

World Book Encyclopedia first appeared in 1917–18 and is revised continuously. It is a twenty-two-volume set with about ten million words, written at a level to enable schoolchildren in the upper elementary grades to use it effectively. Its organization and general treatment resemble those of the basic adult encyclopedias, and its articles meet a high standard of accuracy. It is not "written down" to the elementary-school level, however, and it functions as a family encyclopedia quite successfully wherever there is no adult demand for greater depth. An annual updating supplement is available, and it has been revised annually since 1925.

Compton's Encyclopedia, originally *Compton's Pictured Encyclopedia,* was first published in 1922 for readers in upper elementary grades and in high school. It is a generally excellent work that is annually revised. However, extended periods of very light revision have given various printings stretches of staleness. One of its strong points is a "fact index" that presents with each index entry a capsule of information that often can answer a user's question before he or she turns to the major article itself. Bursts of catching up centering on 1972 and again in the mid-1980s have restored its competitive edge. In its early years, *Compton's* is said to have devised a highly effective if not entirely scrupulous sales method later adopted with enormous success by *World Book:* using a part-time sales force of schoolteachers calling on the parents of their students. *Compton's* is owned (since 1960) by *Britannica,* and in that company's line it fills and upgrades the function long served by the now defunct *Britannica Junior Encyclopedia.*

Encyclopedia International is a high-school-level encyclopedia of high quality introduced in 1963–64 by Grolier, publisher of *Americana.* It is revised continuously.

Macmillan publishes the *Merit Students Encyclopedia,* an outstanding work aimed squarely at fifth- to twelfth-grade students. It seeks to present articles written at the reading level of the grades in which corresponding subjects are taught. It first appeared in 1967.

Note that all the juvenile encyclopedias discussed here feature guides to the pronunciation of difficult or unusual words, a useful reader service disdained by most adult encyclopedias. Note the features of adult and juvenile or young adult encyclopedias indicated in the following tables:

ADULT ENCYCLOPEDIAS

Encyclopedia	Volumes	Pages	Words	Articles	Revision Scheme	Last Major Revision
Academic American	21	9,700	9 mil.	28,500	annual	new
Americana	30	27,000	31 mil.	53,500	continuous	1967
Brtiannica 14th	24	28,700	37 mil.	33,500	annual	1968
Britannica 15th	33[1]	32,000	44.5 mil.	61,700	annual	1985[2]
Chambers's	15	12,600	14.5 mil.	28,000	occasional	1950
Collier's	24	19,000	21 mil.	25,000	continuous	——
Columbia	1	3,000	6.6 mil.	50,000	4th ed.	1975
Funk & Wagnalls	29	13,000	9 mil.	25,000	annual	1983
Lincoln[3]	1[4]	2,500	3.5 mil.	25,000	biennial	1978

Annual Supplement	Alphabetized by	Guide to Pronunciation	Illustrations
no	word	frequent	15,000
yes	word	frequent	21,500
yes	letter	no	22,700
yes	word[5]	no	9,100
no	letter	no	4,900
yes	letter	yes	17,000
no	letter	frequent	0
yes	letter	no	7,500
no	topical	no	1,200

[1] The thirty-third volume is the *Britannica World Data Annual.*
[2] Restructured and *Micropaedia* revised in 1985; major *Macropaedia* revision, 1985–89.
[3] Organization is topical.
[4] Sometimes issued in two volumes.
[5] Alphabetized by letter, 1974–84; by word from 1985.

JUVENILE OR YOUNG ADULT ENCYCLOPEDIAS

Encyclopedia	Vol-umes	Pages	Words	Articles	Revision Scheme	Last Major Revision
Compton's	26[1]	11,000	8.6 mil	10,000	annual	1983–87
International	20	12,000	9.5 mil	30,000	annual	——
Merit	20	12,000	9 mil.	22,000	annual	——
World Book	22	14,300	10 mil.	20,000	annual	constant

Annual Supplement	Alphabetized by	Guide to Pronunciation	Illustrations
yes	letter	frequent	28,300
yes[2]	letter	frequent	12,800
yes[3]	letter	yes	19,200
yes	word	frequent	29,500[4]

[1] Has varied from year to year.
[2] Not related directly to the encyclopedia.
[3] Not related directly to the encyclopedia.
[4] Many large and in rich color.

Up-to-dateness

The purchaser of an encyclopedia is peculiarly vulnerable to the rush of events in the sciences, technology, and world politics. After an outlay of many hundreds of dollars, no one enjoys the prospect of seeing that investment degraded by cosmic events that revolutionize several fields of study in one fell swoop. However, until encyclopedias are not only generally available but also generally consulted via computer terminals, that problem will smite the purchaser of any encyclopedia.

By the time a new encyclopedia is off the press, virtually all of it is out of date by at least a year or two, and it is obviously never going to be as current as the evening news. Encyclopedias are not designed to be consulted for yesterday's stock prices and sports scores—except if yesterday is defined as yesteryear, *i.e.,* history. But great events, whether in world politics or the scientific laboratory, create a problem for both makers and users of encyclopedias. The ability to isolate and manipulate RNA and DNA, for example, revolutionized biology, physiology, medicine, and a lot more, and almost instantly converted many truths to untruths and unknown things to known.

There are two approaches to relieving this kind of problem, and the publisher of *Encyclopedia Americana* was a twentieth-century pioneer at addressing both. Publishers of encyclopedias are often criticized for their relatively high-pressure sales methods, but only a high volume of sales will move enough sets to make reprinting annually economically supportable. And only annual reprinting makes possible annual updating, correction of errors, elimination of obsolete articles, and replacement of badly outmoded articles with new ones. This fact was identified early by *Americana*. (For discussions of yearbooks and computer access *see* in Chapters 3 and 4, respectively.) *Americana* also introduced annual updating supplements decades before its major competitors.

As long as the facts on which an encyclopedia article is founded remain facts, as long as widely perceived truths that inform it remain true, or at least uncontroverted, that article will continue to serve the reader at least fairly well, even while it ignores later developments that may pertain to it. But as soon as the central assumptions of an article are no longer entirely valid it becomes dangerous, a source of misinformation, or at best a source of incomplete information.

Encyclopedia editors and salespersons are subjected to a lot of windy rhetoric about the splendors of past editions. *Britannica*'s eleventh is a major object of such extravagant admiration. It is perfectly true that the eleventh's biographies were excellent and often elegant and that the writing in the whole edition was of as high quality as one can find—in 1911. That edition is still extremely useful for the serious researcher into, especially, the biographies. But the fact remains that its literary excellence is couched in the style of the turn of the century. For all the astute editorial judgment that went into assigning and editing the glorious biographies—"*Britannica*'s crown and glory," a former editor in chief called them—their length was assigned on the basis of their importance to the world of Edward VII and President McKinley.

The remarkable quality of the scholarship reflected in the ninth makes that 1875–89 edition invaluable for kinds of research where timeliness is unimportant. Its articles were long and comprehensive monographs, considering all the aspects of major topics. However, the language of the ninth is that of Victorian England, and it is certainly no place to turn for answering ordinary questions, and especially so for young readers.

Datedness of style and perspective by no means disables the articles in these classic editions, but their value to modern readers is no longer that of an encyclopedia biography, which encapsulates the life of the subject and puts him or her in perspective. That value becomes something different, attractive to the antiquarian, a potential gold mine for the trivia buff, and a source for the perspective of their own time on yesterday's great men—and a tiny sprinkling of women.

Tips for Getting the Most Out of an Encyclopedia

First, don't try to make the encyclopedia work on your terms. You can get some information out of it that way, but if you are looking for anything a bit out of the ordinary you will avoid endless frustration by doing it the editors' way. This can be figured out easily from the prefatory matter in any encyclopedia discussed here. Pay heed to alphabetization and all the other matters discussed in Chapter 1, perhaps especially in the discussion of indexing, inversion of titles, and proper names starting on page 22.

The encyclopedia you are consulting will demonstrate quickly, even if it does not tell you outright, how it transliterates foreign names into English spelling. The systems for Chinese and Japanese are discussed in the preceding chapter. They are perhaps more orderly than those for handling Arabic, and for that matter Hebrew. Vowels play a minor role in both languages, and some vowels are little more than suggested by diacritical marks. In the case of Hebrew, publishers are divided on whether to transliterate the sound for the *ch* in the German and English word *ach* as *h* (*hutzpah*, for example) or *ch* (*chutzpah*), and there are other problems.

Arabic, having only three vowels (long and short *a*, *i*, and *u*) and twenty-eight consonants (three of which are sometimes used as vowel forms), leaves abundant room for confusion in transliterating. Linguists render the Prophet's name in English as Muhammad. But the English conventional spelling has long been Mohammed, and this still is widely used today. (It is one of those survivals from Empire, reflecting that casual British arrogance willing to take the most careless potshot at pronouncing a foreign name—*e.g.*, pee-king instead of bay-jing for Beijing, bu-loin instead of bu-lawn-ya for Boulogne, Jordan for al-Urdunn.) The Muhammad problem is compounded by the fact that many Ottoman rulers were named for the Prophet but in Turkish it is spelled (as always, depending on who is transliterating) Mahmud, Mahmut, Mehmed, or Mehmet.

Spelling the name of the Libyan ruler in the 1970s and 1980s offers even more variations. Muammur or Moammur Qadafi, Qaddafi, Qadhafi, Qadafy, Qaddafy, and Qadhafy all can be found in print, as well as the same set of variations with the initial letters *K* and *Kh*, not to mention *G*.

Under certain conditions the Arabic article usually represented in English as *al*, or sometimes *el*, meaning "the," elides its consonant and adopts the first sound of the following word, which it modifies. This occurs whenever that following word begins with one of the thirteen "sun letters" of Arabic (*t, th, d, dh, r, z, s, sh, ṣ, ḍ, ṭ, ẓ,* and *n*. It's *al* before any other sound (as in al-Urdunn above), but ad-Din, ar-Rahman, as-Sadat, etc. Most newspapers and magazines and some encyclopedias simply use *al* (or *el*) in all circumstances. Some encyclopedias modify the letter correctly but use *e* for the vowel sound, coming up with el-Urdunn, ed-Din, er-Rahman, es-Sadat, etc.

To make matters worse, alphabetizing practice varies. Egyptian statesman Anwar as-Sadat might be listed in any of the following ways, depending on where you look him up:

al-Sadat, Anwar	Sadat, Anwar al-
as-Sadat, Anwar	Sadat, Anwar as-
el-Sadat, Anwar	Sadat, Anwar el-
es-Sadat, Anwar	Sadat, Anwar es-

The point, of course, is to persist. And as soon as you have found where the man is hidden in a particular reference work, you have broken the code for that work, and you will know exactly how to proceed the next time you look up an Arabic word or name in it.

But alas! Encyclopedia editors, who strive mightily—perhaps harder than anyone else—to be consistent, sometimes fail. So if you can't find it by the rules of alphabetizing and transliterating that you have correctly deciphered, try the variations: Ring the changes as above in the case of Sadat, and your lost word may turn up misfiled, as it were.

A common problem encountered by encyclopedia users has to

do with the way kings and queens, emperors, and that lot are handled by encyclopedists. There is a convention of long standing that is virtually always honored by encyclopedists that rulers' names will be entered in the native language of the encyclopedia—in our case, English. Thus King Carlos III is Charles III. Guillaume and Wilhelm are William, Luigi is Louis, Juan is John, and so on. But just to keep you on your toes, exceptions to this rule are usually made for living monarchs—*e.g.*, Juan Carlos of Spain.

If encyclopedists' conventions can create problems for the innocent reader, so can their idiosyncrasies. The titles articles bear often reflect a commitment to scientific accuracy, a passion to educate the reader by forcing him or her to the dictionary to decode some obscure term, a simpleminded reliance on the jargon used in a particular academic discipline and its publications, or sometimes a deliberate effort to prevent an article from resembling too strongly an entry on the topic in another reference work that has been a source for the present article.

Lest this last point seem somehow unsavory, let it be noted that every reference publisher consults, and not infrequently, works of others in the field, and properly so. One of a reference work's prime responsibilities is to make facts and information accessible, and facts and information are not copyrightable. A birth date, the tonnage of wheat exports in a given year, the magnitude of an earthquake, and similar bits and pieces of information are fair game to everyone interested.

But encyclopedists need to fill holes in their own products from time to time—holes that have come to light through inspection by staff members, queries or complaints from subscribers, new developments between revisions, and the like. A first place to turn at such a moment is to other encyclopedias. And when noting facts— for example from a biographic sketch in encyclopedia X—it is all too easy for a writer, and perhaps especially a free-lancer whose pay for such work may be less than ten dollars for a hundred-word entry, to take down some of the connective tissue as well as the salient facts themselves. Most encyclopedias require writers to use multiple sources and to list them, but not all subeditors check all the sources. When one does and occasionally finds a disturbing correspondence between "our" article and the one in brand X, the easiest solution may to be hit the synonym trail and try to disguise the connection.

Probably excessive reliance on the majesty of scientific jargon is the major offender of offbeat titles, however. Examples are "micturition" instead of a straightforward "urination," "integument" for "skin," "lagomorphs" for "rabbits and hares," "lusophone" for "Portuguese-speaking," etc. This is not to assail the propriety of scientific terminology in a scientific work, for each of the arcane forms cited above may be defended as precise and valuable to clarity—among scholars. But the purpose of a general encyclopedia is to inform the lay reader, or the scholar, about disciplines outside his own.

In any case, the point for the encyclopedia user confronted with this kind of jargon in article titles is to know how to find the desired article regardless of how it is titled. Standard practice requires the encyclopedia editor to supply a title cross-reference at every plausible location, as, for instance:

HARE: *see* under Lagomorphs,
and
RABBIT: *see* under Lagomorphs

When, as does happen now and then, the cross-reference is not there, the article has become one of those hidden treasures that prompt the reader to throw down the book in helpless anger. But the anger, thoroughly justified, need not be helpless. Build your own synonym list, and work down it until you find the right one.

Among the irritating conventions of encyclopedias is one that excludes considerable personal detail from biographies. A famous person's marriage or marriages and divorce or divorces are not listed unless the marriage or divorce played an extremely significant role in the subject's career. Ditto extramarital liaisons, venereal diseases, illegitimate children, and homosexuality. One must usually turn to biographical encyclopedias (Chapter 5) or periodical indexes (Chapter 21) to ferret out such information even in many cases in which the scandalous aspect shaped the person's character or affected his or her career.

Nearly all encyclopedias urge their users to begin their search at the index, and that assuredly is where your quest down a synonym list should start, simply because in a multivolume encyclopedia the logistics involved in running down a roster of potential titles at a variety of alphabetical points is just too frustrating. Chase your list of terms down the index, which will clearly distinguish article titles from mere subjects treated (usually by printing the titles in capital letters or small caps or in boldface).

Turning from volume to volume may be frustrating if you're

looking vainly for a title that "just isn't there," but under different circumstances it can be a lot of fun. Browsing. It can be either an unalloyed pleasure or a real thief of time, depending on your turn of mind and the urgency of completing the task that sent you to the encyclopedia in the first place.

If you enjoy browsing, you may be either a serial or a topical browser. The former looks up an article and keeps going down the page and from one entry to the next. A surprising number of people do that, reading encyclopedias from A to Z. Every editor has at least one correspondent who started reading the current edition when it first appeared and is working through the set, sending along periodic notes drawing attention to errors.

The serial browser discovers that the alphabetical order of most encyclopedias carries with it infinite surprises of serendipity, irony, curious coincidence, variety, and a miser's hoard of trivia. The topical browser, on the other hand, can become quite well educated in any number of subjects. One approach to topical browsing is that of the *q.v.* junkie, who starts at one article and goes wherever the *q.v.*s beckon. The other is a systematic one: to follow the reading plan or study guide supplied with several encyclopedias (and built into the *Britannica* with its *Propaedia*). A useful tip if you are a *q.v.* junkie is to put each volume back in the shelf as you move on to another; if you don't after an hour's browse you will be surrounded by a jumble of volumes that will take a half hour to sort. And if you are an inveterate browser who finds it too easy to get lost in the text: When you are in a hurry, set a timer with a loud buzzer.

If not, browse on to the next chapter.

CHAPTER 3

ANNUALS AND SPECIAL AND SUPPLEMENTARY REFERENCE WORKS

Three kinds of reference book are considered here, along with a small mixed bag of odds and ends that fits as well here as anywhere else. These are:

Updating books intended to bring or keep you up to date on facts, events, or other knowledge. They include:

- encyclopedia annuals
- general almanacs
- compendiums of current events
- records of government proceedings
- indexes to newspapers and magazines
- books of general records, trivia, lists, etc.

Books about words and language. Among these are:

- collections of quotations
- joke books
- dictionaries of word or phrase origins
- dictionaries of slang, Americanisms, etc.

63

- rhyming and crossword puzzle dictionaries

- thesauruses and dictionaries of synonyms and antonyms

- dictionaries of abbreviations and symbols

- manuals of style and usage

Books to help you use foreign reference works, specifically English–foreign-language dictionaries, with tips on using foreign-language encyclopedias.

Numerous books that could fit in the first category are treated elsewhere. Examples include annual biographical dictionaries and directories (Chapter 5), detailed sporting records (Chapter 19), proceedings of professional associations (Chapter 7), and books about books (Chapter 21).

ENCYCLOPEDIA ANNUALS

The most tyrannical problem for any general encyclopedia is keeping its contents up-to-date. Since the eighteenth century, as soon as the last volume was finished, the first was out of date. Publishers found it necessary to issue supplementary volumes from time to time in an effort to update the whole set, and supplementary volumes would be added to the last edition so that whole could be sold as a new edition.

The *New American Cyclopaedia* was issued in sixteen volumes between 1858 and 1863, but a year before it was complete its publishers began a yearly updating supplement titled *American Annual Cyclopaedia.* It continued until 1874, when it was taken on by Appleton and published as *Appleton's Annual Cyclopaedia* until 1902, long after the encyclopedia it "updated" had gone out of print. These annuals remain, in the libraries that still hold them, invaluable sources of information and perspective about the whole second half of the nineteenth century in America. A great American reference work, the *New International Encyclopaedia,* was brought out at the turn of the century by Dodd, Mead, which also issued the *International Year Book* as an updating device. When the encyclopedia fell prey to the Great Depression, Funk & Wagnalls bought rights to the set and continued to publish the annual, under the name *New International Year Book.* The encyclopedia was re-created in 1971 but neither it nor the yearbook is any longer in print.

In 1922, five years after the first appearance of its encyclopedia, World Book introduced its *Annual Supplement,* a rather slight paperback meant to be bound with others into a single volume covering several years. Each supplement did its "updating" in several hundred alphabetically organized articles on important topics, places, etc., and included a chronology, a list of obituaries, and many illustrations. In 1962 this was enlarged into the much larger, hard-cover *World Book Year Book* that is familiar today.

The next year (1923), the *Americana Annual* was introduced, in hard-cover and designed to resemble in size and appearance a volume of the encyclopedia itself. Its organization and scope reflected that of the encyclopedia, and it set the general pattern for competing products that emerged over the next two decades, including the enlarged *World Book Year Book.*

Britannica brought out a *Britannica Year Book* that was intended to be an annual in 1913, but that volume was not followed up. It produced a two-volume roundup of the post–World War I world as *These Eventful Years* in 1924, but the company did not actually get into the yearbook business until 1938, when its fourteenth edition was nearly ten years old. It followed the standard format of alphabetically organized topics, each reporting on the past year's major developments in that place or field, plus biographies (and obituaries) of people important during the year.

Gradually a trend developed toward several feature articles of considerable length in the front of a yearbook, meant to elaborate or shed light on important currents in world and national affairs. Special reports began to appear among major subjects in the alphabetical year-in-review sections, variously covering suddenly important subjects not included in the regular alphabetical string, supplying needed background or amplification to certain articles, etc.

The longer an encyclopedia follows a continuous revision policy, the greater the patchwork character of its articles and title list and the less effective the actual updating performed by its yearbook. All yearbooks update by recording major events of the past year, but to a large extent one is as good as another, and often a general almanac (*q.v.*) will serve as well. Having article titles in the yearbook conform to those in the encyclopedia is of some, but limited, benefit.

A number of publishers create "generic" versions of their own encyclopedia yearbooks, which are then made available to other publishers. Among these are Grolier, Macmillan, and Britannica.

World Book and Britannica have developed other yearbooks focused on science and on medicine and health, and Britannica even created a yearbook, *Great Ideas Today,* for subscribers to its set of classics, *Great Books of the Western World.*

The basic formula for encyclopedia annuals has been ubiquitous among publishers, and only two significant variations have occurred in nearly fifty years. When it adopted its new hard-cover format in 1962, World Book began publishing in each *Year Book* several new articles that appeared for the first time that year in the encyclopedia itself. This practice was adopted by Britannica in the 1970s.

In 1985, to coincide with a major encyclopedia revision, that publisher totally reorganized its yearbook and in effect made it a part of the set. So far as possible, all volatile statistical tables and charts were removed from the *Macropaedia* portion of the set and relocated in the annual, now renamed *Britannica World Data Annual.* The move doubled the size of the yearbook, whose familiar alphabetical arrangement of the year-in-review portion was revised to reflect the titles of the revised encyclopedia, and cross-references were introduced from articles in the set to those in the yearbook and vice versa. These changes greatly increased the utility of the yearbook and its correspondence to the encyclopedia.

All encyclopedia annuals have indexes, and the most substantial of them cover several years of the annual, usually from three to ten. Consulting the index is important in any reference work, but especially so in these yearbooks, and first of all see the explanatory box at the head of the index for its particular rules and for the roles it assigns to the various typefaces it uses. An index reference to an article in a previous edition of the yearbook usually will refer the reader to that volume by year, usually by the year's last two digits.

For example, in a 1986 yearbook ("covering events of 1985," as it is sure to say somewhere on the title page), suppose you want to look up the obituary of a celebrated American cook and cookbook author. Here is what you may find:

Beard, James A., obituary, 121

or

Beard, James A., see Obituaries

or

Beard, James A., see Obituaries 86

The first line tells you the article is an obituary and sends you to the page. The second sends you to the obituaries section in the volume you have in hand. The third refers you to the obituaries section in the 1986 volume. But many readers assume the 86 is a page number even though it appears in boldface type and most other numbers on the index page are in lightface. Until you are familiar enough with the index you are using you will be well served to start with the key, instead of waiting until you have already found yourself up a blind alley.

This problem is exaggerated a few years after the death (or whatever event or topic you are seeking). In the case of James Beard, a 1990 index would continue to say "*see* Obituaries 86." The reader turning to page 86 of the 1990 yearbook would be in even worse shape because even if the obituaries happened to be there, he would not find Beard's in the 1990 volume.

GENERAL ALMANACS

The term "almanac" came out of Arabic in the Middle Ages: *al-manakh.* Its original meaning, camels' kneeling place, evolved into camping place, then weather at a campsite, and finally just weather. Star positions were recorded for the days and weeks of the year at a particular place, and from them weather could be projected. Travelers brought the word to the West, where to its calendar framework of astronomy and meteorology was added lore, folk wisdom, and almost anything else.

By the seventeenth century popular almanacs developed in England, and in 1732 Benjamin Franklin patterned his *Poor Richard's Almanack* to some extent on a British model. By the time Robert Baily Thomas launched, in 1793, what became the *Old Farmer's Almanack,* the recipe included all manner of statistical information interspersed with important dates and anniversaries, jokes, health care advice, verse, and more.

A modern general almanac contains an enormous volume and variety of economic, geographic, political, demographic, and other data. Its astronomical roots are not forgotten: Main celestial events of the coming year are listed, along with tables showing star positions throughout the year. A multipage calendar gives sunrise and sunset (and often moonrise and moonset) times day by day for the coming year at each of several latitudes.

There are thumbnail sketches of nations, states, and cities, and thumbnail biographies of political leaders. There are election returns, lists of rulers, political officeholders, vote counts, state capitals, and county seats. Important documents in national history are reprinted, and fairly long sections on world and national history are usually included.

A chronology of the preceding year provides solid, concise summaries of its major events. Outstanding performances and records in major sports are presented; so are world disasters, big lottery winners, and popular and electoral vote counts back to George Washington. The prime focus is on the previous year, but most of the statistical data and many other categories are supplied in tables with ten or twenty prior years for perspective.

Special features, analytical articles on events of extraordinary importance, and various surprises crop up here and there, and a perpetual-calendar section enables you to calculate the day of the week for past and future dates. A busy person with a browser's mentality is at mortal peril on entering such a book with a little time to spare; it is as seductive as an encyclopedia.

The major U.S. almanacs are three, led by the oldest and frequent best seller, *The World Almanac and Book of Facts,* published continuously (except for 1884) since 1868. Its most recent editions have 928 pages, and it is sold popularly in paperback and in hardcover to institutions such as libraries.

The others are the *Information Please Almanac, Atlas and Yearbook* (1947) and the *Reader's Digest Almanac and Yearbook* (1966). All three maintain a high degree of accuracy, comprehensiveness, and accessibility, and their organization schemes are both sound and readily apparent.

There are two British almanacs worth noting that may fall under the ken of American readers. One is *Whitaker's Almanack,* which was established in 1868, the same year as the American *World Almanac*—with which it can be used very well in tandem. *Whitaker's* has two versions, the smaller of which is rather sharply focused on the United Kingdom.

The other, the *Complete Edition,* is, at 1,220 pages, about twice the size (and price) of the U.K. model. It covers the entire British Commonwealth and all significant developments in the rest of the world. It starts out with an index of eighty pages—about half of which contain advertising—and an astronomical almanac for the year for London and six other U.K. cities. In addition to statistics and politico-economic detail in abundance it lists and describes major legislation enacted by Parliament, and it abounds in information about the royal family, the peerage, the constituencies of the House of Commons, and much, much else.

Publication of the second principal British almanac was started in 1897 as a promotional device for Pears Soap. The *Pears Cyclopaedia* opens its ninety-first edition (after a one-page table of contents) with a fifty-three-page "Chronicle of Events" from the origin of Earth (4,600,000,000 B.C.) to May 1, 1982, and the British recapture of the Falkland Islands. It closes with an excellent index. Between are twenty-six lettered sections titled "Prominent People," "Public Affairs," "Political Compendium," "Music," "Science," "Economic Events," etc., to "Cinema" and "Collecting Antiques." As this implies, the work is something of a combination—an extremely concise, topically organized one-volume encyclopedia with the addition of a great deal of recent statistical data, plus careful analysis of both recent and less recent political, economic, and scientific developments, and more.

Almanac or Yearbook?

This question arises: Is a good general almanac as useful as a good encyclopedia yearbook? Yes and no. Yes if you are seeking facts, numbers, very specific bits of fairly recent information. After all, a representative almanac is half the size, a third of the weight, and a quarter of the cost of most encyclopedia annuals.

The encyclopedia yearbook clearly wins if you want any substantial information about last year's coup in country X, including its impact on neighboring countries, military allies, and trade with the United States. If you want no more than two hundred or so words on a catastrophic Mexican earthquake, an almanac will do. For three or four times as much depth, turn to the yearbook.

In one sense an almanac is handier than a yearbook if you are seeking some kernel of historical fact. For example, if you merely want the dates (1864–67) of the French-supported Austrian archduke's reign over Mexico as Emperor Maximilian I, you may be able to ferret them out of an annual if you have its organization pretty well figured out. An encyclopedia yearbook gives you no help at all—unless you happen to luck into an anniversary account. For substantive information on the luckless Maximilian, you will have to turn to the encyclopedia, or a biographic or historical source (*see* Chapters 5 and 8, respectively).

The foregoing Mexican adventure brings up the subject of indexes. All almanacs are fairly well indexed; the remarkable bulk and mix of their contents require it. But no index can contain every interesting snippet buried in such a book. The 1986 *World Almanac*, for instance, has a couple of lines on Maximilian but no index entry, since his situation was so freaky.

You won't find "history" listed under "Mexico" in the index. But if you know that this almanac's basic articles about the countries of the world include a few hundred words of historical review (most do), you will turn there. But how do you know which "Mexico" article to turn to when the index offers you pages 488, 495, 583–584, 899, and 902? You deduce it, correctly surmising that the only article spread over two pages (583–584) is the longest and is apt to be the basic country article, where the history will reside. If you guess wrong, fall back on trial and error.

The *World Almanac* carries its long and generally excellent index at the front of the book. It is organized alphabetically (word by word) by major topic; for example:

Actors, actresses. 393–409
Deceased 404–408
Emmy Awards 33, 355
Films, 1984–85. 360

And so on. It recently added a back page of quick reference index listings of major categories covered, ranging from Abbreviations, State (Postal), to ZIP codes. The *Information Please Almanac* is even more accessible, with both a well-organized topical table of contents and an excellent index.

Books of records and of lists of various sorts comprise another kind of special reference work, falling somewhere between almanacs and indexes. The *Guinness Book of World Records,* the leader in this field, came into existence as a promotional device under the auspices of the brewers of Guinness Stout, by whom it was intended to settle arguments in pubs. It lists records of virtually everything that can be weighed, measured, or counted; indeed, a former title was the *Guinness Book of Superlatives*. Other collections of oddities and trivia include the titles churned out by the Irving Wallace family beginning with *The Book of Lists*. Other books of trivia and general information have proliferated, and several such titles can be found tucked into any library's reference section.

A valuable tool for finding what reference works treat what subject is the *Guide to Reference Books,* published by the American Library Association. It can be found in the reference section of virtually every library—or at the librarian's desk. This work is discussed further in Chapter 21. Important dates in history and various records of sporting events are treated in chapters 8 and 19, respectively.

CURRENT EVENTS

A reliable compendium of current events kept relentlessly up-to-date is indispensable to people whose livings depend on being able to find or verify facts fast. Since 1940 the most widely used U.S. service to meet such needs has been *Facts on File*. Actually, the service is a weekly pamphlet of concise summaries of developments in a wide range of fields, from world affairs to sports and the arts. Each page is a grid, with numbered meridians and lettered latitude markers, so the index can send the reader at once to that column inch on the page where the desired information lurks.

The weekly pamphlets are accumulated in a looseleaf binder. Every second week an index comes with the pamphlet, and once a month a cumulative index appears. Quarterly and annual cumulative indexes also appear on schedule, and the simplicity of the scheme coupled with its breadth of coverage make it extremely effective and easy to use. Its accuracy is famous. It is widely held in the better public and school libraries. Facts on File's orientation is to the United States, but its coverage is worldwide.

A quite similar service is the British *Keesing's Contemporary Archives*, which is a few years older than *Facts on File*. Understandably enough, Keesing's has a British point of view but its coverage is also worldwide.

For anyone whose professional or avocational interest is U.S. national government and politics, an indispensable tool is the *Congressional Quarterly (CQ) Weekly Report*, founded in 1947 by Nelson and Harriett Poynter. Its coverage of congressional floor, committee, and behind-the-scenes activity is assiduous. Its reports and analyses of congressional interactions with the executive and judicial branches of the U.S. government, as well as the political parties, and its lucid interpretations of the sometimes byzantine complexity of the U.S. legislative process have made it must reading in every American newsroom. It is available in most libraries, and each weekly issue contains a table of contents and an index.

Other privately published periodicals cover Congress and other aspects of the national government, and both Prentice-Hall and

Commerce Clearing House provide continuing follow-up service on national legislation. Congress itself publishes the *Congressional Record* daily while it is in session. This thick compendium purports to be a record of what is said (and done) in the House and the Senate, and with limitations it is. However, the right for each member to secure "unanimous consent to revise and extend" his or her remarks is so time-honored that as a general rule the *Congressional Record* can only be assumed to be wholly accurate on vote counts and procedural matters beyond the revision privileges of individual members.

Though some members never avail themselves of the privilege, after a heated floor debate with jangled syntax as well as tempers, it is very tempting to a senator or representative to edit what he or she actually said into sentences and add sparkling afterthoughts before the book-length document is printed overnight. For the flavor of the day's proceedings and the gist of what occurred, it can be useful and sometimes fun. Most substantial libraries carry it. An index is prepared periodically, but not all libraries subscribe to it.

Newspapers and newsmagazines also, of course, are records of current events, but their bulk and the degree to which their reportage is interrupted by advertising make poring through them the hard way to look up anything. The most effective way to use newspaper resources in researching anything (apart from computer access; *see* Chapter 4) is through the bound annual indexes of a few major newspapers of record.

For all practical purposes in U.S. libraries this means *The New York Times*, although the bigger and better libraries will also have *The Wall Street Journal* and *The Times* of London. All three indexes are supported by microfilm files of back issues, which in the case of *The New York Times* goes back to its founding in 1851. However, it was not until the early twentieth century that *The New York Times* became the great newspaper of record it is today, and its early files are not widely held. Most good libraries have *The New York Times* on microfilm since World War II.

Even without access to the microfilm files, however, these newspaper indexes are useful reference tools in that approximate dates of events—and deaths, book reviews, theater and film openings, *et al.*—can be located in them, making it possible for you to find coverage of the event in other newspapers or magazines. To use this approach conveniently, you need to know the time of the event within a few years, because the index volumes are cumbersome, but once you find the date of a *New York Times* story you know the event probably occurred on the previous day.

The organization of these indexes is essentially similar and is explained clearly near the front of each. Categories—*e.g.*, Golf, Missiles, and Ships and Shipping—are interspersed along the alphabet among the names of persons, countries, or the key words in major stories, along with lucid cross-references.

All three papers publish indexes for the current year in pamphlet form, usually bimonthly, for accumulation in looseleaf binders, so if you are seeking a story less than a year old you may have to rummage through quite a batch of monthly or quarterly indexes to find it.

Magazines and professional journals rarely publish indexes to their own contents, but there are across-the-board indexes that cover most U.S. periodicals for the twentieth century and with less completeness and convenience the nineteenth as well. The most generally useful of these probably is the *Readers' Guide to Periodical Literature*, published since 1900 by the H. W. Wilson Company.

Readers' Guide covers more than 180 magazines of general interest (including the Sunday magazines of major newspapers). It is issued in semimonthly paperbacks, which are replaced successively by monthly and quarterly issues, also paperbound, each organized alphabetically by subject area and each indexed by article title, author, and a coded passage indicating the magazine's volume number, page, and date of issue. For instance, "136:31 N 18 '85" indicates that the article appears in Volume 136 beginning at page 31 in the issue dated November 18, 1985. An abridged *Readers' Guide* is found in some smaller libraries.

American periodicals of the nineteenth century (1806–1902) are indexed—by subject or title only—in *Poole's Index to Periodical Literature*. The last decade of the century is much more completely indexed in the *Nineteenth Century Readers' Guide to Periodical Literature*, and in 1970 an *Author Index for Poole's* appeared. Although your library may not have it, it is worth asking for, just in case.

The Wilson Company also publishes a variety of specialized periodical guides that normally are available only in college, university, and public libraries. These index journals in the following fields: agriculture (since 1964 biology and agriculture), art (visual arts), business, the humanities, law, science, applied science and technology, and the social sciences. Two additional indexes cover more or less general magazines that *Readers' Guide* does not, and publications of various social and political movements. These are the *Popular Periodical Index* and the *Alternative Press Index.* However, few libraries carry the magazines indexed in them, despite the fact that serious journalism appears in them frequently, as for instance *Playboy* and *Rolling Stone.*

BOOKS ABOUT WORDS AND LANGUAGE

Dictionaries of quotations began to appear in England before the end of the eighteenth century. The first and most famous of that genre in America was published in 1855 by John Bartlett, a clerk and eventually proprietor of the campus bookstore at Harvard University. Bartlett had a natural head for "quotes," and he augmented his memory with an extensive notebook to facilitate answering the unending requests of his patrons for an apt quotation for this situation or that. He finally put the collection in print as *Familiar Quotations,* and after fifteen editions and repeated and extensive expansions and revisions it remains the U.S. standard.

The modern Bartlett's opens with an alphabetical index of authors, followed by their quotations (some 115,000 of them) grouped by author in chronological order, except that quotations from such religious works as the Bible and the Koran appear in a separate following section. The final element is an index of key words occupying a good one third of the 1,800-odd-page volume. It is done with such care that, for example, fourteen of the thirty-five words in the final passage of Emma Lazarus's sonnet at the base of the Statue of Liberty are index entries (italicized in the text below):

> *Give* me your *tired,* your poor,
> Your *huddled masses* yearning to *breathe* free,
> The *wretched refuse* of your *teeming* shore,
> Send these, the *homeless, tempest-tossed,*[1]to me:
> I *lift* my *lamp* beside the door.

Oxford University Press has produced an outstanding rival to Bartlett's in its *Oxford Dictionary of Quotations.* It is a smaller work, of

---

[1]Not "tempest-tost," as in the original.

fewer than fifty thousand quotations, but its range is a bit broader than the Bartlett in foreign quotes, and its indexing is superb. Foreign quotations appear both in the original language and in excellent translations, and the index carries key words in both English and original languages. For its extensive quotations from the Greek classics it has a separate index in Greek. (Latin quotes are incorporated in the main index.) Both indexes locate the quotes by page and item number. The quotations themselves are organized alphabetically by author.

There are numerous other general and specialized works in the field. *Brewer's Dictionary of Phrase and Fable* is good for pre-twentieth-century English literature. Burton Egbert Stevenson has compiled the general *Home Book of Quotations, Classical and Modern,* as well as special-focus works in the *Home Book of* series dealing with the Bible, Shakespeare, and others. There are dictionaries of quotations from American presidents, other politicians, Canadian and other national writers and speakers, Catholics, Jews, business leaders, and so on and on. Look them up in the card catalog at your library under "quotations" in the "Subject" section, or go directly to the books themselves in the reference department (Dewey Decimal System number 016).

A tip to seekers of quotations: It is obvious that you must look in a recent edition for any fairly recent quotation. Much less obvious is that sometimes you have to find an old edition to look up the source and context of an old quote. Every reference work, to make room for new material, is obliged to retire some of the old. Editors try to hang on to the best, or the most likely to be looked up, but something has to give way.

A famous lecturer of the late-19th to early-20th century, Russell H. Conwell, had a standard oration that once every schoolchild was obliged to read if not deliver. You could look up its title—"Acres of Diamonds"—in Bartlett's twelfth edition, but not in the thirteenth. Whenever you are frustrated in finding a famous old line that "just has to be there" but isn't, try an earlier edition.

To a degree, the concordance resembles a quotation dictionary except that it is focused entirely on a single work or body of works instead of an entire literature. A concordance indexes every phrase in a work, or, put another way, every important word within its context. Shakespeare's works are the subject of concordances. Computerized access to a body of text such as an encyclopedia is by means of what in effect is a concordance, for the computer will scan the entire body for the word or phrase you assign it and deliver every instance—unless you (prudently) modify your request to pin it as closely as possible to the exact context you want.

For most readers, the Bible is the most familiar work with which concordances are associated. Here there is a major caveat because of the enormous array of different biblical translations in print. A concordance is keyed to a particular translation. If you are dealing with the King James and want to look up the story of Moses parting the Red Sea for the Children of Israel, fine: You will find several references to the Red Sea cited under the Book of Exodus, and these will take you straight to the story.

But if the Bible you are consulting is the Jewish Publication Society's new translation of the Jewish Bible—known to Christians as the Old Testament—or the New International Version of the Christian Bible, your King James concordance will be a blind guide indeed, because these translations (and some other newer ones) place the episode of the parting waters in the Sea of Reeds.

Match the concordance to the translation you are using and you will have no problem, for a properly matched concordance is marvelously easy to use in that it presents every appearance of the word, arranged sequentially (in the case of the Bible) from (Christian Bible) Genesis to Revelation, each passage with enough context to identify the setting clearly.

"Joke books" represent another variation on the quotation dictionary. They are particularly useful to anyone who, unaccustomed to doing so, has to prepare a speech or function as a toastmaster and needs to find a few anecdotes that are both entertaining and to the point. They will be found among the rest of the genre, usually under titles such as *Speaker's Handbook of Epigrams and Wit*, and often such material will be incorporated in a work of larger purpose—*e.g., The Speechmaker's Complete Handbook*, which includes model speeches for various occasions.

Texts of actual speeches notable for content or style, or with a particular focus, are also collected in book form. Examples include Charles Hurd's *A Treasury of Great American Speeches; Inaugural Addresses of the Presidents* published by the U.S. Government Printing Office; the more general *Speech Index* in various editions; and the even more general *Treasury of the World's Great Speeches*. The periodical *Vital Speeches* publishes noteworthy current speeches biweekly, and has done so since 1934.

Etymological dictionaries deal with the origins of words and phrases. There are etymologies of almost every language on Earth, but here we can confine the scope to the English language and especially its American version. Any good general dictionary, as noted in Chapter 2, supplies some etymological information, though none so well as the *OED*. Frederick Bodmer's *The Loom of Language* from the 1940s is an excellent general etymology that treats English in the context of world languages.

H. L. Mencken's *The American Language*, edited for decades after his death by Raven I. McDavid, is an excellent, broad, and authoritative work on Americanisms and their origins. A massive project is under way, albeit at a snail's pace, in the *Dictionary of American Regional English*, usually known as *DARE*, whose first volume, covering A–C, was produced in 1985 under the editorship of Frederick G. Cassidy. Apparently this will be a long time coming but worth the wait.

Dictionaries of slang are somewhat similar to the regional-language case. Outstanding in this field is Eric Partridge's *A Dictionary of Slang and Unconventional English*, revised by his colleague Paul Beale. Considerably squarer are Mitford M. Mathews's *A Dictionary of Americanisms on Historical Principles* (1946) and *A Dictionary of American English on Historical Principles* (edited) by Sir William Craigie and James R. Hulbert (1936–44); much newer (1975) is Harold Wentworth and Stuart Berg Flexner's *Dictionary of American Slang*. Others are *Dictionary of Afro-American Slang* by Clarence Major (1970) and *Dictionary of Contemporary Slang* compiled by Jonathan Green (1984, 1985). Browsing through the section in your library will pay dividends; you will find your own favorites.

In 1805, after several years in pursuit of an avocational idea, the English physician and philologist Peter Mark Roget (1779–1869) completed a small compendium of key words and their synonyms organized by the ideas they represented. Near the end of his busy career, Dr. Roget, upon his retirement as secretary of the Royal Society, at last found time to complete and publish a greatly expanded version of that early work, under the title *Thesaurus of English Words and Phrases* (1852).

This work was updated and revised for many years by the author's son and grandson and, having long since passed into the public domain, its basic plan and content have been massaged by various revisers into alphabetical order in dictionary form and various other ways. One of the most useful of these adaptations has been the expansion of the index, begun by John Roget in 1879. Most versions preserve Roget's approach, grouping synonyms under subject headings and differentiating carefully among various nuanced connotations. Each class of ideas—*e.g.,* "Intellect"—embraces subdivisions, such as "Intellectual Faculties," where key words ("intelligence") and their synonyms appear, with an appropriate set of antonyms nearby.

Other approaches to a dictionary of synonyms and antonyms exist, of course. A case in point is *Webster's New Dictionary of Synonyms* (Merriam). Its structure is like that of a conventional dictionary, setting down synonyms, analogous terms, and antonyms. Most lexicographic publishers have variations of their own. There also is an *Encyclopedia of Homonyms, "Sound-alikes": The Only Complete Comprehensive Collection of "Sound-alike" Words Ever Published; a Reference Book for Everyone* by Dora Newhouse (1976).

Another variation on the basic dictionary is one listing rhyming sounds. There are several versions of this, most of them following one basic method: organization by number of syllables in the rhyming word, and alphabetically within each grouping. Monosyllabic, bisyllabic, and trisyllabic rhymes are covered. Typically, the single-syllable entries range from long *a* as in *affray, agley,* and *allay* to long *u* with a *zh* sound, as in *rouge* and *Bruges.* Bisyllables run from *A'al* as in *betrayal* and *defrayal* to *u'zur,* as in *transfuzer* and *user.* Trisyllables start with *conveyable* and *defrayable* and end at *muzziness* and *wuzziness.* These works are accompanied with text on versification techniques, rhyming patterns, the kinds or divisions of poetry, and the like.

Crossword puzzle dictionaries are rather truncated and specialized versions of the general dictionary, listing words in wide general use accompanied by lists of the arcane terms in which crossword constructors so delight. They are nearly as popular as crossword puzzles themselves, which is to say very.

There are also dictionaries of nonwords, or substitutes for words, *viz.,* of abbreviations and symbols. Although nearly all regular dictionaries list a considerable number of standard abbreviations and most encyclopedias carry lists of the abbreviations used in their pages, there remains a market for similar treatments at greater length. The market includes such works that identify general, scientific, commercial, medical, and other abbreviations, ordinarily numbering from fifteen thousand or so to twenty-five thousand or more. Some of these works also illustrate and define scientific, mathematical, and other symbols, as their titles make plain: *Scientific and Technical Abbreviations, Signs and Symbols* and *Dictionary of Abbreviations and Symbols,* for instance. Gale Research Company publishes an *Acronyms, Initialisms & Abbreviations Dic-*

tionary. (An initialism is an acronym using only the initial letters of a phrase, as in "snafu" or "UNESCO"; acronyms may also combine larger word elements, as in "intercom" or "Politburo.")

No discussion of books about language would be complete without taking note of manuals of style and usage. These may be as concise as William Strunk, Jr., and E. B. White's *The Elements of Style* (usually referred to as Strunk and White), which presents elementary rules of usage, the principles of composition, and illustrations of misused words and phrases in fewer than a hundred pages. They may be as voluminous as Fowler's famous *Modern English Usage,* with its range from capsules to lengthy essays examining good and bad usage. Dating to 1926, it has been more or less continuously revised and updated, and while its orientation is to British English, its exploration of real and imagined pitfalls, such as split infinitives, is not only instructive but also often delightfully witty.

An American work of comparable scope, authority, and wit is Wilson Follett's *Modern American Usage.* Actually the work was begun by Follett but completed after his death by Jacques Barzun and a half dozen other stellar collaborators. Its own prose is a little leaner than Fowler's, which only improves its utility for contemporary Americans. Like Fowler, its short to medium-length essays are organized alphabetically, after the fashion of a dictionary. Another popular and readable manual is the *Dictionary of Contemporary American Usage* by Bergen and Cornelia Evans, and there is an excellent newer entry, the *Dictionary of Contemporary Usage,* by William and Mary Morris (second edition, 1985). There are more—enough for every appetite and purse.

This usage-and-style genre may also be quite explicit, addressing style in the sense of preparing manuscripts for publication. This variety is exemplified by the definitive *Chicago Manual of Style* of the University of Chicago Press.

FOREIGN-LANGUAGE DICTIONARIES

There are three basic kinds of foreign-language dictionary: those written in the foreign tongue, generally useful only to people at home in the language; "one way" dictionaries that translate from, say, Chinese to English or vice versa but not both; and the more familiar "two way" dictionaries—*e.g.,* French–English and English–French. The latter is likely to be most helpful to readers of this book, and we shall concentrate on it.

Apart from using them to extend a traveler's limited foreign vocabulary, or to translate the odd foreign word or phrase that shows up in one's reading, these two-way dictionaries can also be used to unlock reference books—for instance, biographical dictionaries and even encyclopedias—in a foreign language you do not speak.

This is probably not true at all if you have neither a head for nor any interest in or experience with languages other than English. However, many millions of Americans have at least a smattering of another language or two, acquired from travel, relatives, or half forgotten from school.

If you are searching for background on some event, person, or place that has great importance in a foreign country but little or none in your own, it may well be worthwhile to try a foreign source. Many libraries in fairly large cities carry reference works in several languages. In such a situation a decent foreign-language dictionary is usually essential.

A lot of nonsense is heard about the inadequacies of common foreign-language dictionaries. Nearly all of the familiar ones are really inadequate only to the linguist—who wouldn't touch the genre with a ten-foot pole. Depending on their size and recency, their word lists may be limited, but the same is true of any dictionary.

The intelligent lay reader may encounter two problems in employing one of these standard two-way dictionaries to dope out the essence of, say, a foreign encyclopedia article. One is that a needed word may be missing; in that case consult another dictionary. The other problem is that many of the words—especially verbs—you look up will not be in the form in which they appear in the dictionary. In Spanish, for example, one of the meanings of the verb *deber* is "must" or "ought." As an auxiliary with *ser* ("to be"), it is used in the indicative mode and imperfect tense as *debía ser* to mean "must have been." You can figure these things out by a combination of hunch and checking the supplementary matter on grammar, irregular-verb tables, etc., which are supplied with all the better bilingual dictionaries.

If you are using a bilingual dictionary to translate from English into the other language, a good deal of caution is indicated. This is one of those areas in which looking the word up is not necessarily the same thing as finding out its meaning. Idiomatic uses and the ambiguities built into every language present plenty of pitfalls. A couple of examples: In French, *pêche* means "peach." It also means "fishing." *Pêcher* means "peach tree," and it also means "to fish." *Pêcher en eau trouble* means "to fish in troubled waters," but what it really means is playing around with somebody else's spouse. And *pêcheur* ("fisherman") dangerously resembles *pécheur* ("sinner"). Proceed carefully.

Fortunately, most languages have one or more dictionaries of idiom that can steer one safely over these linguistic shoals; consult your librarian. Unfortunately, perhaps, they are almost never bilingual. A good general rule, when translating from English to the other language, is always to retranslate to English when you have finished, to see if something ludicrous or ambiguous has crept in. If so, back to the drawing board, or, alas, possibly the wastebasket.

CHAPTER 4

COMPUTER ACCESS

Most of the look-it-up functions addressed in this book can be conducted sitting in front of a personal computer. Thus far, most maps and photographs have been off limits, but this is due to limitations in the way databases can be stored and not to any shortcoming in the capabilities of computer hardware or software.

Database, hardware, software . . . already this chapter is sprinkled with computer jargon, and if you find that distressing, you're in good company. It will be kept to an irreducible minimum, but a few terms are essential, and they will be defined briefly.

But first a look at the research functions you can carry out by computer and at those you cannot and the reasons why. Because of the costs involved, of which more later, it would be silly and wasteful to use a computer to consult a dictionary. Moreover, only a few of the general encyclopedias are available by computer, so your choice of access to those reference works is limited.

Illustrations are few in computer-accessible reference material. It has been an expensive proposition to place a photograph in a computer storage file. This is so because a photograph is not made up of a small number of standard characters like those that compose a book—twenty-six letters, ten numerals, and a handful of commas and such. Each point of light or shadow in a halftone photo reproduction, a point far smaller than a period, has to be located in the computer's memory almost as though it were a word.

In this sense the old adage about a good picture being worth a thousand words comes true the hard way. Storing photographs eats up more disk space than storing words, and that's why reference works accessible by computer have not been heavily illustrated. The relatively poor resolution of most computer screens has limited picture quality, too. Both these considerations are changing rapidly, however. Resolution—*i.e.*, the ability to depict extremely fine detail on the screen—has been improving greatly, and the development of the laser/videodisk offers a revolution in storing high-resolution graphics.

The fact is that the computer is an idiot, with no intelligence of its own. Its saving graces are its willingness to do the dullest of repetitive chores (it doesn't want to be a vice-president) and its speed. Its world is one of black and white, yes or no, off or on, and it must run back and forth doing thousands of those off-on errands just to type a sentence on a screen. It does this dog work at nearly the speed of light. If the messages had to be carried back and forth by some vehicle powered by coal or oil, it would take a month for the machine to type a paragraph, and you could fly to Paris on less fuel.

With the help of some simple programming, computers can "talk" to each other if they are wired together. But to communicate over telephone lines they need special assistance because the computer does not employ electrical energy the same way the telephone does. The computer's pulses of energy—on, on, off, off, off—must be converted into a continuous wave of electromagnetic radiation, which is what our voice is converted to when we talk on the phone. The voice, passing through an electronic device at this end, modulates the electrical wave and distorts its shape in a distinctive way. At the other end, an electronic device has to read those distortions or modulations and convert them back into sound waves like those of the human voice. Similar modulation transmits the computer's off-on pulses over the electrical wave flowing steadily through the phone line. And, as in the phone conversation, the modulation has to be reconverted to pulses at the other end.

This process, reversing what the modulation did, is called demodulation. A special electronic instrument attached or built in to the computer at each end handles both modulation and demodulation necessary for communication between computers. The computer mavens made the word "modem" out of modulation-demodulation. Sooner or later new developments will make modems unnecessary, but until then, for your computer to get access to anybody's database over telephone wires, there must be a modem at each end to do this translating.

Hooked up in this fashion, from your computer at home or office, you can look up every kind of thing that this book addresses. The commonest and easiest way to do this is by establishing a connection with a database distributor, generally called a computer information service. There are several of these, among which the most generally known probably are CompuServe, Dialog, Dow Jones News/Retrieval, EasyLink, Nexis, NewsNet, and The Source. In addition, there are many academic and other specialized services with less familiar names.

Once in contact with one of these services, you can order up a table of contents—a "menu" in computerese—of all the various databases that service has to offer. You can select an item from that menu and immediately establish contact with it—access it, as the computerheads have it. Having done that, you can describe the specific word or passage you want to look up, and you will shortly learn whether it is there or not. If it is, you can call it to your screen and browse through it at your own speed, on pages of normal width but only twenty-five lines deep (the depth of a standard computer screen).

By simple keyboard commands you may choose between browsing page by page or having the text unroll before you as on a scroll. If you find the passage you are searching out, you may read it on the screen or press another button and have it typed on paper by the printer connected with your own computer while you are looking at it.

The promise of being able to look up every *kind* of thing this book addresses is not open-ended; it does not mean every single thing, every book cited here. Relatively few of the books in your public library are likely to be part of some database and thus accessible to your computer. But many major reference works are available, along with a very high proportion of modern scholarly and scientific writing in every discipline.

All you need do to find out what's available and where, and at what cost, is to survey the existing computer communication companies and find out the databases and other services offered by each of them. If you decide to use a computer in this way, the instruction manual that comes with your modem will give you names and telephone numbers of some of the principal services. Computer magazines put out lots of information on what services are available where, and professional and scholarly associations will supply information on how databases dealing with their fields are accessible.

If you pursue this course, there are a couple of other technical obstacles you will have to pass before you can "go online," as they say. Many of the computer information services can be reached only through a data communication network. This is a company that rents or operates high-capacity telephone lines interconnecting major cities and specializes in connecting the computer information services themselves with their customers. There are several of these networks—*e.g.*, the CompuServe Network, Sourcenet, Tymenet, Telenet, and Uninet.

Modems operate at different rates of speed, and practically speaking, yours must be able to send and receive at the relatively modest speed of either 300 or 1,200 baud. "Baud" is not computerese, by the way. It comes from the name of a French electrical experimenter and inventor, Jean-Maurice-Émile Baudot (1845–1903). He invented a system of telegraphy that supplanted Morse Code because it was faster and cheaper. It used short pulses of energy—combinations of dots instead of Morse's dots and dashes. One baud was established as the length of time required for a single dot, or a single nondot, to be transmitted. Since the computer works in pulses (dots and nondots) the baud was an ideal unit for measuring its speed of transmission.

When you have gotten over the various technical hurdles, you are ready to roll. Some of the computer information services are quite specialized—sending "electronic mail" back and forth, for instance, or supplying financial and stock market data and related research material. Two of the general services, however, Dialog and Nexis, make a wide range of extremely sophisticated resources available to you.

The information services offer you access to the databases of major newspapers and assorted magazines and journals. These files are not simply today's paper but a whole archive covering many years and in some cases many decades. All the companies except Newsnet and Nexis have an online encyclopedia, Grolier's *Academic American.* Dialog has *Academic American* and the English-language version of a European work that is no longer updated called *Everyman's.* But it also has millions of abstracts, journal articles, books, and scientific and technical reports in many fields of medicine, engineering, science, and scholarship. Dialog is owned by Lockheed Aircraft Corporation.

Nexis is associated with a slightly older and highly specialized service called Lexis, which has an enormous computerized library of law—the text and legislative history of every law, federal and state, court decisions, an incredible array of legal information and record. Lexis and Nexis are owned by Mead Data Central, a spin-off from Mead Paper Company, which was early to see the computerized handwriting on the wall about the printing paper market in an electronic future.

Nexis has *The New York Times* and *The Washington Post* and other major newspapers; the national wire services; the major newsmagazines; the BBC's world news summary; selected English-language coverage from the Soviet news agency TASS; and a staggering array of other scholarly, scientific, technical, and journalistic reference sources. It also acquired access to the entire text of *Encyclopaedia Britannica* in the late 1970s.

There are hundreds and hundreds of databases that are online somewhere, many of them available through several of the commercial information systems named here, and others only through smaller consortiums of scholarly organizations, etc. In the realm of basic reference works, the entire *Public Affairs Information System* (*PAIS International*), all of the *Educational Resources Information Center* (*ERIC*), *Books in Print, American Men and Women of Science, Ulrich's International Periodicals Directory* index, and the entire *Dissertation Abstracts Online* of University Microfilms are available, as well as scores of other bibliographic, biographical, directory, and other reference materials.

Many of the databases of individual scientific associations are available directly from the organization or through one of the computer information services discussed earlier. Among them are the Medline file of the National Library of Medicine, covering medicine, nursing, and dentistry; the complete *Merck Index of Pharmaceuticals,* the whole *Kirk-Othmer Encyclopedia of Chemical Technology,* and (largest of all) the entire database of the American Chemical Society. Also available are the online service of the National Institute of Mental Health, the *Zoological Record,* the *Biosis* database, the *Biological Abstracts,* and nearly countless others. The social sciences have enormous computer-accessible files. The world of business and finance is covered from top to bottom, including every major financial publication, and the full text of every tax information publication of the Internal Revenue Service.

Virtually all the publications and services cited in this list are discussed elsewhere in this book as major reference resources in their guise as bound books. With a couple of exceptions they are no less valuable to the researcher at home or office via computer. One such exception is when you get intrigued with what you are looking at and want to browse in it indefinitely. Another is the situation in which you want to prop the book open on the library table and move back and forth between it and the stacks or the reference librarian's desk or the photocopy machine.

In any such situation, your bill for the service is going to mount very rapidly. Therefore, a word about the costs associated with computerized research. All this, mind you, comes after the very substantial costs of a computer, a modem, a printer, and such other peripheral equipment as you may desire. To be permitted access to some of the computer information systems you must have equipment that meets a certain standard, notably compatibility with the brand of modem that set the industry standard (Hayes), and the appropriate speed of 300 to 1,200 baud mentioned above. Incidentally, a modem sending and receiving at 300 baud can take an eternity to handle a lengthy document; at 1,200 baud it's four times as fast. And when it comes to printouts, many computer printers are notoriously slow.

For the more substantial of the information services you will face three kinds of charge. There is a monthly fee that, measured in 1988 dollars, will range from twenty-five or thirty dollars to about $125 for a service as specialized as Lexis. The latter, of course, is an infrequent choice for home research.

Next, you have a time charge for the minutes you actually spend connected to the database you are using. This will range, again in 1988 dollars, from about thirty to fifty dollars per hour—fifty to eighty cents per minute—in "prime time"—usually from 7:00 A.M. to 6:00 P.M. Monday through Friday, and perhaps 25 percent less for "off prime" time. In addition, there is frequently a search charge for each topic you look up; in the case of Nexis this ranges from three to thirty dollars.

The higher your monthly fee and hourly charge, the more scrupulous the service is likely to be about billing you for only time actually spent in the database. You are not charged while you are scanning directories of what's available, for example, by the likes of Nexis, but you probably will be charged "portal to portal" by some of the lower-fee services.

Finally, there is a document-access charge that varies with the resource you select, and it may range from, say, seven dollars for connecting with the actual text of a particular issue of a major newspaper to $180 or so for "accessing" some exotic scientific document.

The popular-priced services will cost significantly less in several ways. Usually there is a one-time "initiation fee" of twenty-five or fifty dollars, and an annual maintenance fee of a similar amount. The per-minute charge ranges from around twenty-five cents to about a dollar.

To make matters worse, all the time you are connected to somebody else's database the meter continues to run on your own phone bill and on the computer information service if you're using one as a means of access. Many computer-search users find they spend more on telecommunication costs than anything else.

So, you see, it is not hard to envisage running up a fairly substantial bill, especially if you're in one of the "top of the line" services and get intrigued with what you are reading and stay hunched over the tube as you would a book in the library.

There are copious resources in print about the resources and procedures of online research. The following list is merely a sample, but a good one.

Answers Online

Bowker's Software in Print

Business/Professional Microcomputer

The Complete Handbook of Personal Computer Communication

Data Base/Electronic Publishing: Review & Forecast

Dictionary of Special Libraries and Information Centers

Directory of Online Databases (monthly)

Encyclopedia of Information Systems and Services

Guide to a Selection of Computer-Based Science and Technology Reference Sources in the USA

Information Industry Market Place

International Guide to Library, Archival, and Information Science Associations

An Introduction to Automated Literature Searching

Libraries, Information Centers and Databases in Science and Technology

Online Bibliography of Databases

Online Research and Retrieval with Microcomputers

Videotext: The Coming Revolution in Home/Office Information Retrieval

Okay, you've seen the future. Now figure out whether it works for you. If so, it can make your life easier and greatly extend your reach in looking things up. If not, salvage some of the jargon and say, "For me, it's just not online."

The tremendous information-storage capacity of the technology known as CD-ROM has opened up a new indexing device accessible only through a personal computer. The initials stand for compact disk–read only memory. Data filed optically (by laser) on a compact disk cannot be written over as on a magnetic disk, hence "read only." Wilsondisk and DialogDisc are a couple of services through which libraries can subscribe to super-directories of publications. This approach is also known as optical offline technology.

So online or offline, you've seen the future. Now figure out whether it works for you. But keep this in mind: It won't go away.

CHAPTER 5

HOW TO LOOK UP PEOPLE

Finding a particular biography that you've been seeking is always a relief and sometimes a sheer delight. The objective of this chapter is to make it easy for the nonprofessional researcher to know, or to find out easily, where and how to locate the volume needed to answer questions about the person being tracked down. Not under consideration here is the full-scale biography in a whole volume or many volumes of one person. We are concerned here mainly with collections of biographic sketches, long and short.

Much good biographic material, especially of contemporaries, appears in magazines and newspapers. Apart from the periodical indexes discussed in Chapter 3, there are published helps to locating such material. Basic is the *Biography Index,* a continuing series published by Wilson. A benefit for one contemplating rummaging through a number of *New York Times* indexes is the *Personal Name Index to The New York Times, 1851–1974.* For the most part, however, biographical dictionaries is the name of the game.

The world of the biographical dictionary is enormous, and it can answer research questions about anyone of note from the earliest English kings—indeed, even from Asian rulers whose reigns are lost in prehistoric myth—to this year's sensations in rock music. There is a *Who's Who* for every country of consequence in the world and for a few of almost no consequence. Some collections of biography go into vast detail; others are mere summaries of public records. One publication, *Biographical Dictionaries Master Index,* lists dozens (but not all) of them.

One word of caution for the user of this great body of information: Very few biographical collections take pains to verify facts. The norm for the field is pretty much the approach employed by

Who's Who in America; its publisher invites individuals selected by the editors as being of some "research interest" to fill out question-naires supplying all the desired information, including education, employment history, books published, honors received, etc.

Nearly all respondents are both honest and careful. They are, after all, people of substance and some station in life, and most of the information they supply is exactly right. But not always, as occasional hoaxers have demonstrated over the years. One man figured out a way to get a fictitious biography of his dog into the volume. The A. N. Marquis Company, publisher of *Who's Who in America* and some two dozen regional and occupational spin-offs, even has a few phony entries of its own, to enable it to keep track of who's using *Who's Who* as a mailing list.

Although the information "they," the subjects of the biographies, supply is usually accurate, it is not always complete. For example, think of a prominent person you know to have been imprisoned for some criminal offense—perhaps mail fraud or bribery. Look up the name in any *Who's Who* and it is virtually certain you will find no record of the conviction or sentence (unless, of course, it should be an honorable imprisonment, as for instance for violating a "whites only" ordinance in the civil rights campaigns of the 1960s).

There aren't many technical problems threatening the people-researcher. Probably the most common is figuring out which name a person will be alphabetized under. Japan's great postwar prime minister, Yoshida, had the given name Shigeru. Japanese practice (albeit grown a little ambiguous in the late twentieth century) is to write and speak the full name family name first, as Yoshida Shigeru. American journalists and editors, however, refer to him Western-style, as Shigeru Yoshida. How then, should he be "alphed"? Certainly under Yoshida, with or without a comma.

To make matters more confusing, general practice in the West is to treat Chinese names in proper Oriental style, so that while Mr. Yoshida is Shigeru Yoshida, China's paramount post-Mao leader, Mr. Deng, is addressed and alphabetized as Deng Xiaoping.

There is more: For generations, Western scholars (and the press) used the Wade-Giles style of romanizing Chinese names so their pronunciation could be written using Western alphabets. According-ing to that system, Mr. Deng's name was written Teng Hsiao-p'ing. Then the People's Republic of China adopted Pinyin (the word means romanization), and suddenly, though pronounced exactly the same way, it is written Deng Xiaoping.

Roman history has lots of name pitfalls—as its great men had lots of names. The first general Scipio, for instance, had four: praenomen (given name), nomen (the name of his clan), cognomen (his family name), and agnomen (surname, *i.e.*, an epithet or byname; some heroes had several). In full he was Publius Cornelius Scipio Africanus. Look him up at Scipio Africanus.

Spanish names offer another problem, because the matronymic or mother's maiden name often is listed last but the patronymic or father's family name in much of Latin America, listed second, is what the person is called and how he is alphabetized: Mario Vargas Llosa is Mr. Vargas, and in a biographical dictionary you should find him as Vargas Llosa, Mario.

Other European-language names can be tricky, too. A famous French historian is named Emmanuel Le Roy Ladurie. You could look for him all day in vain under Ladurie. He is Mr. Le Roy Ladurie and is found in biographical dictionaries as Le Roy Ladurie, Emmanuel. When frustrated in seeking any such name, first double-check spelling and capitalization, then ring the changes on all the possible combinations, and you will find the guy (or gal) at last.

German *von*s and Dutch *van*s also create problems. Capitalization can be a key. If you can't find Van Dyck, Anthony (as you should be able to do), try Dyck, Anthony van. But the same work that gives you Van Dyck is apt to give you Gogh, Vincent van, and Goethe, Johann Wolfgang von.

Finally, pseudonyms or bynames of various sorts are always with us, whether they be noms de plume, noms de guerre, aliases, or plain old nicknames. Biographical information about writers, revolutionaries, criminals, athletes, and defunct Japanese emperors, among others, often can best be found under a byname. In the best of all possible worlds, there would always be a cross-reference, but in this world, be prepared for a little legwork.

The information in major collections of biographical sketches such as that splendid British institution *Dictionary of National Biography* (usually abbreviated *DNB*) and its younger and smaller counterpart *Dictionary of American Biography* (*DAB*), as well as the *Dictionary of Scientific Biography* and others of its type, whose articles are individually and professionally researched and written and then carefully fact-checked, are generally completely reliable. In such publications when a fact or date simply cannot be obtained it will be omitted or offered tentatively, perhaps by a question mark.

Biographies in major general encyclopedias are equally trustworthy when they are signed with the name or initials of a scholarly authority. Unsigned short biographies in such publications, however, usually are written by staff members or free-lancers, and their facts are almost always drawn from secondary sources. When these sources are completely dependable—the *Dictionary of National Biography*, for example—the encyclopedia entry will be as sound. But in short encyclopedia entries there is no way for the reader to identify the sources unless a bibliography is included (as they sometimes are). So be careful about placing bets on your findings in this kind of research. However, you may be confident that accuracy is the norm. *Almost* all of what you look up will be correct.

The present tense in the title of works of the *Who's Who* type makes clear that they deal with living persons. This won't help much if your target is a historical figure, but most publishers in this field collect at least the most prominent of their deceased subjects into *Who Was Who's* covering stated periods. Marquis, whose *Who's Who in America* series goes back to 1899, assembled (in the early 1960s) a *Who Was Who in America: Historical Volume* that covers 1607 to 1896 to augment the more recent volumes.

The U.S. Government Printing Office does no less for members of Congress. The *Congressional Directory* (formerly *Official Congressional Directory*) includes biographic sketches of all members of the Senate and House of Representatives, and the *Biographical Directory of the American Congress* extends the treatment all the way back to members of the first Continental Congress of 1794. However, in both the current annual directories and the historical one, biographies of members elected or reelected after 1866 were supplied by themselves and contain virtually no unflattering information. Although essentially truthful in what they do relate, they are hardly objective. A revision by more rigorous editorial standards is under way at last. Other biographical directories exist for the legislative and executive branches.

Can a biographer accurately and fairly evaluate a living contemporary and the importance of his or her work? The question has agitated biographers and editors for ages. William Smellie, who compiled the first edition of *Encyclopaedia Britannica*, refused to edit the second because its publishers decided that biographies would be included. (He did, however, agree to write for the third edition a biography of his late friend Lord Kames.) Not for more than a century would the notion of *living* biographies be seriously considered.

The issue is still disputed. A number of biography collections large and small—*e.g.,* *DAB* and *DNB* (lengthy) and *Webster's Bio-*

graphical Dictionary and *Webster's American Biographies* (concise)—cover only persons who had been dead for a number of years at the time of publication. For most of the twentieth century, however, most of the general encyclopedias and a number of the biographic dictionaries have treated both historic and contemporary people of importance. Encyclopedia yearbooks present obituaries of influential world figures who have died during the year covered, and most of them carry thumbnail sketches of living people who were prominent in the news of the year.

Surely the preeminent biographical collection in the English language is the stately *Dictionary of National Biography*. *DNB* began to appear in 1885 under the editorship of Sir Leslie Stephen. By 1901 Sir Sidney Lee had become Stephen's colleague and later became his successor, and the work numbered sixty-three volumes. In 1903 an index and a two-volume supplement were added. The whole, including the supplement, was reissued in 1908–9 in twenty-two volumes, and in 1917 it was given by the original publisher to Oxford University, whose press republished it in 1938 and adds supplementary volumes from time to time. Since the third supplement (published in 1927), each supplement contains a cumulative index to all supplements back to the first.

DNB became the model for the *Dictionary of American Biography* (*DAB*)—and for a considerable number of other national collections (see later). The American Council of Learned Societies originated the *DAB* project and it began to appear in 1928, one volume at a time, reaching completion with Volume 20 in 1936. Allen Johnson, a U.S. historian who had edited *The Chronicles of America,* turned out the first seven volumes, and the rest were edited by Dumas Malone, who went on to become a distinguished Jefferson scholar. Occasional supplements began appearing in 1944, most including some famous Americans from early times and many who had become eligible by dying since the set—or the last supplement—was complete. *DAB*'s prose, reflecting the era of its writing, is serious enough but nowhere near as musty as that of *DNB*.

Having successfully launched *DAB,* the American Council of Learned Societies turned its attention to the scientific community, and not only in the United States. With a grant from National Science Foundation, it sponsored the creation of a biographical dictionary of the great scientists from all the world and from all ages. The result was the *Dictionary of Scientific Biography,* completed in fourteen volumes in 1970 and published by Scribner's. Two supplementary volumes, one an index, were added later. The work contains some five thousand long and nicely written sketches of the preeminent men and women of science from the time of Archimedes and before to the age of Einstein and his successors. (It does not include living persons.)

In fact, in a 1978 supplement this excellent work goes back far before Archimedes to the ancient Chinese, Indians, and Egyptians, among others. The supplement, Volume 15, treats the scientists of those cultures, whose personal names and identities are lost in antiquity, in seven extended essays summarizing the scientific knowledge and discoveries of each set of these ancients. In addition, the supplement is augmented by names omitted from the original fourteen volumes.

A smaller dictionary of scientific biographies, shorter than *DSB* but considerably longer than the *Who's Who* type and limited to American scientists, is Cattell's *American Men and Women of Science* (formerly *American Men of Science*), now published by R. R. Bowker Company in seven volumes and divided into categories of the physical, biological, and social sciences.

Several other sources of biographical information bear special mention. A concise one is the three-volume *New Century Cyclopedia of Names,* last revised in 1954 but still in active service in most decent libraries. It is not limited to biography, but its names include many hundreds of actual people along with places, literary and other artistic works, literary and mythological characters, U.S. Supreme Court decisions, organizations, institutions, etc. The concise entries in this work show an excellent international balance, with plenty of North Americans but also a good many Asian, European, and Latin American names difficult to find elsewhere.

Another invaluable work, especially for some of the lesser lights in U.S. history, is one likely to be found only in fairly large libraries. It has been out of print since the early 1970s, but it remains eminently worth consulting when you're having trouble finding your man or woman elsewhere. This is the *National Cyclopaedia of American Biography,* initiated in 1892 in two series. Numbered volumes treat only historic figures, and lettered volumes cover people alive at the time of publication. These volumes—numbers 1–53 and A–M—cannot be used without consulting the accompanying indexes because they are organized in an impenetrably random fashion, certainly not alphabetically, chronologically, or geographically. A revised bound index appearing in 1969 supplanted the looseleaf indexes that prevailed originally. The sketches in this set are fairly long and usually contain interesting and helpful family background on the subject. They are staff-written and therefore probably less reliable than *DAB* and *DNB*, but the old *National Cyclopaedia* set, when you can find it and when the volume you need isn't lost, is a jewel.

Appleton's Cyclopaedia of American Biography is another old-timer that contains outstanding biographic sketches of the leading figures of eighteenth- and nineteenth-century America. The original, completed in 1900, included a list of pen names and nicknames and an analytical index. It also, alas, contained quite a number of absolutely phony sketches, but the real ones were great. It was revised and reissued by another publisher in 1915, and supplementary volumes VII–XII were issued gradually up to 1931. Yet another publisher, Gale Research Company of Detroit, put the set out again with a revised index in 1969.

One marvelous source of information about the lives of people who have attained celebrity status in the United States since the 1940s is something of a hybrid: a monthly magazine that is rebound every year as an annual collection, constituting an encyclopedia of biography from 1940 to date. This is *Current Biography*, a publication of the H. W. Wilson Company, which divides with R. R. Bowker Company and Gale Research Company most of the spoils in the American bibliography world.

Each monthly issue of *Current Biography* provides twenty-five or thirty professionally written biographies of famous literary, entertainment, sports, scientific, or otherwise prominent figures of the day. The authors of these admirable, always revealing, and often pleasantly breezy profiles, which run from two to four pages and include a careful bibliography, usually interview the subject personally to resolve ambiguities and questions. Each issue of the magazine also carries obituaries of former subjects who have died, and each has a cumulative index for the year to date. The bound set has an index for each volume, cumulative indexes by decade appearing in each decennial year, and occasional omnibus cumulative indexes in separate volumes—*e.g.*, 1940–80. Although the style is far more relaxed than the quite sedate *DNB* and the nearly as proper *DAB*, *Current Biography*, like them, is presented in narrative style and is a pleasure to read. This can be a pitfall for the inveterate browser, but that's a peril busy readers face all the time.

You have doubtless noticed that writers are the protagonists or central characters of a disproportionate share of fiction. Writers, knowing writing, write about writers. It seems to be the same in the world of biographical dictionaries. There seem to be as many collections of authors' biographies as of all other callings combined. The most massive such compendium is *Contemporary Authors* of Gale Research Company, with scores of volumes and revisions now covering more than eighty-five thousand authors who are alive or who have died since 1960.

These are long and careful biographies, quite professionally done, of nontechnical authors in all genres of literature. There is nothing quite like *Contemporary Authors,* but don't even think of approaching it except through the index. There are dozens and dozens of smaller but quite solid works out there covering authors of a particular period, nation, genre, or, especially of recent years, race.

It was noted earlier that there are either *Who's Who*'s or, in several cases, full-blown dictionaries of national biography for scores of countries. An international multivolume work is *The McGraw-Hill Encyclopedia of World Biography* (twelve volumes, 1973). It is illustrated and has a substantial bibliography. There also are several truly international *Who's Who*'s, including the *International Who's Who,* published in London by Europa and covering the world since 1930; *Who's Who in the World* (Marquis); and others. Here is a generous sampling, but only a sampling, of the national *Who's Who*'s. Countries marked with an asterisk (*) also have a much larger dictionary of their national biographies.

Africa (general)	Italy*
Australia	Japan
Austria	Netherlands
Belgium	New Zealand
Canada	Norway
China	South Africa
France*	Spain
Great Britain and the Commonwealth (the prototype of the genre, *Who's Who*)	Sweden
	Switzerland
India	U.S.S.R.
Ireland	West Germany*

Other kinds of specialization can be found; continental focus, for one: the *African Historical Biography* by Mark R. Lipschutz and R. Kent Rasmussen (1978). In addition, either carefully prepared collections of short biographies or dictionaries of the *Who's Who* type cover almost every academic and occupational specialty. A partial list of categories follows.

aeronautics and space pioneers

arts, visual: architects

arts, visual: engravers

arts, visual: painters

arts, visual: sculptors

association executives

automobile, including motor sports

booksellers

broadcasting (radio and television)

business: advertising, banking and finance, insurance, real estate, etc.

conservation

education: administration, teaching (elementary, secondary, higher)

engineering (civil, electrical, mechanical, etc.)

ethnic groups: blacks, Italian Americans, Polish Americans, etc.

foundations

geographers

government and politics: by activity (*e.g.*, diplomats), or country and activity (*e.g.*, rulers, party officials, state and local government officials. U.S. Congress, British Parliament, etc.)

government and politics: by country

government and politics: by political groupings (British Commonwealth, non-Communist Asia, Communist countries, etc.)

government and politics: United Nations

historians

industry: data processing, durable-goods manufacturing, electronics, etc.

journalism: newspaper, radio, television

labor leaders

lawyers

librarians

literature: fiction, nonfiction, plays, poetry, etc.

mathematicians

medicine: dentists, medical and surgical specialties, M.D.s, psychiatrists

military commanders

music: general, as well as separate works for composers, conductors, instrumentalists, vocalists, jazz performers, concert, opera, popular performers, etc.

mythological figures

natural sciences: life or biological sciences, biology, botany, paleontology, zoology; earth and atmospheric sciences, geology, oceanography, etc.; astronomy, chemistry, physics, etc.

Nobel laureates and other prize winners

nobility

philosophers

poets

publishers

religion: biblical characters, Judaism, Protestant Christianity, Roman Catholicism, popes, saints, Islamic leaders, etc.

scholarship (*e.g., Dictionary of American Scholars,* and in many cases by academic discipline) sciences: general (*e.g., American Men and Women of Science,* with similar works for other countries or continents, *e.g.,* British and continental European scientists)

social sciences: *e.g.,* anthropology (general, and specializations such as Egyptology), political science, psychology

sports (participant): camping, fishing, hiking, hunting, jogging, etc.

sports (spectator): *e.g.,* baseball, basketball, boxing, football, golf, tennis, horse racing, track and field

theater and entertainment: dance, motion pictures, opera, stage, etc.

trade associations

transporatation: aviation, railroads, motor vehicle, marine

watch- and clockmakers

women (by country, region, or occupation)

GENEALOGY

Genealogical research is as old as the earliest beginnings of civilization. The American image of that calling probably could be aptly caricatured by a middle-class Midwesterner (like the author) chasing around in libraries trying to establish some plausible link between himself and this or that ancient king, or at least his bastard son the earl. Actually, the profession of genealogist would have somewhat similar trouble tracing its own roots to any academic discipline, for it has no claim to scholarly credentials. Yet what genealogy is all about is really the stuff of history. "There is properly no history, only biography," Emerson wrote. Carlyle, at about the same time, agreed, calling history "the biography of great men."

If you are coming cold to genealogical research and think of pedigree as a concern limited to pet and livestock breeders, it may amuse you to learn that genealogy is the science of pedigrees. The latter word comes from the Latin for "crane's foot." Early European genealogists used an arrowlike sign resembling a crane's foot to point out the line of descent on genealogical charts. So the genealogists of cats and cows borrowed the pedigree from tracers of people's bloodlines.

The oral traditions of genealogy were brought to wide attention in the 1970s when Alex Haley accomplished a stunning research feat by tracing his ancestors in West Africa. His best-selling book *Roots: The Saga of an American Family* and the ensuing television special series related the role of the *griot* or oral historian in serving as a sort of public memory for his preliterate people. The written tradition of genealogy is ancient, too—as witness the extensive genealogies in the Old Testament, especially in Numbers, and in the New Testament as well.

If you are immersed in working out your family tree, take comfort in the fact that people who are not famous still leave a considerable trail. Genealogy has been an increasingly popular pursuit in recent years, and this has spurred a fairly substantial stream of publications designed to be helpful. Every decent public library has at least a small section on genealogy. There are how-to kinds of books (see Chapter 20), and the subject is also treated in all the major encyclopedias. Resources abound for the amateur as well as the professional.

Major public libraries, including such privately supported ones as the New York Public Library, usually have excellent genealogical collections under the charge of a librarian who can answer amateurish as well as sophisticated questions and suggest sources. Naturally, smaller libraries usually have more modest holdings.

If your resources of time and money permit travel to special libraries, that of the Mormon church—the Church of Jesus Christ of Latter-Day Saints—in Salt Lake City is unparalleled for its holdings in microfilm of genealogical records from Europe, including the British Isles, and these records are accessible to non-Mormons. The Church has a large branch library in Chicago's northwestern suburbs. In Chicago itself the private Newberry Library, also open to the public, has vast holdings of interest to the genealogist. Any of the how-to books will list other major libraries as well as print sources beyond those touched on in following material.

A sampling of genealogy sources includes four publications of the Burke's Peerage people, the famous chroniclers of the titled persons of the British Isles. These are *Burke's Genealogical and Heraldic History of the Landed Gentry, Burke's Genealogical and Heraldic History of the Landed Gentry of Ireland, Burke's Genealogical and Heraldic History of the Peerage, Baronage, and Knightage,* and, perhaps of most immediate help to Americans, *Burke's American Families with British Ancestry.*

There are other peerages—DeBrett's and the successor to the famous *Almanach de Gotha,* for example, *Ein Genealogisches Handbuch des Adels.* For Americans the *Guide to the Records in the National Archives* is potentially invaluable. And an *Index to American Genealogies* is excellent up to the dawn of the twentieth century for listing such fundamental elements of genealogical records as local histories compiled for communities all over America.

A final cautionary note: The amateur genealogist should take pains to work consistently back into history, generation by generation. It is a fool's errand to start with, say, a British family of a couple of hundred years ago that has your own surname, and research forward, hoping to find your own great-grandfather. This kind of search is nearly always a wild goose chase that saps your enthusiasm and the cooperation of your librarian.

And if you should decide to make the trip to London or Salt Lake City or Washington, D.C., to track your forebears, look first at the following chapter. Bon voyage!

CHAPTER 6

How to Get There from Here: Looking Up Places

Finding a map of a country or region or an important city is easy enough: Look in any atlas—once you have deciphered its mode of organization. One of the purposes of this chapter is to help the innocent reader do just that. Another is to guide you as effortlessly as possible to gazetteers and guidebooks that are available in public and school libraries and that go well beyond the usual bookstore selection of two or three different guides to each important tourist country.

Tourism, though it may be the most frequent reason people turn to travel guides, is far from the only one. Other motives include getting an understanding of what life is like in an ancestor's homeland, acquiring a feel for the location of a book or movie or news story, and contemplating a possible job transfer. Sometimes people are moved to conduct such research to one-up, or at least to avoid being snowed by, a boastful, widely traveled friend. Armchair travel is an ancient and honorable pastime and one that often precedes a decision to make the trip in real life.

And even for planning actual travel, access to a variety of resources in a decently appointed library can be an excellent way to start. There one may find the kind of geographic information needed to make a sound decision about whether to visit the place or not, or which countries to include on a trip.

But atlases and guidebooks are not the only reference works that may be helpful in such a quest. Major encyclopedias have outstanding treatments of the countries and the cities of the world and often supply historical background, lore, and insights into government and social mores at greater depth than many of the travel guides. William Benton, who owned and published *Encyclopaedia Britannica* for thirty years before his death, used to take a number of friends on occasional chartered sea cruises or other extended trips. Required reading for every guest was a hard-bound book of several hundred pages that he would have his editors make up of duplicate pages from the *Britannica's* articles on all the countries, physical features, and great cities on the itinerary. But even if you're not a millionaire publisher you can enjoy most of the benefits of that kind of costly present by doing the research at home or in the library beforehand.

There is a potential wild goose chase that can be avoided by the individual interested in this kind of information and background. Books with *Geography* in their titles may seem to be a resource, but actually they are unlikely to be of much help to the prospective traveler. The professional geographer is as much concerned with political and economic geography—statistical information about production and trade, gross national or domestic product, and the like—as with maps. You could rummage through the geography section of a large library for an hour or two without learning much about a country's cultural life and customs or finding maps or descriptions of its cities, countryside, and daily life. For the prospective traveler or the reader interested in local character, culture, sights, sounds, and smells, the place to turn is an atlas, gazetteer, guidebook, or some congenial combination of them. Indeed, there are special regional and national encyclopedias in many libraries—*e.g.*, the *Encyclopedia of China Today*, the *Encyclopedia of Latin America*, and the *Dictionary of the European Economic Community*.

A word of caution applies to looking up geographical names anywhere in the world. Most modern reference publishers *usually* adopt the local spelling of a place name. However, especially in Asia and other places where the Latin or Roman alphabet is not used, conventional spellings long in general use in the Western world predominate. The capital of the People's Republic of China, for example, is conventionally spelled Peking, although the Pinyin spelling used by the Chinese government represents the way the Chinese pronounce it: Beijing. It has formerly been spelled (in the West) Pekin and Peiping. When you are looking in older books, if you don't find it your way, try the alternatives. Arabic place names also are a trial for Americans who aren't steeped in the language and the history and traditions of the Middle East.

There are several possible approaches to solving this problem when you encounter it. First, libraries have books of place names, such as the *Illustrated Dictionary of Place Names, United States and Canada* or the *Geographical Etymology: A Dictionary of Place-Names Giving their Derivations.*

Alternatively, of course, you can look up your first-choice spelling in a good general encyclopedia. You should find an indication of alternative spellings, which will reveal where to turn in your geographic source. Another is to look up the latest report of the U.S. Board of Geographic Names, often called simply BGN. This is an interagency organization of geographers and others who come to agree on which place names should be rendered in the local spelling or its transliteration and which should continue to be spelled in the old, conventional way. BGN reports also reveal the range of possibilities for spelling names about which there is ambiguity or confusion.

ABOUT ATLASES AND GAZETTEERS

Early cartographers often decorated their maps with drawings of Atlas, the Titan of Greek mythology who was condemned to hold the heavens and Earth apart. Atlas was at first depicted bearing a celestial globe on his shoulders, *i.e.*, a globe representing the heavens. Later mapmakers sometimes rendered his burden as a terrestrial globe, and the notion of that overworked Titan "bearing the weight of the world on his shoulders" passed into the popular culture. Atlas decorations become a universal fixture on maps by the mid-sixteenth century when Mercator, the Flemish geographer and cartographer, is thought to have first used the name "Atlas" for a bound collection of maps. It quickly became universal.

A gazetteer is, by definition, a geographic dictionary, supplying concise information about cities and towns, populations and boundaries, and such natural figures as lakes and mountains. The word itself originally meant something like "newspaperman," a reporter on one of the gazettes that arose in late-sixteenth-century England patterned on the Venetian *gazzetta*, or gossip sheet, so named for the Venetian coin that was its price. One of the first newspapers in England took that name—the *Oxford Gazette*—in 1665. Early in the eighteenth century, an English gazetteer named Lawrence Echard published an alphabetical descriptive list of places—thus a geographic dictionary—under the title *A Gazetteer's Interpreter*.

The idea of such geographic dictionaries or indexes was already twelve centuries old, first known in Byzantium, but after Echard the name "Gazetteer" stuck and came to be synonymous for the genre. Early famous ones came from nineteenth-century Britain, the Scottish *Johnston's Gazetteer* and *Blackie's Gazetteer* (both 1850) and the English *Longman's* (1895). *Lippincott's Gazetteer* (1865) was the first great American one, and its descendant, the *Columbia Lippincott Gazetteer of the World*, remains one of the most popular and important in the United States. It presents, in alphabetical order, the cities and towns of the world, along with physical features such as lakes and rivers, and practically every important geographical name on Earth in its 130,000-odd entries. It locates each place precisely by longitude and latitude, and (big help!) shows pronunciation of all tricky names.

Something like a gazetteer is the authoritative and widely used *Statesman's Year-Book*, an annual compendium of political and economic geography published in London and running to more than sixteen hundred pages. Its four sections cover, in order, international organizations including the UN, Great Britain and the Commonwealth, the United States (including every state and territory), and the rest of the world. It is effectively indexed.

In the developing world, having a national gazetteer is as important a badge of esteem as having a national biographical dictionary, and judging by the comparative incidence of them, more important even (and a lot less expensive) than a national airline. Increasingly, maps are being published according to guidelines established by the UN Conference on Geographic Names, a helpful step toward uniformity in place names. About thirty U.S. states have official state gazetteers, and there is a national one.

As a rule, an official gazetteer does not contain any significant number of maps, and an atlas *per se*, while it should have an index to places on its maps, does not include a gazetteer. Earlier in the twentieth century, some publishers began producing combination volumes, often under the title "atlas and gazetteer," or sometimes such a formulation as "encyclopedic atlas." Gradually the distinction blurred, and today most atlases are actual combination volumes with a good deal of gazetteer-type information, often augmented with photographs, in addition to the maps and index.

Whenever changes occur in political boundaries, or the names of countries, or highway or rail lines, etc., revision is obviously required. What is less obvious is the relative frequency of such changes. Early-twentieth-century atlases, for example, show West African kingdoms called Yatenga, Ouagadougou, and Gourma. By the end of World War I they constituted most of the French colony of Upper Volta. In 1947 Upper Volta became an overseas territory of France. In 1958 it was an autonomous republic within the French community, and in 1960 it became the independent Republic of Upper Volta. Succeeding changes of government kept the name until 1984, when it was retitled Burkina Faso, meaning "Country of Honest Men." Revision at every step: a political necessity, but a publisher's nightmare.

Even the elevations of mountains and the depths of lakes change from time to time as more precise measuring instruments are developed, or being developed, and are brought to the top of the mountain. Thus the atlas publisher, like the encyclopedist, is always behind.

Most countries produce their own national atlases, probably more often than not without the wealth of gazetteer data now usual in commercial atlases. (The gazetteers are usually issued separately.) This is not only a matter of prestige but also a practical necessity for national governments and their political subdivisions. In the world of commerce, publishers of periodicals and reference works frequently issue atlases or atlas-gazetteers under their own names, sometimes works created by their own staffs, but often what might be called generic brands prepared by professional map publishers and offered for sale under other names. In the United States most such generic atlases, or at least the maps for them, are produced by one of the two principal map publishers, either Rand McNally or Hammond.

Besides the general and current geographic altases referred to earlier, there are many other varieties focused on a particular subject, such as the world in classical times, international trade, the Bible, and several kinds of historical atlas.

Of current conventional or general atlases, several merit comment. The *Britannica Atlas,* published by the encyclopedia company, appeared in the late 1960s with maps by Rand McNally (as are those in the encyclopedia itself). The atlas attempted an interesting design that many users find extraordinarily frustrating. It is organized to view large chunks of Earth as they would appear from space, then zooming in on regions for closer looks. For example, after a view of the United States and a bit of Canada, instead of individual states regional clusters appear, as for instance the Mississippi Valley, containing Missouri, Arkansas, Louisiana, and Mississippi; plus most of Illinois and Alabama; parts of Iowa, Tennessee, Kentucky, and Georgia; and slivers of Nebraska, Kansas, Oklahoma, Texas, Florida, Ohio, and Michigan. There are no separate maps of individual states.

Goode's World Atlas, another using Rand McNally maps, is designed mainly for students and pronounces as well as lists some thirty thousand place names.

Hammond, one of the two major U.S. cartographic publishers, puts out an array of atlases using maps from its vast store of world, national, regional, and city maps in a variety of combinations, augmented with appropriate selections from its gazetteer-type data and indexed in detail. The *Hammond Medallion World Atlas* is perhaps the best known of this company's long list of publications. It has individual maps of the states of the United States and the provinces of Canada.

The National Geographic Society uses its own extensive and famous cartographic resources to publish the *National Geographic Atlas of the World.*

Rand McNally, the other principal American map supplier, produces, like Hammond, numerous general and special atlases. The *Rand McNally Cosmopolitan World Atlas* is the most important of its general atlases. It includes separate maps of each U.S. state and Canadian province.

After World War II *The Times* of London issued an outstanding world atlas in five volumes that is frequently revised. *The Times Atlas of the World* is one of the best in the world, large in size, minute in detail, and divided into regional volumes (*i.e.,* the world, Australia, and East Asia; India, the Middle East, and Russia; northern Europe; the Mediterranean and Africa; and the Americas. There are more than two hundred thousand place names, and each volume has its own index.

Something of the range of specialized atlases is reflected in the following abbreviated list. The historian James Truslow Adams in the early 1940s edited a comprehensive *Atlas of American History,* published by Scribner's.

Hammond's Historical Atlas is a combination of three earlier separate works, treating American history, Bible lands, and a sort of anthropological atlas, *The Races of Mankind.*

Atlas of the Classical World by A.A.M. van der Heyden and Howard Hayes Scullard is a British publication that can be found in larger and better libraries. It is an excellent companion piece to serious or casual researches into the cradle of Western civilization, ancient Greece and Rome, and the vast reach of their armies. *Muir's Atlas of Ancient and Classical History* is a similar American work also addressing Greece, Rome, and the Middle East. Facts on File is publishing a new group of schematic atlases on subjects such as the classical world.

The Economist Intelligence Unit of the *Economist* of London is one of the World's premier economic and geographical research entities. It has assembled the economic content of many outstanding atlases in various parts of the world, including Canada and the United States.

The West Point Atlas of American Wars was compiled by the Department of Military Art and Engineering of the U.S. Military Academy, and published (in 1959, so it excludes the Vietnam War) by Praeger.

As noted, the foregoing illustrations are only a fragment of what's available in special-focus atlases. See what is held by your own library in these and other categories. One note of caution: The text portions of some of the more esoteric ones may be hard going if you're not a linguist. If, for instance, you get into the *Oxford Classical Dictionary,* which apart from being a dictionary of important archaeological discoveries, etc., is an excellent source of geographical information about the ancient world, you will encounter many untranslated passages in Greek and Latin. It is really addressed to scholars and serious students of the classics and has little patience with the rest of us. A comparable work is the *Princeton Dictionary of Classical Sites.*

BAEDEKER'S GUIDES AND BAEDEKER'S SUCCESSORS

Travelers' guidebooks are often called Baedekers, after the German publishing house that produced the first classic series of utterly reliable guides to most of the countries of the world. Karl Baedeker was a printer's son who, in his mid-twenties, set up his own publishing house in Koblenz in 1827. A couple of years later he turned out a guidebook to Koblenz, which proved so popular that he carried the idea into other towns and regions. His objective came to be providing in text a guide to the place covered that was so accurate and comprehensive that the traveler would not need to engage a professional guide to get around town or hinterland and take in all the sights.

Baedeker's guides were well received because they were so complete and so dependable. He provided excellent and minutely detailed maps of cities. He starred the outstanding sights and the most reliable hotels, often checking the latter himself while traveling incognito. After supplying ample cultural and historical background on the area at hand, he set forth in detail specific tours through city and countryside. Eventually the *Baedeker's Guide* series came to include all of Europe and much of the Near East plus the United States.

Karl Baedeker's sons and their successors carried the firm into the twentieth century, and the guides—in English as well as various continental European languages—were revised from time to time. The old series was supplanted in the 1950s by more up-to-date *Auto Guides*. However, various editions of the old ones are still held by the bigger and better libraries, where even though seriously outdated by changes in hotels, restaurants, and air travel, they are invaluable for their wealth of detailed information on scenic views, castles, cathedrals, and other old buildings; and where to find great works of art (in museums but also in town halls, parish churches, wayside chapels, and the like). In recent years a Baedeker grandson has succeeded to editorial responsibilities and a new series has been initiated. More may yet be heard of the old name.

Travel guides by other publishers abound, usually in series with dozens or scores of other guides. One of the best resources for lore and local history of the American states is a relic of the Great Depression. It is the *American Guide Series*, a work that covered, in separate volumes, all the then-forty-eight states and Alaska (but not Hawaii) and was created by the WPA Writers' Project. The books appeared from 1937 to 1950, the more recent dates being revisions under the imprints of a variety of publishers. While they are no help in dealing with such modern developments as international airports and an interstate highway system that wasn't begun for more than a decade after the last of the *American Guides* appeared, they are beautifully written, often sprightly and engaging, and worth reading just for pleasure. And they are a treasure-house of local, regional, and state color and tradition. The titles usually are such formulations as *Alabama: A Guide to the Deep South; Illinois: A Descriptive and Historical Guide;* and *New Jersey: A Guide to Its Present and Past.*

The *Blue Guides,* started between the world wars, are a series covering most of Europe; the series was revised and expanded after World War II. The focus varies from national (*Blue Guide to Sweden*) to regional (*Blue Guide to Southern Italy*) to metropolitan (*Blue Guide to Paris*). They go into somewhat less detail than the Baedekers and are written in more contemporary language and thus are a bit easier to take in. They, too, have an abundance of quite good maps of cities and regions, and their indexes are excellent.

The Swiss publishing house of Nagel produces (in English as well as the principal West European languages) a worldwide line of bulky and authoritative guides that are as detailed as the original Baedekers. They are aptly titled the *Nagel Encyclopaedia-Guides,* for while they will fit easily into a suitcase or a fairly good-sized briefcase, they surely aren't pocket guides.

The Nagel guides cover well over a hundred countries, many of them in well over a thousand pages. In the case of the Japan guide, for instance, a general introduction takes up nearly three hundred pages and covers geography; history; government; architecture and the other visual arts; performing arts; sports and recreation; the economy; customs; food; and the Japanese character. The next 650 pages offer a "portrait of the country," with tour itineraries; descriptions; and copious, detailed maps. The last 170-odd pages supply practical information about transportation, communication, shopping, hotel and restaurant information, a travelers' glossary, and an extensive index. Guides to various countries differ in length, but in each case the organization is essentially similar and extremely effective. The better libraries will have a collection of Nagel guides, and even though they may be out-of-date they usually are worth consulting.

For the American states and adjoining Canadian provinces, the *Mobil Guide* series, published by the U.S. oil production and marketing company, is an important asset to motor tourists (and others). The series is divided into seven regional paperbound volumes: *California and the West, Great Lakes Area, Middle Atlantic States, Northeasern States, Northwest and Great Plains States, Southeastern States,* and *Southwest and South Central Area.*

Each of the five books is divided into states and alphabetically within each state by city and town. There are background articles on every state and prominent tourist region as well as a description of each locality and its attractions and points of interest. Most decent hotels, motels, and restaurants are not only described but also rated with a system of stars from one ("good, better than average") to the rarely bestowed five ("one of the best in the country"). The guides are revised and reissued annually. The research reflected in this series is of high quality and their level of reliability is tops for community and tourist information as well as on food and lodging.

The *Mobil Guides* are essentially an American takeoff on the famous French *Guides Michelin*. These guides, covering Western Europe, are published by the Michelin tire people and for some years have been available in English as well as their native French and other West European tongues. They are revised annually, and each year's list of five-star restaurants is watched anxiously by the proprietors and chefs of the finest restaurants on the Continent to see who has been added and who dropped. The *Guide Michelin* is the international arbiter of which European restaurants are really great.

There are many other series of travel guides that address the more important tourist countries. Among these are the books of Eugene Fodor, Temple Fielding, and Doré Ogrizek. All are similar but each has its particular strengths.

Apart from these full-fledged and sharply focused books of information for travelers is that separate genre of travel writing characterized by the work of such contemporary writers as Paul Theroux. He exemplifies a long tradition that can trace its way back through Bernard Berenson to Mark Twain to—well, Marco Polo. They wrote for armchair travelers rather than the Baedeker and timetable set. But more to our point here, their work was impressions and perceptions and not the stuff of reference material. Thus it is outside our purview—but not a bad way to kill a few hours. So into the armchair, and bon voyage!

CHAPTER 7

THE WORLD'S ORGANIZATIONS AND INSTITUTIONS, AND HOW TO FIND OUT ABOUT THEM

There are directories to every kind of institution from advertising agencies to zoological gardens. Some list nothing more than the name, address, and phone number of the organization along with its stated purpose and a few words about its program. Others add information about budget and staff. Still others go into great detail about purpose and programs.

The management, organization, principal products, and usually sales and financial information are on record and accessible for almost every major business in the world. Similar information is available about trade and business associations. The world's labor unions also are a matter of record, and information on their history, membership, and leadership are accessible in your library, along with breakdowns of the industries or trades covered by each.

An immense volume of statistical data on the population, economy, legal system, political structure and subdivisions, and much more is on record for every government on Earth, although outside the large Western democracies these are not always reliable beyond the barest basics. Directories list intergovernmental organizations at every level, from associations of mayors or state attorneys general to the United Nations. There are directories of philanthropic foundations as well as compendiums of successful applications for foundation grants.

BASIC SOURCES OF INFORMATION ABOUT ORGANIZATIONS

Even a classified telephone directory can be helpful if all you need is the correct formulation of an organization's name and its address and phone number. (But you will have to spell some words the directory's way—*e.g.*, disc, not disk; theatre, not theater.) Sometimes that's enough. In addition to such familiar classified lists as those of lawyers or attorneys, hospitals, restaurants, etc., the *Yellow Pages* carry an alphabetized but otherwise unclassified list of *associations* under that title. *The World Almanac* carries slightly more data about more than a thousand societies and associations, including, in addition to name and address, the year of incorporation and the number of branches, chapters, or members. Although the phone-book list is alphabetized strictly by the first word of the association's name (omitting "the"), *The World Almanac* lists the groups alphabetically by the key word in the name—*e.g.*, Bluebird Society, North American.

In any search for current data about organizations, don't waste time with general encyclopedias. Their treatment of business corporations and various associations is limited to general background about a relative handful of the largest and most famous. Their factual information—*e.g.*, on sales volume or number of employees—is inevitably limited, and where it appears, inevitably out-of-date.

This is where specialized and usually annual publications about organizations shine. A convenient way to consider these directories is by the kinds of organization they describe or list. There are three principal sources for these books. Most of them are produced by commercial publishers. Next come the many associations that publish directories of their own members. The other major category is that of government agencies—national, state, and local— and by stretching the definition a bit also including international organizations.

Whatever kind of organization you are looking up, the most direct path to information about it may lie in an association. In America virtually every organization belongs to one or more association, and that applies to associations themselves. In the 1830s Alexis de Tocqueville noted in *Democracy in America* the ubiquity in the United States of associations "of a thousand kinds, religious, moral, serious, futile, general or restricted, enormous or diminutive. . . . to give entertainments, to found seminaries, to build inns, to construct churches, to diffuse books, to send missionaries to the antipodes; in this manner they found hospitals, prisons, and schools."

It is just as true today, and the surest way to find an association in the United States is to look it up in the *Encyclopedia of Associations,* an invaluable reference tome first published in 1956 by Gale Research Company. Now a multivolume work, this superdirectory identifies more than twenty-three thousand American associations, including international ones based in the United States, and an additional twenty-five hundred or so international associations headquartered outside the United States. They range from household words such as "Red Cross" to tiny groups so arcane that they would have startled Tocqueville. The information supplied includes name, address, phone number, name of the responsible executive, and date of founding. It lists the number of members and the occupation or interest that brings members to the organization. The general and specific program objectives of the association are cited, along with the names and frequency of publications, affiliation with other organizations, frequency and often dates and place of meetings, whether the group maintains a library, and sometimes budget.

The scheme of organization of this resource makes it accessible from any direction. Volume 1 is itself in three huge parts, each a volume. Parts 1 and 2 cover U.S. organizations arranged by seventeen general subject categories—*e.g.,* Trade, Business, and Commercial Organizations; Health and Medical Organizations. Part 3 of Volume 1 is a name and key-word index to Parts 1 and 2. The three volumes or parts of Volume 1 are all that many smaller libraries buy.

The rest of the set, found in virtually all substantial general-purpose libraries, comprises three more books. Volume 2 contains two additional indexes, one geographic and the other of the names of executives. Volume 3 is a quarterly cumulative update service for U.S. national organizations. Finally, Volume 4 lists and indexes international organizations situated outside the United States. It is updated by semiannual supplements.

The range of this encyclopedia is so wide that it includes numerous associations that are members of other associations that it also lists, which fact of course accounts for its tremendous bulk. At the other end of the scale are narrowly focused directories that list only the organizations in a particular category, such as companies that rebuild automobile parts, or black-owned businesses in U.S. cities or in a given state.

To find one of these very specific directories, turn to the *Guide to American Directories,* produced by B. Klein Publications of Coral Gables, Florida, or to Gale's *Directory of Directories.* There also is a *World Guide to Abbreviations of Organizations*—invaluable in this sort of research. And in case you remember an association's publication but not its name you should be able to match them up in Bowker's *Associations' Publications in Print.* In the United States many states have directories of associations within their borders.

This chapter opened with an implied promise to locate information about advertising agencies and zoos as well as what's in between. The guides just cited could take you straight to a source for ad agency information: the *Standard Directory of Advertising Agencies.* It lists U.S. advertising agencies, and advertisers and their products. Zoos are easy enough to find out about: the major ones are described in good general encyclopedias, and tourist guidebooks to states or cities cover all of them. There is also another approach, discussed in the following section.

CULTURAL INSTITUTIONS

"Cultural institution" can be defined to mean almost anything. Here it refers to such institutions as libraries, museums of art or natural history, aquariums, planetariums, botanical gardens, and zoos. One publication lists all such establishments in the world, along with higher educational and research institutions. It is *World of Learning,* which is also discussed in Chapter 13.

"Cultural" also embraces the performing arts, which are treated in Chapter 10 and not addressed here. Religious and educational institutions, inescapably part of the cultural scene, are covered in Chapters 11 and 13, respectively. Other categories, which we shall include arbitrarily, are philanthropic foundations, research and scientific institutions despite their identification with the world of education, and the fields of conservation and human relations.

If you are looking up one of these entities and can't find it in your own library, there are many volumes in the reference section that can put you on the trail of another library that has the resource you need. One of the basics in this class is Bowker's *American Library Directory* and its companion guide, *Subject Collections.* The former is organized by state and city, the latter by subject area, with the libraries described listed alphabetically by state within each subject. The American Library Association's *ALA Membership Directory,* published by Bowker, is an international guide to the professional associations of librarians and archivists and others in the information sciences.

Gale's *Directory of Special Libraries and Information Centers* and its companion, *Subject Directory,* do about the same job for special libraries, which term embraces the libraries of universities and colleges, corporations, associations, museums, and other institutions. Some of these are restricted to faculty and students or employees, others are open to the public, and still others are open on a case-by-case basis to what appear to be serious inquirers. Quite a few special libraries participate in interlibrary loan programs, so it pays to inquire.

The *Directory of Special Libraries* lists libraries alphabetically by the name of the library or its parent institution, with a geographical breakdown in Volume 2. For this reason you may find *Subject Directory* easier to use. Bear in mind when you turn to these directories that they describe the libraries' collections and do not contain actual lists of books. The state library in your state may also be a useful resource even though you are not near the capital city where it is situated. A high level of cooperation between state and individual public libraries is the norm.

Museums, both of art and of natural history, are well documented in directories, and finding them poses no particular problem. Some of these are published under the auspices of professional groups—*e.g.,* the *Official Museum Directory* of the American Association of Museums. Other standards include Kenneth Hudson's *Directory of Museums and Living Displays* and *World Art in American Museums.* Finally, the *Directory of Unique Museums* covers such special museums in the United States as the Circus World Museum at Baraboo, Wisconsin.

Aquariums, botanical gardens, and zoos (formally zoological gardens or parks) often are listed together. You can learn a good deal about the world-class institutions in this group in any good general encyclopedia. Individual books or sets, however, often go into much greater detail. If that's what you want instead of a quicker look, turn to a popular work such as *Lions and Tigers and*

Bears, a guide to zoos, visitor farms, nature centers, and marine life displays in the United States and Canada, or the more formal *Zoos and Aquariums in the Americas,* which extends its net to Latin America as well. It is sponsored by the American Association of Zoological Parks. Botanical gardens are addressed in, among others, the *Handbook of American Gardens—A Traveler's Guide.*

Whatever the reason, even given the interest in astronomy generated by the space probes and other advances of recent years, planetariums get short shrift from the publishers of directories. Although a planetarium is in effect a museum of astronomy that interprets what the astronomer "sees" to the layman, and an astronomical observatory is a serious workplace for the professional, there are far more directories of observatories than of planetariums. The latter are described in travel books and city guides. One book can be recommended: *U.S. Observatories: A Directory and Travel Guide.* Although its name implies concentration on observatories, it specifically lists and describes planetariums.

For U.S. philanthropic foundations, the *Foundation Directory* is the standard work. Updated annually and available in almost every library, it is organized by state and lists the essential information, including founder, trustees and officers, fields of interest, approximate endowment, and sizes or range of sizes of characteristic grants. Coming the other way at the "philanthropoid mind," there are several books useful to grant-seekers. Factual information about a foundation's track record can be found in, *e.g.,* the *Annual Register of Grant Support.*

Others, such as *Grantsmanship: Money and How to Get It,* coach would-be recipients on approaching the goose that might lay the golden egg. In a loosely related field, there is a plethora of books listing prizes, awards, and scholarships, many of which topics also appear in various books of lists and records.

Science and research associations are amply treated in general directories such as the *Encyclopedia of Associations* and the *World of Learning.* The latter is also good on scientific and research centers as distinct from societies. The comprehensive, multivolume *Research Centers Directory,* revised annually, is organized by field of activity and thoroughly indexed. The U.S. National Academy of Sciences publishes *Scientific and Technical Societies of the United States and Canada,* and a good many other similar works are published by UNESCO and various commercial publishers.

There are specialized directories for conservation and environmental organizations. American government agencies and private groups concerned with ecological issues are covered authoritatively in *Environment USA: A Guide to Agencies, People, and Resources.* Some bodies publish their own—*e.g.,* the National Wildlife Fund's *Conservation Directory*—and the subject also is addressed in many of the general directories and in yearbooks such as *Europa.*

Societies of Afro Americans, and other agencies addressing the interests of American blacks are listed in *The Black Resource Guide,* among others. Various specialized directories identify civic and charitable organizations—*e.g.,* the *Community Resources Directory* and the *Social Services Organizations and Agencies Directory* (covering both public and voluntary agencies). Others concentrate on agencies using volunteers, as does *Volunteer: The Comprehensive Guide to Voluntary Service in the United States.*

A miscellany of interests remains, embracing such human-relations concerns as ethnic identity, interfaith or ecumenical activity, interracial and intercultural understanding, social and fraternal organizations, service clubs, private clubs, and organizations focusing on the concerns of women and of youth. Some categories of wide general interest are treated separately in this book—*e.g.,* business, commerce, finance, and industry, which are addressed in Chapter 17. All of these categories also can be found in *Encyclopedia of Associations* and similar works.

LABOR ORGANIZATIONS

General encyclopedias treat the researcher somewhat better in this field than they do in the business world. However, more consistent coverage is found in more specialized resources. For American unions, one of the best is the U.S. Government Printing Office, especially its *Directory of Labor Unions* and *Handbook of Labor Statistics,* both from the Bureau of Labor Statistics. The directory *National Trade and Professional Organizations of the United States,* generally known as *NTPA,* has a somewhat broader reach, as its title promises.

The easiest sources for information on labor organizations in the rest of the world are found under the heading of economic geography. An outstanding example is the worldwide trade union coverage in *Europa Year Book,* discussed in more detail in the following section. It has an excellent list of labor organizations, with names, addresses, etc., in its section on each country.

Foundations and commercial publishers produce reference material about labor with lists of unions and key personnel. They also disseminate a very large volume of studies, critiques, polemics, and histories by individual scholars and other authors. The latter are accessible through various directories and library card catalogs. Finally, unions of course are also covered in general works such as the *Encyclopedia of Associations* and various handbooks and yearbooks in the category of economic geography.

INFORMATION ABOUT GOVERNMENTS

As suggested earlier, statistical and personnel information supplied by the large Western democracies and their various subdivisions are generally both available and reliable and are regularly updated. All these countries produce a flood of information in the form of annual reports, summaries, and studies that reveal much about the personnel and operations of their governments.

For example, the United States issues its *U.S. Government Organization Manual* detailing departments and key people in the whole executive branch. The *Congressional Directory* (for some bureaucratic reason formally listed as *Official Congressional Directory* though even its cover doesn't engage in that bit of overkill) supplies similar exhaustive coverage of the legislative branch. There is an infinitude of like information on every aspect of government right down to a *Directory of Federal Regional Structure* and a directory of federal information services in *Information USA*. As noted, other major Western governments do likewise. Don't worry for the Public Printer. That worthy—accompanied by an enormous staff—will never go out of business.

However great their number and variety, the federal publications leave a few gaps, and private publishers have moved aggressively into those niches. The *Congressional Directory* gives almost no information about the staffs of senators and representatives and their committees, so a former congressman brought out the *Congressional Staff Directory*, listing staff assignments and biographies of key staffers along with House and Senate committee and subcommittee assignments and much more. The same company parlayed the formula into a successful and useful *Federal Staff Directory*, going into similar detail for the top levels of the federal bureaucracy in general.

In the United States it is simple enough to locate information about any state. The *National Directory of State Agencies* is useful in such a quest. So is the *State Information Book* and *State Elective Officials and the Legislatures*, the latter produced by the Council of State Governments. And if you want to find out which state officeholders run the machinery by which their elective officials get elected, the Federal Election Commission issues the annual *Election Directory*.

Another important resource found in the bigger and better libraries is in effect a government-watcher's guide to periodical literature, a semimonthly looseleaf subject index universally known as *PAIS*, formally the *Bulletin* of the Public Affairs Information Service. It covers English-language publications anywhere in the world that address economic, political, and international affairs. Issues are cumulated quarterly and are bound at year-end with an annual index of authors.

It is also fairly easy to find out about municipal governments inside the state in which you are looking them up. Every state produces lists of its state, county, and local offices and officeholders, usually in the state's *Blue Book*. And a resource for locating them is produced by the Council of State Governments: *State Blue Books and Reference Publications*. Finding this information about a city or county across the country, however, often is less simple. Still, there are a few publications that may help, including the *Book of the States* and the *Municipal Year Book*.

Outside the United States, all the big Western democracies have something analogous to the American crop, and the best way to seek it out in a library is to turn to "government" in the catalog and riffle through the alphabet there until you come to the country you want. Watch for the word "directory" (if that's what you are seeking) to minimize wasted time. That is to say, don't stray into "trade statistics" or "public transportation" or extraneous stuff of that sort.

There are important privately published reference works on foreign countries that also contain directories. The best of these is the *Europa Year Book*, mentioned previously under "Labor Organizations." This is a two-volume product of the London-based Europa Publications. Volume 1 covers continental Europe, the United Kingdom, and international organizations. Volume 2 addresses the rest of the world. Coverage is country by country and across the board, embracing constitution; structure of government; legislative representation; political and diplomatic information; news media; and much else, including lots of statistical matter.

A couple of U.S. publishers also put out solid compendia of information on the countries of Western Europe. These are Facts on File and Washington, D.C.'s Stryker-Post Publications. Both are titled, logically enough, *Western Europe.*

Traditionally, completely accurate and relatively up-to-date information has been much less available outside the West. There are two reasons. States in the Communist world have long treated economic information, and also the identity and background of officials below the topmost level, as something of a state secret, releasing only as much as meets the political need or objective of the moment.

This tendency to hoard information is not particularly Marxist. In the case of the Soviet Union, for example, it is Russian, inherited from the bureaucracies of the czars. More than that, it seems to stem from the essence of bureaucracy itself. Things are beginning to change, however. Such information is slowly becoming available about the Soviet Union and a few other countries in its bloc, and also on China. Though still far less complete than in the West, this trickle of data appears to be increasingly accurate, much more so than before the advent of Gorbachev and Deng Xiaoping.

Many governments, including most of those in the Third World, will not release current and accurate economic information because of their great concern to reflect an upbeat national image, and they are quite unconcerned with such Western notions as freedom of information. Indeed, it was to maintain control of information that the developing nations sponsored UNESCO's ill-famed move to create a "New World Information Order" to license journalists and publishers, an idea that was abandoned in England before 1700.

Because so many countries have been so sparing in letting out facts, the best information about them often comes from other countries, in part through academic research and partly by courtesy of various intelligence and counterintelligence agencies. The Central Intelligence Agency publishes an annual called *The World Factbook,* which is available in most substantial libraries.

A long series of *Area Handbooks* on countries mostly in the Third World was prepared under the supervision of American University in Washington for publication by the U.S. Government Printing Office beginning during the Cold War. These titles, of which *Albania, Iraq, People's Republic of China (Communist China),* and *Zambia* are representative, are still extremely useful in many situations. In their original form they are no longer in print, but these publications have been continued, and in many cases revised, under the title *Country Studies.* (If you were familiar with them, the green bindings are now white.) The whole collection, green or white, is held in many libraries.

The United Nations and many of its agencies such as UNESCO publish voluminous statistical and other information about the world at large and about individual member states. Although their overall studies—*e.g.*, the annual *World Economic Survey* of the UN Bureau of Economic Affairs—are generally excellent, the data on particular countries ordinarily come from the states concerned, so accuracy is not guaranteed.

The International Monetary Fund's *International Financial Statistics Yearbook* is a standard work for economic geographers. Most other international organizations put out annual or periodic reports containing similar information. An example is the Organization for Economic Co-operation and Development (OECD) with its periodic *Economic Surveys* on particular countries, among other reports. Good libraries, even fairly small ones, will have a decent collection of this kind of resource.

Needless to say in this public information age, international and intergovernmental organizations issue a lot of printed matter about themselves. The UN's own *Yearbook of the United Nations* reports its own actions and is well indexed. Even the North Atlantic Treaty Organization puts out an annual *NATO Handbook,* published in Paris by the NATO Information Service. Private publishers are active here, too. One such U.S. work is *International Organizations: A Guide to Information Sources.* Another, published in Munich, is the *Yearbook of International Organizations.*

National, regional, and local population figures, land and water areas, and crude economic data are usually reported in national gazetteers and are usually accurate if not always up-to-date. More sensitive matters, such as agricultural production and public health, may be dissembled or omitted. It is difficult for many Westerners, especially Americans, Canadians, Australians, and New Zealanders, given their ready access to kinds of official information that are kept strictly secret in the rest of the world, to appreciate how rare such freedom is. This is also true of Britons but a little less so because of the Official Secrets Act, and of residents in most of the other Commonwealth and Western European countries in varying degree.

You can find out about political parties by consulting encyclopedias or broad-gauge yearbooks such as *Europa* under the country and the name of the party concerned, if you know it. Remember that, particularly in a non-U.S. reference book, a foreign party may well be alphabetized by its name or initials in its own language. For instance, Germany's Social Democratic Party is really the *Sozialde-mokratische Partei Deutschlands* or SPD, not the SDP. Gale Research Company publishes an annual directory helpful for searching out a foreign party: *Political Parties of the World.*

There are also sources for political interest groups that are not parties *per se*, such as lobbying organizations—e.g. (in the United States), *Washington Representatives* or the *Washington Lobbyists/Lawyers Directory.* In any such search, keep in mind that almost every trade, labor, professional, and special-interest association—and certainly any with a Washington address—is at least in part a lobbying organization.

Organizations and individuals interested in foreign affairs—*i.e.,* international politics—can also be located in a library search. The Foreign Policy Association (FPA) issues a directory of Americans active in the leadership of nongovernmental organizations such as the U.S. Association for the United Nations (or the FPA, for that matter): *U.S. Citizens in World Affairs.* There also is a directory titled *Voluntary and Transnational Organizations of the United States.* Groups whose international interests focus on world peace can be located in such resources as the *Peace Resource Book* or the *International Peace Directory.* Do your inclinations run to war? There's an organization for you; just name your war and look it up in the *Encyclopedia of Associations.* How about 1812?

CHAPTER 8

Human History: Looking Back in Time Without Wasting Time

This chapter is intended to help you fill in gaps in what you learned or remember of history, and not at all to be a guide to a whole do-it-yourself course in any aspect of history. There are at least three circumstances in which you may find it useful. One is a healthy curiosity for background on the disruptions in today's headlines or the bomb smoke on the nightly news, a desire to understand the ancient times and conditions that spawned and conditioned the peoples and places of today's devastation.

Second, most of us know someone who has a phenomenal grasp of history, whose occasional historic allusions or quotations pique our curiosity. These pages are intended to help you play catch-up, to locate and understand what was behind the obscure currents of history: what sent Hannibal and his handful of elephants across the Alps, or how Emperor Hirohito's grandfather was able to wrest control of Japan away from the last *shōgun*, or why the Dreyfus affair tore French society apart for more than a decade.

And third, travel or reading often sparks a new area of interest in which one is moved to set out on a systematic quest for new knowledge about a particular place or time.

Unless you are thoroughly familiar with the work you are searching in and the period you are looking up, in any historical search you must be prepared to spend a few minutes of unproductive time figuring out the names to look under. Iran or Persia? Germany or Prussia? German Confederation? Hapsburg (or Habsburg) Empire? Holy Roman Empire? In a conventional book of history the table of contents may be helpful; if not, the index surely will. In a regular encyclopedia or a historical encyclopedia or dictionary, cross-references will put you straight. But don't let a minute or two of this sort of backing and filling irritate you into giving up the quest in disgust. The internal consistency in a given book's treatment of names is necessary to prevent chaos. Some arbitrary choices are necessary, too, where an area has had different names and been occupied by different peoples down the course of history.

The nonprofessional historian engaged in historical research is surprised from time to time at coming across a statement or interpretation he or she "knows" is not true, that is contradicts what one has "always known." If you find yourself in that situation, here are a few words of comfort. First, discovery and invention change "facts" and overturn the common wisdom: "If God had meant man to fly, He would have given him wings."

Second, every historian sees, understands, interprets, and writes through a certain set of biases and viewpoints, a particular *Weltanschauung* or world view. Since World War II a school of revisionist historians has emerged that holds the view that U.S. imperialism and greed are essentially responsible for poverty and hunger. This view is widely held on the political left and often is used to interpret modern history by left-wing historians. It is ardently opposed by right-wing historians, some of whom lay every social ill to Marx, Lenin, or Mao. Most historians fit somewhere between the extremes and try very hard to keep their narration of events objective. A historical viewpoint is inevitable when one is interpreting history and not merely reciting events, but most historians try to make that viewpoint a calm and reasoned one, avoiding either subtle propaganda or polemics.

When, in your historical browsing, you encounter a statement or judgment that clashes with what you always knew, a simple way to evaluate it is to look up what other writers have to say about the subject. This kind of search, if you have the time for it, can be absorbing and good fun. You quickly discover that there are hardly two historians who present exactly the same interpretation of a particular event or situation, yet their summaries are not likely to clash. Instead, the slightly different angle from which each sees and reports creates that three-dimensional effect that makes history come alive before your eyes. Where there are real conflicts of view and sharply differing interpretations, you simply have to choose sides or adopt a neutral position. Base your decision as you would in a jury room, on the weight of the evidence and the credibility of the witness.

FINDING FACTS

Facts and dates are only part of the grist of history, but they get argued about a lot and they are easily forgotten. If you are only looking for a quick fact, or to confirm a date, like what the casualties were in the Second Battle of Bull Run, or when the first manned space flight took place, there are several approaches you can take. One is *The World Almanac* or any other book that includes a compendium of memorable dates.

For U.S. history, one of the handiest of many historical dictionaries is Richard B. Morris's *Encyclopedia of American History*. It is well indexed and is organized chronologically within topical subdivisions—*e.g.*, "Business Cycles and Price Trends." Sometimes the topical headings themselves are grouped chronologically—*e.g.*, "American Foreign Relations, 1899–1917." This title was revised in 1976 by Morris and his son, Jeffrey. Other encyclopedic works on U.S. history include Scribner's *Dictionary of American History* (eight volumes, revised edition, 1976) and the abridged *Concise Dictionary of American History* (1983).

Richard Morris and Graham W. Irwin compiled a world history similar in design to Morris's U.S. encyclopedia cited above, the *Harper Encyclopedia of the Modern World*. There are others on narrower topics—wars, for example. *The Marshall Cavendish Illustrated Encyclopedia of World War II,* edited by Peter Young (1972), was produced originally for mail-order sales in twenty-five slim volumes. Any good narrative history that has an excellent index can be used as nearly as easily as an encyclopedia of history. An outstanding example of the latter is Samuel Eliot Morison's *Oxford History of the American People*. There are many more.

TRY A GENERAL
ENCYCLOPEDIA

General encyclopedias also excel at supplying the fast fact. They are a reliable resource, easy to use, and available everywhere. They may serve you even better in a search for something broader than mere facts. History is a subject that is treated extremely well by the good general encyclopedias, and you really couldn't do better than to start your quest there. In turning to them, simply remember that in terms of bulk, what you see is what you get—*i.e.*, the smallest encyclopedia will give you a quick, accurate summary with little detail. The largest will have an extremely long account with much detail.

World Book features concise entries on specific topics, and its treatment of complex historical issues is necessarily short. *Academic American*'s articles will be longer and at somewhat greater depth and with more details. *Collier's* and *Americana* will go further in that direction: The articles of both will be longer and will bring a bit more sophistication to the topic and demand it of the reader.

The *Britannica*, characteristically, will supply massive detail at extensive length, and the very large treatment in the *Macropaedia* volumes will be synopsized in a few words in the *Micropaedia* portion of the set. All five encyclopedias represent the cream of the four visible segments of the field—*i.e.*, young readers (*World Book*); bright senior high school students and moderate-demand general use (*Academic American*); full-fledged general adult and family use (*Americana* and *Collier's*); and large, costly, and complete treatment (*Britannica*).

As an illustration, selected randomly, consider the history of Iran and focus on the period from the beginning of recorded time through the first great Persian empire, which was conquered by Alexander the Great. This covers nearly three thousand years and includes the kingdom of the Medes and the emperors Cyrus the Great, Darius the Great, Xerxes, and his successors named Arta-xerxes.

In *World Book* the period is handled in about 450 words. Biographic sketches of the leading figures of the time give additional detail, but this is true of all the encyclopedias. *Academic American* gives the history of the same span in approximately eight hundred words. It gets on the order of three thousand words in *Americana* and *Collier's*.

The *Britannica* uses nearly seven thousand words for its *Macropaedia* coverage of the same time span; the *Micropaedia* article on Iran has about a hundred words on this period in its five-hundred-word précis of Iranian history. All five of the substantive articles are well illustrated, the *Britannica* one in this case somewhat more generously than usual in the sparely illustrated *Macropaedia*.

It is entirely possible that your curiosity about ancient Persia will be fully satisfied by your encyclopedia search. If not, all the sets mentioned here have good bibliographies, in detail roughly proportional to the size of the article, that will point out the best sources for further study and describe the treatment you can find in the various ones. The recommendations in each of these bibliographies are, as you would expect, geared to the general depth and level of difficulty of the encyclopedia's own coverage.

But there are a couple of other avenues to pursue if you still have questions left after getting out of the encyclopedia. Perhaps the best of these is the Cambridge University series, most of which can be found in the better suburban and small-city libraries; all of them are available in nearly every big-city and college or university library.

THE CAMBRIDGE HISTORIES

The *Cambridge Ancient History* is a work of seventeen volumes, five of which are filled with maps and plates. It was begun in 1923 and completed in 1939. Each section of the text was written by one of that period's leading historians of the region and era. Each volume ends with an excellent bibliography organized by chapter. This is not a work for one seeking a quick, casual review of a long and complex period. But for the user of the present book it excels in two ways. One is to flesh out with richer details an episode you have found sketched only briefly in an encyclopedia (or other) account. If, for instance, you read that Artaxerxes III was poisoned by his eunuch Bagoas, and you want to seek out additional detail on the role and character of Bagoas, you can find what you need here.

On the other hand, if, *e.g.*, the background you picked up from the encyclopedia (or elsewhere) makes you want to read at some length on the reign and legacy of Cyrus the Great, here, too, the *Cambridge* can serve you well.

However, in neither case will the search be as simple as in an encyclopedia. Before using the *Cambridge* you need to know something about its organization. The set is devoted to the ancient world of classical history—*i.e.*, those parts of Europe, Asia, and Africa lying within a sweeping semicircle focused approximately on Sicily and embracing the basins of the eastern Mediterranean and the Aegean, Black, Caspian, and Red seas and the Persian Gulf. In time it begins in prehistory and runs all the way to A.D. 324, the eve of the Council of Nicaea and the dawn of the medieval period.

Thus inevitably the *Cambridge* volumes switch back and forth in time as well as geography to tell the story from different perspectives, notably in the case of our example those of the Persian Empire and its great rival, Greece.

As noted, *World Book* has about 350 words on Persian history up to Alexander the Great; the *Britannica,* nearly seven thousand. The *Cambridge Ancient History* has well over a hundred pages and sixty-five thousand words on the same period. Each volume of the *Cambridge* has its own index. To locate Bagoas and Artaxerxes III (d. 338 B.C.), you can find them indexed in Volume VI (Macedon, 401–301 B.C.). In your search for Cyrus the Great, once you know that he lived c. 590–529 B.C., you find you must look him up in Volume IV, where there are thirty-eight index entries for him. Only a few of them supply the context, so without actually looking, you won't know just what part of the long and fascinating story of Cyrus is being told at that point. Encyclopedia indexes will send you to fewer places, but generally with more accuracy and therefore ease. For instance, the *Britannica* on Cyrus indexes twenty-six references, long and short, that are spread across fourteen of the set's twenty-nine text volumes. The index (new in 1985) supplies the context for each of the references, so it is fairly simple to know where to look for the kind of information you want.

There is another kind of complication that is easy enough to handle if you are forewarned. It is illustrated in the case of Artaxerxes III, whose personal name was Ochus. While the encyclopedias will also reveal that fact, the *Cambridge* work uses "Ochus" and "Artaxerxes III" interchangeably in its narrative, so if you are not alert to that fact it is easy to become confused.

The next chronological step in the series is the *Cambridge Mediaeval History,* in eight volumes, started in 1911 and completed a few years ahead of the *Ancient History,* in 1936. It treats the history of Europe, mostly Western Europe, from the declining years of the Roman Empire to the eve of the fifteenth century and the Renaissance. Here, too, each section is written by a major authority, and like the *Ancient History* it has outstanding bibliographic material, in this case concluding each section.

The *Cambridge Modern History* takes up where the *Mediaeval* leaves off and comes down to the years after World War I. The first six of its fourteen volumes trace the history of Western Europe from the Renaissance to the exploration and colonization of America. The seventh deals with the United States, and the last six resume the history of Europe and the modern world. The fourteenth volume is an atlas. The *Cambridge Modern History* was begun before the others, in 1902, and not completed until 1926. Like its counterparts, it was published in England by Cambridge University Press and in the United States by Macmillan.

A completely new work on modern history was published by Cambridge University Press (in both Great Britain and America) in fourteen volumes in 1975, under the title *A New Cambridge Modern History.* Unlike the three earlier works, this one has a separate index volume.

OTHER WORLD AND NATIONAL HISTORIES

An old and excellent large general history on a quite different plan still found in most bigger libraries is the *New Larned History.* Its "newness" goes up to 1924, when it was last published, in twelve volumes, a revised and expanded version of what had been a five-volume work in its first appearance in 1893–95. It was compiled by a Buffalo, New York, librarian named Josephus N. Larned, whose library of the Buffalo YMCA was the first in the United States to adopt the Dewey Decimal System of classification. He was something of a self-made historian who compiled several other historical works and was highly regarded for his scholarship and authority. Larned assembled in this work many thousands of entries embracing the whole of human history, virtually all in quoted excerpts from other historians. The work is arranged in alphabetical order with abundant cross-references, and the source of each of the historical excerpts is supplied.

If you find it difficult to envisage a sprightly book in world history, you might look up William L. Langer's *An Encyclopedia of World History,* first published in 1952 by Houghton Mifflin. Its fifth edition appeared in 1972 in a single fat volume of compact capsules on people and events. Its basic organization is chronological, and its time periods are subdivided where appropriate into countries or regions. It is both comprehensive and well supplied with maps, tables of rulers, *et al.,* and its organization makes it extremely easy to use.

There are a couple of interesting sets of parallel treatments of world and American history to be found in the libraries, works executed by some interesting and consequential people. In 1936 Grossett brought out the *Dictionary of Events: A Handbook of Universal*

History by George Palmer Putnam and his father, George Haven Putnam. These gentlemen were the grandson and son, respectively, of the George Palmer Putnam (1814–72) who founded the publishing house that became G.P. Putnam's Sons. Both compilers of this unusual history were important figures in the history of the publishing house and both were writers, the father also a serious student of history. The son, who was married to aviation pioneer Amelia Earhart, saw to the completion of the work in 1936, a few years after his father's death.

The Putnams' *Dictionary of Events* is arranged like a *hexapla* Bible, in which parallel columns present six different biblical translations, verse by verse so that the different shadings of meaning in the various versions can be compared for each passage. In this case the columns are topical and regional, with the date in the left margin. The columns, left to right across each two-page spread, carry headings such as: "Progress of Society, etc."; "United States"; "Great Britain"; "France"; "Austria, Prussia, etc."; and "The World, elsewhere." There are genealogical tables and an index.

Gorton V. Carruth (father of poet Hayden Carruth) took a similar physical approach to organize information somewhat differently in editing *The Encyclopedia of American Facts and Dates* (sixth edition, 1972). This work uses four columns across each two-page spread to present, year after year in the vertical dimension, important or unusual or intriguing events. The four columns across the horizontal dimension are divided into loosely related groups of topics, as follows:

Science; Industry; Economics; Education; Religion; Philosophy	Sports; Fashions; Popular Entertainment; Folklore; Society	Politics and Government; War; Disasters; Vital Statistics	Books; Painting; Drama; Architecture; Sculpture

Collections of documents important in the history of various peoples are as old as documents and libraries. William MacDonald, a great historian, political scientist, and writer-editor, assembled the fourth and last volume of his *Documentary Source Book of American History, 1606–1926* in the latter year. Large libraries still hold it, and it is worth perusal if your interest lies in getting into the documents themselves. Another distinguished historian a couple of decades later, Henry Steele Commager, published his *Documents of American History* in 1949, taking the story from Ferdinand and

Isabella's charter to Columbus down to the creation of the North Atlantic Treaty Organization (NATO) in 1949, and subsequent revisions have updated it from time to time. Many other such collections have appeared before and since, including the *Annals of America,* assembled by Mortimer Adler for the Britannica company.

In 1965 the writer Milton Viorst used that approach for world history in *The Great Documents of Western Civilization.* He covers the span from the time of Christ to the 1960s, and he prefaces the text of each document with an explanatory headnote describing the setting, circumstances, and import for the society of the time.

Oxford University Press is famous for (among many other works) its *Oxford Companion* series to such subjects as English literature, the theater, etc. These are single volumes organized in dictionary form with a long alphabetical roster of concise articles. It also publishes histories in English art and literature as well as a multivolume work of general history, the fourteen-volume *Oxford History of England,* which takes the story up to the outbreak of World War I. Oxford also publishes an American history in the *Companion* series, the *Oxford Companion to American History,* edited by Thomas H. Johnson and issued in 1966.

It goes without saying that this brief review of various conveniently usable histories of various kinds is only that: a brief list. Every country that has any history to speak of has a long list of books recounting that history from one perspective or another. In the library some time when you are in a mood to browse and rummage, simply get into the card catalog or its computerized or microform equivalent and look up history and its various chronological, regional, national, state, and local manifestations.

While you are in the catalog, don't fail to note the historical associations. Apart from the major professional associations—the American Historical Society and the Association of American Historians—every state and an astonishing number of counties, cities, and towns have their own historical societies. Many of them have museums that also house excellent libraries where rare and fascinating books often can be found. These associations are important assets for amateur and professional genealogists, by the way.

Yes, and in the catalog don't forget ethnic, racial, religious, and tribal entries; and topical as well. Minorities, for example. Interest today is high in the history of minorities of various definitions. It is high in terms of publishing as well as reading. The list of minority histories grows almost daily. For this reason the field is not represented here with standard works. If your look-it-up inclinations run this way, look over your library's own holdings and discuss your particular approach with a reference librarian.

One last word: Don't overlook the "New Books" shelf.

CHAPTER 9

LOOKING UP THE EARTH AND ITS CREATURES

The subject matter of this chapter is literally as old as the hills. It was an ancient topic in the fourth century B.C. when Aristotle wrote his four tracts on biology, cataloging and describing the animals, their parts, and their reproduction. Four centuries later, in about A.D. 77, Pliny the Elder devoted to it more than one third of the Western world's first encyclopedia, his *Historia naturalis,* thirty-seven volumes treating the natural universe. Thus this vast topic can be seen as the foundation of modern general encyclopedias, and it still constitutes a great portion of their bulk. By and large the modern general encyclopedias handle the world of nature extremely well, as do the general scientific encyclopedias, *McGraw-Hill* and *Van Nostrand.*

Today there is a variety of specialized encyclopedias that focus entirely on one or another of the several parts of this world. We may think of these parts as the three traditional "kingdoms": animal, vegetable, and mineral. The scope of these parts can be put somewhat more precisely: The "mineral kingdom" must have room for all the Earth sciences, going far beyond mineralogy alone. The life sciences of biology embrace botany and zoology, both of which incorporate kinds of life we don't always think of under the "vegetable-animal" rubric. Then there is paleontology, in effect the science of former life, which relates to both Earth sciences and biology but which will be treated here with the former.

Gradually theoretical frameworks developed for continuing scientific inquiry into the planet and its inhabitants, evolving into three full-fledged scientific disciplines, each with a number of subdisciplines. These are the geologic, hydrologic, and atmospheric sciences.

To minimize wasting time as you carry out your search, you will do well to figure out ahead of time what kind of information you are looking for. It is always important to distinguish the subject of a science from the science itself. For instance, if you want to find out the names and characteristics of particular kinds of stone, a straightforward heading like "rocks and minerals" is the place to start. But if your aim is to get some understanding of the study of rock, to learn something about that science and its objectives and procedures, your target is petrology (from the Greek *petros*, "rock").

If you were not familiar with that term, it would only take you one extra step to find it. You know that as rock is part of Earth, the particular study of rock is part of geology. The introduction of any encyclopedia article on geology will list its subdisciplines and will make clear that petrology is the study of rock. It also will show that mineralogy is closely related and may be worth a look. Furthermore, a careful browse through the library card catalog itself would bring the same result.

THE SCIENCES OF EARTH

The three principal areas of study about Earth are the geologic, hydrologic, and atmospheric sciences. Geology (literally "Earth study") deals with the structures of the planet and the knowledge of its origins and evolution as recorded in the composition and shapes of its physical features. The relatively new discipline of geophysics is concerned with how Earth got the way it is—*i.e.*, with physical forces such as those of plate tectonics that, for instance, pushed Africa eastward away from the Americas. Mineralogy's subject is obvious from its name: the composition and occurrence of the minerals that make up Earth's crust. Volcanology (sometimes spelled vulcanology), also obviously, is about understanding volcanos—finding out how and where they erupt, and constructing, then testing, theories to explain why and when.

Another of the geologic sciences is paleontology (from the Greek *paleo*, "ancient"). This is the "ology" or study of ancient things specifically of the fossil remains of Earth's animals and plants. While they were alive, the creatures that turned into fossils were the subject of biology; paleontology is essentially the biology of the past. But today they are rock replicas of their former plant and animal selves, and paleontology is treated as an element of geology.

Other geologic sciences are petrology (discussed previously) and geochemistry, which has to do with the role of chemical processes in the abundance of minerals, in volcanic action, etc. Geodesy (Greek *geodaisia,* the divisions of Earth) is concerned with the shape of Earth itself, and geomorphology (Greek *morph,* "form") with shapes or landforms on Earth.

The hydrologic sciences look into the behavior and effects of water on Earth—in glaciers, in streams and rivers, and in lakes and oceans. Hydrology (Greek *hydro,* "water") addresses the quantity and quality of water. The other hydrologic sciences are glaciology; limnology (Greek *limne,* "pool"), the study of fresh waters; and oceanography.

The atmospheric sciences address Earth's envelope of air and its assorted gases. Everybody knows that meteorology is the study of weather, but not necessarily how it got that name. In eighteenth-century English usage the primary meaning of the word "meteor" was one that dictionaries now list as archaic or obsolete: any strange object in the sky not part of the sky itself. Thus rain was a meteor. Its white and flaky cousin was identified in an early-eighteenth-century encyclopedia as "snow, the well-known meteor." Lightning was a meteor; so was an asteroid or a chunk broken off some passing comet and fallen to Earth. The latter, of course, is our own well-known "meteor," or as we sometimes say, as fancifully as the ancients with their "meteors," our shooting star. Hence meteorology: the study of foreign objects in the sky.

The focus of climatology is self-evident: the study of weather and weather patterns and their effects over a sustained period. Other atmospheric sciences are aeronomy ("nomy" from the Greek *nemein,* "to distribute," thus knowledge about the air and its distribution) and various practical applications such as weather forecasting.

General and science encyclopedias have been suggested as starting points in looking up general reading about the Earth sciences. Every subfield has at least one "dictionary" whose content is actually encyclopedic. Usually they are a lot more accessible to the lay reader than many of the texts, and they are entirely reliable. For example: *Dictionary of Environmental Sciences* compiled by Robert W. Durrenberger, *A Dictionary of Earth Sciences* edited by Stella E. Stiegeler, and *Dictionary of Geology* by John Challinor.

For minerals see works such as the following: *Encyclopedia of Minerals* edited by Willard Lincoln Roberts, George Robert Rapp,

Jr., and Julius Weber; *How to Know the Minerals and Rocks* by Richard M. Pearl, one of McGraw-Hill's *Field Guide Series;* and *A Field Guide to Rocks and Minerals* by Frederick Pough.

On paleontology there is the *Encyclopedia of Prehistoric Life* edited by Rodney Steel and Anthony P. Harvey. Also see *Index Fossils of North America* by Harvey W. Shimer and Robert R. Schrock. (Index fossils are so called because they can date geologic eras easily and accurately; they are abundant, widespread, and easily identified.)

And don't forget the card catalog.

THE SCIENCE OF LIFE:
BIOLOGY

The dictionary tells us that biology deals with living organisms and their vital processes. The subject, then, is as broad as the immense diversity of living things on Earth. It studies the structure and function of organisms, from microscopic single-cell creatures to the largest and most complex. Its major subdivisions have been botany and zoology (those kingdoms again) and morphology and physiology, the studies of forms and function, respectively. But modern knowledge has opened new frontiers such as molecular biology and cell or cytobiology (Greek *kytos,* "hollow vessel" or cell). Biophysics and biochemistry reflect the increasing interdisciplinary overlap in biology today. Marine biology deals with life in all kinds of water—fresh and salt, moving and still.

Heredity and genetics also are part of biology, as is ecology (from the Greek *oikos,* "house," thus household or environment). Physical anthropology (Greek *anthropos,* "human") studies the origin and evolution of man. An original and central part of biology was taxonomy (from the Greek *taxis,* "arrangement" or "system," and *nemein,* "to distribute," thus distribution or classification system). This is what Aristotle and Linnaeus and others were about as they developed systems to name, describe, and organize into classes all the things of nature, identifying the relationships among them. Linnaeus's system differed sharply from Aristotle's, but the key similarity was the idea of systematic classification.

Finally, the classic divisions of old: botany and zoology. Botany (from the Greek *botanikos,* "of herbs") is the study of plant life, and zoology (Greek *zoe,* "life") of animal life. Although bacteria are plants (or were long thought to be) and amoebae are animals, both are now treated under microbiology, along with bacteria, viruses, and other microorganisms, once called microbes. Among modern biologists the old distinction between botany and zoology is blurred. A biological scientist may think of himself or herself as a cell biologist, for example, or a geneticist, and explore cytology or genetics across the boundaries of the vegetable and animal kingdoms.

Here again, for a good general understanding of biology and its scope and elements, an excellent starting point would be your favorite general or science encyclopedia. As an alternative, locate an introductory-level book in your library's card catalog. There is the *Dictionary of Life Sciences* edited by E. A. Martin and the *Encyclopedia of the Life Sciences*. Also helpful is the *Dictionary of Biological Terms* by I. F. and C. F. Henderson and edited by J. H. Kenneth. A standard recent taxonomic work is *Synopsis and Classification of Living Organism* by Sybil P. Parker. David Attenborough's *Life on Earth* and much other literate and richly informative writing on the natural sciences in recent years make this category fun to browse in at your library, and indeed at your favorite bookstore.

There is an enormous body of journals and other periodicals in the field; the mainstay reference to them is *Biological and Agricultural Index,* issued monthly (except September) and cumulatively indexed. *Biological and Agricultural Index* has been published since 1964, when the biological content was added to *Agricultural Index,* which had been published since 1919. *Biological Abstracts,* published since 1926 under the auspices of the Union of American Biological Societies, is an excellent source for literature from the whole world in theoretical and applied biology. Anyone doing research in the life sciences periodical press should keep in mind the general science magazines, such as *Scientific American.* Nearly ninety magazines addressing relatively broad spectrums of science are covered in Wilson's *General Science Index,* which was initiated in 1978.

BOTANY

One of Aristotle's disciples, Theophrastus, is considered the father of botany. Aristotle's work in taxonomy was in classifying the animals; Theophrastus worked out a classification system for plants that remained the standard for hundreds of years. But it was the monumental *Species plantarum* of the Swedish naturalist Linnaeus, published in 1753 and elaborating his earlier work, that fully opened the door to modern botanical taxonomy, and his system of classification remains the basis for present-day botany. In that work

Linnaeus presented the so-called binomial nomenclature for identifying plants, with one name identifying the genus and the second the species. For example, poison ivy is *Rhus toxicodendron:* the generic name from the Greek *rhous,* "sumac," and the specific name from Greek meaning roughly "poison tree." Other members of the genus *Rhus* have different specific names, such as *Rhus vernix,* the sumac.

General surveys of the science of the vegetable kingdom can be found in encyclopedias and individual books variously under such headings as "plant life," "flora," and, of course, "botany." Major areas of study within the discipline include, as with biology, morphology (form), physiology (function), and ecology (interrelationships). The subdiscipline of systematics embraces classification and taxonomy. Other specializations within botany include bacteriology, mycology (from the genus *Mycota,* fungus), algology, also called phycology (algae), and bryology (Greek *bryon,* "moss," the study of mosses and liverworts). Others are pteridology (Greek *pterid,* "feather," the ferns, from their feathery appearance), and paleobotany, where biology overlaps with paleontology, the study of fossil plants.

The classification work of Linnaeus and his successors has, of course, been modified from time to time by international agreement among botanists, notably through the International Botanical Congress. Its revisions and updatings are published in the *International Code of Botanical Nomenclature,* which is issued after each assembly of the Congress at which such changes are adopted. Classifications compiled by individual scholars are often published in regional collections, such as *Gray's Manual of Botany,* itself a hardy perennial now well into its second century and whose title suggests universal coverage but whose content is limited to the central and northeastern United States and neighboring Canada. Standard works of taxonomy are the *Index Londonensis* and the *Index Kewensis.* Other useful works found in many good libraries include *Plants of the World* (three volumes with few technical terms) by H.C.D. De Wit; *Dictionary of Botany; Including Terms Used in Biochemistry, Soil Science, and Statistics* by George Usher; and *Encyclopedia of Water Plants* by Mirko Vosatka.

ZOOLOGY

Aristotle's classification of animals, transmitted to future generations in Pliny's *Historia naturalis* and other sources, served as the basis of zoological knowledge through the Middle Ages. Crusted with myth at the outset, Pliny's encyclopedia gathered additional accretions of myth and mistake with each new manual transcription. The emergence of printing in the fifteenth century opened the possibility of standardization, and in the mid-eighteenth century the French naturalist Buffon began the publication of his enormous work of natural history, *Histoire naturelle, générale, et particulière*.

That multivolume compendium, which Buffon did not live to complete, described plants, humans, and minerals as well as animals, but its systematic accounts of animals and the *histoire des animaux* brought significant reform to zoology. A few years later, Linnaeus, though a botanist at heart, published in his *System naturae* his classification of animals and minerals as well as plants using binomial nomenclature; *Felis tigris* denotes that the tiger's genus is *Felis* (cat) and its species is *tigris* or tiger. The precision of the system enabled relations among species and within genera to be set forth accurately and consistently, and it revolutionized taxonomy.

The overlapping of the "turf" of zoologists with that of botanists is widely noted today. But for all that, botany and zoology remain disciplines, and if you are looking up things zoological it will pay you to be able to recognize its subdisciplines. Among these are several whose names are common with botany, such as morphology (or anatomy), physiology, cell and molecular biology, taxonomy (also called systematics), genetics, and ecology. Specializations particular to zoology include embryology (or developmental studies), evolutionism, and ethology (from the Greek *ethos,* "character," thus the study of character, or, in zoology, of animal behavior).

A veritable encyclopedia is *The Invertebrates*, six volumes by L. H. Lyman. For insights into early physiology, *Lectures on the History of Physiology During the 16th, 17th, and 18th Centuries* by Sir Michael Foster (a founder of modern physiology) was a 1901 classic that was reissued in 1970. In *The Double Helix*, J. D. Watson tells his own story of discovering the molecular structure of DNA, a landmark of biophysics.

A big, well-illustrated set of books for lay readers, fun for adults but easy for eighth- and ninth-graders to use and not "written down" to them is *Grzimek's Animal Life Encyclopedia* edited by Bernhard Grzimek and presenting animal life in thirteen fairly large volumes, from lower animals to insects to mammals (three volumes). A few years later the same man put together *Grzimek's Encyclopedia of Evolution* (1976).

Zoology abounds in popular works on all divisions of the animal kingdom, perhaps most of all birds. But everything is covered one place or another. For illustration, there are scores of books in print on entomology explicitly for fly fishermen. The following list only ticks off a few of the standard nontechnical works in this whole field.

Of insects, there is the *Dictionary of Entomology* edited by A. Leftwich. Of fishes: the *Book of Fishes* edited by John Oliver La Gorce for the National Geographic Society; the *Encyclopedia of Aquatic Life* (not limited to fishes) edited by Keith Banister and Andrew Campbell. Also see the *Encyclopedia of Reptiles and Amphibians* edited by Tim Halliday.

When it comes to birds, Roger Tory Peterson is in a class by himself. His *A Field Guide to the Birds* and *A Field Guide to Western Birds* are constantly in print; see also his (with others) *A Field Guide to the Birds of Britain and Europe*. Peterson's entire *Field Guide* series is not only classic, it is also celebrated by scientists and ordinary "birders" as absolutely reliable. Other standard works are *Audubon Guides: All the Birds of Eastern and Central North America* and *Audubon Western Bird Guide*, both edited by Richard H. Pough; the *Encyclopedia of Birds* edited by Christopher W. Perrins; and the *Illustrated Encyclopedia of American Birds* by Leon A. Hausman.

There also is the *Audubon Encyclopedia of Animal Life* edited by Ralph Buchsbaum *et al.* Of quadrupeds: *The Animal Kingdom* by Frederick Drimmer (three volumes), the *Encyclopedia of North American Wildlife* by Stanley Klein and edited by Tom Aylesworth, and the *Encyclopedia of Mammals* edited by David Macdonald.

MICROBIOLOGY

As early as the thirteenth century the idea arose that disease and death were caused by things invisible. A couple of centuries later the microscope was invented, and soon natural philosophers could see through it ugly little creatures swimming about in their water. By the late seventeenth century, Leeuwenhoek perfected the microscope and meticulously recorded his observations of "animalcules" living in animal and human tissues, and the way was paved for the eighteenth-century realization that these microscopic organisms affected life and health. Microbiology emerged in Europe near the end of the nineteenth century, and in America a decade or two later, and from then on improvements in instruments and intercommunication gave the young discipline unprecedented importance.

Microbiology is by its nature interdisciplinary. Its own subdisciplines make this evident. One is bacteriology, another protozoology, and a third virology. Some authorities still classify bacteria as primitive plants; protozoa are primitive animals; viruses are probably neither but perhaps meaner than either. Other categories of microbiology that find their way into indexes and card catalogs involve techniques: microscopy, cultivation (of microorganisms for study), and staining (to make the transparent microorganisms visible under the microscope).

A standard work on the development of the field is Ruth Moore's *The Coil of Life*. Other highly useful books in the realm of microbiology range in tone from wry to poetic, including Theodor Rosebury's *Life on Man* and Lewis Thomas's *The Lives of a Cell*. The taxonomic authority is *International Code of Nomenclature of Bacteria and Viruses*, published by the International Association of Microbiological Societies. A good general reference source is *Dictionary of Microbiology* by Paul Singleton and Diana Saintsbury.

It is, of course, obvious that but for the technological advances that created microscopy and then revolutionized it with the electron microscope, and so on down the course of science, microbiology would not even exist. The newer developments of modern scientific technology have built on knowledge from microbiology to establish a new field of tools for interdisciplinary life science, namely biotechnology. There is an excellent but hardly elementary survey in *Biotechnology: Principles and Applications* edited by I. J. Higgins, D. J. Best, and J. Jones. Some of its impacts are examined in *The Gene Factory: Inside the Genetic and Biotechnology Business Revolution* by John Elkington.

The computer has played an increasingly important role, too, of course, and access to computer databases on the biological sciences have broadened the access of every scholar. Some of these resources are touched on in Chapter 4, on computer access.

CHAPTER 10

LOOKING UP THE ARTS

Nowadays "everybody," that slovenly stylist, defines "art" to mean painting or drawing or sculpting or something arty like that. But "the arts" carries a much broader and more diverse meaning. The word "art" comes to us straight from the Latin *ars, artis,* where it meant "skill," especially skill in some special pursuit, such as war or politics, or singing or oratory or, eventually, painting or sculpture. From Latin it found its way into French and then English, still meaning a skill requiring special knowledge or training.

Liberal arts (*arts libéraux*) originally meant the *trivium* and the *quadrivium* of the medieval university: grammar, rhetoric, and logic; plus geometry, arithmetic, music, and astronomy; all were necessary to liberate the person to use his or her intelligence in pursuit of knowledge and wisdom. A work of art (*ouvrage d'art*) was something created by an expressly human agency and not by nature. Our phrase "fine arts" is the French *beaux arts, i.e.,* the higher or more noble ones. Sometimes we still hear the phrase "the agreeable arts": These were the *arts d'agrément* of music, dancing, etc. The lively arts were the popular arts, from Punch and Judy to the comic strip.

Although at one time or other each aspect of the arts has been put down as dangerous to public morality, every recorded society has given special status to its artists. Small wonder, perhaps, since often enough it was the artists who were doing the recording. In any case, the modern reader seeking information on any or all of the arts faces a problem of selectivity.

By and large, the major general encyclopedias treat the arts brilliantly, in both text and color illustrations, and in length and detail approximately proportional to their size. And the arts are a kingdom unto themselves for multivolume special encyclopedias and other reference works. But each of these works is devoted to a single art. Interestingly enough, in all this wealth of coverage there is no single major encyclopedia devoted solely to all the arts. Only in the general encyclopedias will you find comprehensive treatment of both the arts in general and the several particular arts. In addition to the large encyclopedias, the *New Century Cyclopedia of Names* is unexcelled in its coverage of individual works of art in every field—paintings, literature, musical compositions, plays, etc.

Also note that the yearbooks associated with all general encyclopedias cover each year's important developments in the arts quite thoroughly, as, in varying degree, do the major general almanacs.

This chapter will address the arts in the following order: literature, performing arts, visual arts, and decorative arts. Like every classification of art, this one is arbitrary. Borders between particular art forms are often invisible. (We treat opera under music, but it can't exist without major contributions from literature, theater, dance, painting, and the "practical" arts of design and costume.) The nature and history of the art, individual works, and economic and other aspects of the art will be considered under the same heading as the actual practice of the art. For instance, famous individual paintings, schools of painting, the sale of paintings, and the techniques and media of painting will all be treated with the art of painting.

Biographical sources about painters are conspicuously absent from this example. In the main the present chapter will omit them because the finding and use of biographical reference materials is taken up in Chapter 5, "How to Look Up People." Where biographical works are cited here it is because they include an additional element such as history, critical comment, or bibliography.

LITERATURE

Although it derives its name from the Latin for "letters," what we call literature is older than writing and older than pictograms. It is precisely as old as the first storyteller, and if you want to look up oral literature do it under "folk," specifically under "folklore."

The general encyclopedias handle literature well—perhaps better than anything else—because that is the basic calling of encyclopedia editors. The individual variations in the encyclopedias' approach to subjects—alphabetizing, comprehensiveness vs. particularity, etc.—is explored in Chapter 2. Briefly, the newer, *i.e.*, younger, encyclopedias, specifically *Academic American, Americana, Collier's* and *World Book*, treat both the large subject—*e.g.*, literature—as a separate entity and also carry substantial articles on its various components, such as essays, poetry, novels, children's literature, and American and assorted other national or regional (*e.g.*, Latin American) literatures.

The fourteenth edition of the *Britannica* does so, too, as also does the *Micropaedia* section of the fifteenth. But in the fifteenth edition, for *Britannica's* fullest treatment on major elements, such as the whole concept of literature, one must turn to the *Macropaedia* volumes, where virtual tomes such as "Literature" (some 115,000 words in 140 pages) address the overall subject, including its various genres and the important subtopic of children's literature, leaving Western literature, English literature, French literature, American literature, Japanese literature, and many others to other *Macropaedia* articles in other hundreds of thousands of words.

Here are brief identifications of some of the more important special encyclopedias and encyclopedialike books on literature in general. *Cassell's Encyclopedia of World Literature* has three alphabetically organized parts: articles on national literatures, genres, etc., and on famous works in various languages; and biographic sketches of (Part 2) nineteenth-century and (Part 3) twentieth-century authors. The *Reader's Adviser,* edited by Barbara A. Chernow and George A. Vallasi (thirteenth edition, 1986), is a three-volume lay reader's guide organized by country and literary genre, continuing a line begun in 1921. Other resources are the *Encyclopedia of World Literature in the 20th Century,* W. B. Fleischman, general editor (three volumes 1967) and the *Dictionary of Literary Terms* by J. A. Cuddon (1977). A pair of important guides to important national literatures is *The Oxford Companion to English Literature* and *The Oxford Companion to American Literature.*

The various genres of literature are extensively addressed by the vast literary reference world. For novels, check under both "novel" and "fiction" in the library catalog or bibliography you consult. (Much more on bibliographies is contained in Chapter 21.) There are assessments of American and English and historical and other varieties of fiction. Wilson's *Fiction Catalog,* for one example, lists novels, short stories, and other forms in dictionary format. Many reference books concentrate on novels and other long fiction. Some—*e.g.*, the Wilson *Short Story Index*—concentrate on the short story. This work, first published in 1923 and long revised by a succession of editors, is now kept up-to-date in annual supplements.

Special tastes are catered to; for the Baker Street Irregulars, there is always *The Encyclopaedia Sherlockiana; or A Universal Dictionary of Sherlock Holmes and His Biographer John H. Watson, M.D.* compiled and edited by Jack Tracy. In the fairly extensive literature on folklore such titles as these can be found: *Encyclopedia of Black Folklore and Humor* compiled by Henry D. Spalding; *Dictionary of Medical Folklore* by Carol Ann Rinzler; and *Encyclopedia of Comic Book Heroes* by Michael L. Fleisher, assisted by Janet E. Lincoln.

Dramatic literature is usually so cataloged, and writing for the theater as well as critical and other writing about dramatic literature can be located there. Valuable treatment of theatrical writing is given by three general works on theater, which are discussed later, in the section on theater. They are *The Oxford Companion to the Theatre,* Allardyce Nicoll's *World Drama: From Aeschylus to Anouilh,* and *The Reader's Encyclopedia of World Drama.* Joseph T. Shipley's *Guide to Great Plays* presents historical background, plot summaries, and critical comment on more than 650 plays in many lands and times. Indexes of plays and such collections as the "Best Plays of . . ." are abundant.

Poetry is the subject of innumerable anthologies, usually in national literatures but also often in such categories as love poems, ballads, the English Restoration, etc. Important reference works include the *Encyclopedia of Poetry and Poetics* edited by Alex Preminger with Frank J. Warnke and O. B. Hardison, Jr., a book of history and commentary, often delightfully witty, that is arranged topically by various aspects of poetry. *Granger's Index to Poetry* first appeared in 1869, and in its sixth edition it remains a major resource, with a three-way index that embraces authors, subjects, titles, and first lines. Frank N. Magill brought out in 1984 a useful *Critical Survey of Poetry.*

The latter author and editor, an educator and an indefatigable cataloger, has left his imprint on a very large variety of literary reference works. Probably the most universally familiar is *Masterpieces of World Literature in Digest Form.* This work originated as *Masterplots,* in four volumes appearing in 1949–52. Annual updating supplements were started in 1954 and eventuated in 1977 in a twelve-volume *Survey of Contemporary Literature* under the *imprimatur* of Magill's own Salem Press. It is known almost everywhere as *Masterplots.* For Harper & Row Magill compiled his

Cyclopedia of Literary Characters, describing the major characters of some thirteen hundred novels and plays in world literature, organized by the titles of the works and indexed by the name of character.

An earlier approach to the same service can still be found in many larger libraries: William A. Wheeler's *Explanatory and Pronouncing Dictionary of the Noted Names of Fiction,* covering world literature to the date of its publication, 1893. A couple of decades later Lippincott published William S. Walsh's *Heroes and Heroines of Fiction* in two volumes, one identifying characters in works originating before and during the Middle Ages, the other thereafter and up to the early twentieth century. The *Reader's Encyclopedia* is a one-volume work by William Rose Benét naming and explaining titles, characters, terms coined in various books, etc., along with many citations in the visual arts, music, and classical mythology.

Literary criticism is another aspect of literature that is well represented. Here again we find Frank Magill's fingerprints, with *Contemporary Literary Criticism.* Another is *Twentieth Century Literary Criticism* edited by Dennis Poupard. For most of us such farther shores of criticism as the 1980s vogue of "deconstructionism" are a lot less important than the humble book review. Publishers know it, too, and there are several indexes and digests of reviews in various literary genres. The standard covering the general-interest field is *Book Review Index.*

A valuable new survey of modern literature is Frederick Ungar's five-volume *Encyclopedia of World Literature in the 20th Century.* For research into particular literatures, the *Oxford Companion* and the *Cambridge History* series are invaluable in their quite different ways. As noted in Chapter 8, on history, the Oxford series is comprised of fat single volumes arranged in dictionary style, with thousands of informative and relatively concise articles on authors; individual works, literary genres and concerns; subjects much written about such as mythic figures; and much, much else. In the realm of literature they are: *The Oxford Companion to American Literature, The Oxford Companion to Classical Literature,* and *The Oxford Companion to English Literature.*

The Cambridge histories are multivolume works that treat their subjects exhaustively—*e.g.,* from the origins of English literature through the end of the nineteenth century. Each period is addressed in a chapter written by a world authority on that era. The full-scale literary sets are *The Cambridge History of American Literature* in three volumes and *The Cambridge History of English Literature* in fifteen volumes. The latter is no longer in print but still widely held. There is also a single-volume abridgment, the *Concise Cambridge History of English Literature*. Another highly useful research tool from the same source is the *Cambridge Bibliography of English Literature,* in four volumes plus a supplement. Its scope (thirteen centuries) and organization (in chronological periods subdivided into genres and general topics) makes it a richer resource than its title implies.

Smaller but still quite comprehensive introductions to various national and regional literatures abound. A good example is the *Penguin Companion to European Literature* edited by Anthony Thorlby. All the major European languages have literatures covered thoroughly by the various dictionaries, encyclopedias, and guides or companions. Jewish literature fares similarly, and Latin American literatures are the subjects of increasing attention. In the latter connection, bear in mind the two distinct groups of Brazilian and Spanish American literature. Brazil's huge population and its vital literary tradition contribute greatly to the Portuguese language's status as the world's fifth-most-widely-spoken tongue.

Anthologies and other collections of literary works themselves are ubiquitous on the literary scene. In the late nineteenth and early twentieth centuries, the collected works of major individual authors were widely published and aggressively peddled to adorn the shelves of families wishing to manifest an air of culture. The door-to-door flogging of these handsomely bound sets of Fielding and Thackeray and Dickens and the Brontës—and Mark Twain and presidential memoirs and Civil War histories—established the pattern later adopted by encyclopedia publishers.

In 1909 this vigorous approach to publishing and marketing came to a happy marriage with classical literature under the auspices of an Irish immigrant publisher, P. F. Collier, and an illustrious president of Harvard University, Charles W. Eliot. Collier had started out publishing Roman Catholic religious books peddled on the installment plan and later added various sets of classical works and *Collier's Weekly* magazine. Eliot, a mathematician and chemist who became a classical scholar and the most famous U.S. educator of his day, was ending a forty-year reign in which he virtually remade and enormously expanded and enriched Harvard.

As a part of his campaign to advance the humanities and sciences in American general education, he saw to the selection and editing of the *Harvard Classics,* which Collier's promoters quickly made famous as "Dr. Eliot's Five-Foot Shelf of Books." In the year of its publication, Eliot retired from Harvard, and Collier died and was succeeded by his son, Robert. The fifty-volume collection of the great works of the English language and translations of the classics of Greek and Latin and various European and Oriental languages quickly became famous throughout America, sold for generations, and still is found in most public libraries. Its elaborate indexing, including even the first lines of poetry, made it an extremely useful resource.

A later educator-celebrity, Robert M. Hutchins, while president and chancellor of the University of Chicago, introduced new emphasis on the classics there and also persuaded *Encyclopaedia Britannica* to publish a new collection focused somewhat differently from the Harvard version (Hutchins was a Yalie). Hutchins and his philosopher colleague Mortimer J. Adler then edited the fifty-four-volume *Great Books of the Western World* (Hutchins thereafter called Adler "the Great Bookie"). This set was promoted and sold as widely and aggressively as its Harvard precursor. Its unique and uniquely useful attribute is a two-volume "Syntopicon" created by Adler, which indexes and interrelates the 102 "great ideas" that the great books address and elaborate.

For readers seeking a specific classical allusion, any of several classical dictionaries may be a godsend. Among these are the *Oxford Companion* cited earlier; the *Oxford Classical Dictionary;* and the venerable *Harper's Dictionary of Classical Literature and Antiquities,* which originated in 1897 but which still can be widely found, usually trimmed down to pretty narrow margins with repeated rebinding.

WHERE DID YOU HEAR THAT TUNE? LOOKING UP MUSIC

The classic reference work on music is so good that you should start there, instead of in the general encyclopedias, to find the answers to musical questions. It is at once complete, authoritative, and accessible to the nonmusician, in some cases more so than the encyclopedias. This is the definitive *Grove's Dictionary of Music and Musicians.* It's really an encyclopedia in twenty volumes, as the *New Grove's* in its most recent editions under the editorship of Stanley Sadie. While the original work was on the press (in nine volumes appearing from 1879 to 1889), its original editor, the English musicologist George Grove, became Sir George and was made the first director of the Royal College of Music. There also is an abridged version of the newer *Grove's*.

The musical coverage of the various general encyclopedias is excellent: sound and generally well and accurately written. Other special works on music are a good deal smaller than the Grove, but there are outstanding books among them. Theodore Baker's *Biographical Dictionary of Musicians* is one of the best, its seventh and other recent editions revised and edited by the brilliant American musicologist Nicolas Slonimsky. Its two-thousand-odd pages of relatively fine print convey grand fascinating lore about the musical genres in which the great names worked that goes beyond what might be expected of an ordinary thumbnail biography, and for that reason the Baker is discussed here instead of under biographies in Chapter 5. Slonimsky also has an outstanding one-volume musical encyclopedia under his own name; and the *New Oxford History of Music*, in ten volumes in chronological order and compiled by a succession of editors, also is worth consulting.

Other outstanding compact general musical reference sources are the *Concise Oxford Dictionary of Music* by Percy Scholes, and Oscar Thompson's *International Cyclopedia of Music and Musicians*. The *Britannica Book of Music* was put together by one of the *Britannica* editors who was a musician and musical scholar, Benjamin Hadley, from the entire musical coverage, updated, of the encyclopedia's fourteenth edition after it was supplanted by the fifteenth in 1974. It is a comprehensive, concise encyclopedia of about nine hundred pages. Others include *Encyclopedia of American Music* by Edward Jablonski and *Dictionary of Contemporary Music* edited by John Vinton. Books on composers come with and without music: *Dictionary of Composers* edited by Charles Osborne and *Dictionary of Composers and their Music: Every Listener's Companion: Arranged Chronologically and Alphabetically* by Eric Gilder and June G. Port.

Books of narrower focus address the various genres of musical composition and performance. Each one cited below is merely one, if one of the best, among many. For folk music: *Encyclopedia of Folk, Country, and Western Music* by Irwin Stambler and Grelun Landon.

Hymns: A great old work that was revised and brought up-to-date in 1977 is John Julian's *Dictionary of Hymnology*. It has short articles on nearly all the English-language hymns in use as well as those in many other tongues. This fat book (nearly eighteen hundred pages) is well indexed by author, translator, and first line.

Jazz: The *Encyclopedia of Jazz,* compiled by Leonard Feather, is mostly a compendium of biographies of a thousand or so major jazz artists, but it is augmented most usefully with bibliographic and historical material. It was last revised and enlarged in 1960 but has been updated by Feather in sequels, *Encyclopedia of Jazz in the Sixties* and *Encyclopedia of Jazz in the Seventies.*

Instruments: The standard work is the *History of Musical Instruments* by Curt Sachs, published by Norton. It covers the whole range of instruments from the earliest times. It is well illustrated and has excellent bibliographic information on individual instruments. Another is *Musical Instruments Through the Ages* edited by Anthony Baines.

Symphonic music and the symphony orchestra: Robert Simpson's two-volume *Symphony* and Paul Henry Lang's *Symphony, 1800–1900.* Various aspects of classical music are treated in numerous other books that can be found in catalogs, directories, and bibliographies under categories such as chamber music or music of particular eras—Baroque, Romantic, etc.

Opera: the most complete is Gustave Kobbé's *The New Kobbé's Complete Opera Book.* It was first issued in 1919, the year following his freakish death when his sailboat was accidentally run down by a taxiing U.S. Navy seaplane. The revision reflected in the title presented here was done by the Earl of Harewood and brings the work up-to-date through such composers as Benjamin Britten and Gian Carlo Menotti. The work gives the history of particular operas, background on their composers, plot outlines, and the musical notation of important melodies. There are other works, including *Encyclopedia of Opera* edited by Leslie Orrey.

Popular music is covered in every variation. Key works include: *A History of Popular Music in America* by Sigmund Spaeth (1948); *Country Music U.S.A.: A Fifty-Year History* by Bill C. Malone (1968); Charles Boeckman's *And the Beat Goes On: A History of Pop Music in America* (1972); Irwin Stambler's *Encyclopedia of Pop, Rock and Soul* (1977); and *The Devil's Music: A History of the Blues* by Giles Oakley.

Songs: *Song Index* by Minnie Earl Sears, published in 1926, with a supplementary volume in 1934, the two reissued as a single volume in 1966. This work indexes almost twenty thousand songs taken from some two hundred collections. Indexing is by author, composer, title, and first line.

"Discography" has emerged as a term for bibliography of musical recordings in the various media of phonograph, audiotape, and compact disk. When you are seeking that kind of information, try it if you don't find it in the catalog under "records," "phonograph," or "recordings." The major U.S. and British periodical discographies cover every kind of recorded music, from acid rock to chamber. Penguin, among others, has a number of record and cassette *Guides,* and there is an *Index to Record and Tape Reviews.*

THE WORLD OF THEATER

Musical comedy, with a leg in both the world of music and that of theater, offers an easy transition to the latter. David Ewen's *The Complete Book of the American Musical* describes more than three hundred productions, including composers, authors and librettists, original casts, and plot summaries. Also see the *Encyclopedia of the Musical Theatre* by Lehman Engel.

The legitimate stage and the world of drama, comedy, tragedy, farce, and melodrama: As in the other arts, the *Britannica* provides near-book-length treatment in its *Macropaedia,* devoting about a hundred pages and some ninety-five thousand words to survey articles on the art of theater, the history of Western theater, and theatrical production. Theater in the non-Western world is addressed in *Macropaedia* "arts of" titles under Africa and East and Southeast Asia. Meanwhile, the *Micropaedia* has concise articles on particular theatrical topics, such as acting, black theater, Comédie-Française, directing, environmental theater, footlights, and Grand Guignol, all the way to Yiddish theater and zanni (the stock servant character of the *commedia dell'arte*).

The other general encyclopedias do likewise, in most cases, throughout their alphabetical strings, intermingling among the shorter pieces relatively long and comprehensive articles on the larger topics. Examples are "Theater," which in *World Book,* for instance, encompasses children's theater and in *Collier's* incorporates drama. Among these other sets titles usually coincide but sometimes vary slightly: It's "Musical Comedy" here and "Musical Theater" there, but, especially given the high general quality of cross-referencing, these tiny differences pose no problem for an IQ above 95 or so.

One bibliography worth mentioning cites books across the whole spectrum of the performing arts. It is *Performing Arts Books in Print,* published by Drama Book Specialists. Samuel French publishes the scripts of individual plays for use by schools, local theater groups, and others. More specialized reference works on theater alone include the *Illustrated Encyclopedia of World Theatre*, and a standard historical source, *The Oxford Companion to the Theatre* edited by Phyllis Hartnoll, author also of *A Concise History of Theatre*. Encyclopedic treatments include the illustrated *McGraw-Hill Encyclopedia of World Drama* (four volumes) and the classic *Encyclopedia of Theatre* by George Jean Nathan (1940, reissued in 1970).

THE DANCE

The general encyclopedias offer, at their various levels of length and language, quite satisfactory treatments of the history of dance, dance as an art form, and dance in its various modes—ballet, modern, and social or ballroom dancing. Readers desiring to look further into history, theory, or technique have ample resources available. There is one general encyclopedia of the dance, covering all its various aspects, but with slightly heavier emphasis on ballet. That is *The Dance Encyclopedia* edited by Anatole Chujoy and P. W. Manchester. There also is *Encyclopedia of Dance and Ballet* edited by Mary Clarke and David Vaughan.

The following works are representative of the best in treating the respective forms of dance. Ballet: *The Concise Oxford Dictionary of Ballet* by Horst Koegler; *A Dictionary of Ballet* edited by G.B.L. Wilson. Modern dance: *Borzoi Book of Modern Dance* by M. Lloyd covers the early years; *The Complete Guide to Modern Dance* by Don McDonagh adds another eventful generation to the story. For further insights into the continuing development of this still new art form consult biographies of, periodical interviews with, and occasional writings by such pioneers as Martha Graham, Hanya Holm, Ruth St. Denis, Merce Cunningham, Alvin Ailey, and Twyla Tharp. Social dancing: *Social Dance: A Short History* by A. H. Franks.

WIDE SCREEN AND SMALL
SCREEN: MOVIES AND
TELEVISION

When you look up either motion pictures or television in a library or an encyclopedia index, beware of a few modest pitfalls. Is it film? cinema? movies? motion pictures? Start with the latter and work your way back until you pick up the trail. If you are not trying to find a particular book whose title has slipped your mind, it may be a good idea simply to find the section of the reference department where books on movies are stored and browse there. It is both easier and more fun to browse among actual books on the shelf in front of you than to poke around in the catalog. If you don't already know where the section is, either ask the reference librarian or look up the classification number of an obvious title in the card catalog. (Try the latter first: It will increase the ease of using the catalog for future searches.)

In tracking television as an art medium, you often encounter what seems to be a stubborn resistance in the catalog to helpful cross-referencing. TV is treated in two principal ways there: as a technical phenomenon and as a commercial, especially an advertising, one. It is, of course, both, but it also is the medium for some fine drama and for popular entertainment whose appeal has changed the whole nature of the entertainment business. It took several varieties of theater, cabaret, carnival, concert, and pageant to deliver the range of entertainment that television does today. If you are looking through a card catalog for TV drama, persist. Skip around a bit, too. Probably you will find it under television plays. There are, however, books dealing with the techniques of television (and cinema) such as *The Focal Encyclopedia of Film & Television Techniques* (First American edition, 1986). *The Oxford Companion to Film* edited by Liz-Anne Bawden is a standard resource.

Even if there were no other evidence, the universal popularity of motion pictures would be evident from the literature about that art form. It is enormous and comprehensive. You can find more than one source to look up every motion picture ever made professionally. The field is wide enough so that no two small- to medium-size libraries may have exactly the same combination of yearbooks, catalogs, and compilations of film criticism. A major reference is the *American Film Institute Catalog of Feature Films,* which describes U.S. feature films since 1893. After an initial volume covering 1893–1910, it devotes a single, thick, atlas-size volume to every succeeding decade.

The *Film Review Index,* the *Film Daily Yearbook of Motion Pictures,* the *Macmillan Film Bibliography,* and *The New York Times Film Reviews,* among others, perform similar functions in slightly different ways, as does the *British Film Catalog 1895–1970* for British films. Roy Pickard's *The Oscar Movies* is only one example, but a good one, of books describing Academy Award-winning movies.

For all the difficulty of finding it on the shelves, there is a substantial body of writing on television arts, *i.e.,* drama. Collections of critical comment on radio plays are numerous, too. Elders will remember the golden days of radio. People who grew up in the video age can't remember that in radio, like print fiction, the listener (reader) is the casting director, costumer, and set designer. The hero or heroine is just as gorgeous as your own fevered brain chooses to make him or her. For this reason dipping into some of the collections of radio plays and critical comment about them may be a most beguiling way to kill an hour or two, or a lot more. As in the case of TV, drama on radio is likely to be found under radio plays.

The general encyclopedias treat the artistic aspect of the broadcast media fairly well, but probably not as carefully as they do the technical and commercial aspects. The yearbooks discuss last year's programming, but the best critical comment is to be found in the press—newspaper and magazine reviews. Don't overlook the terse and pithy comment of *Variety*, the weekly bible of show biz. As in the case of theater and film, TV reviews are collected. Sources include the *International Television Almanac* and Vincent Terrace's *Encyclopedia of Televison Series, Pilots & Specials*.

Les Brown has compiled *The New York Times Encyclopedia of Television*. In addition, there are several paperback books describing regular motion pictures now available on television, under such titles as *TV Movies and Video*. These make a handy guide for parents anxious about what their younger children may be watching. Also, of course, they are handy for kids wondering whether a particular flick is raunchy enough (or bloody enough) to stay up late for. *Chacun*, as the French say, *à son goût*.

THE VISUAL ARTS

The visual arts, or plastic arts as they are sometimes called, are elegantly presented in the general encyclopedias, in good part because the quality of modern color reproduction makes for stunning as well as instructive illustrations that demonstrate graphically what the text has to say about a painter's or sculptor's style, technique, use of light and color, and the like. The various fields involved—painting, drawing, printmaking, sculpture, architecture, *et al.*—usually are indexed straightforwardly in just those terms, although the *Britannica*'s full-length treatment in the early years (1974–84) of the fifteenth edition was lumped under "Visual Arts,

Western." (It was broken apart into the familiar elements of painting, etc., starting in 1985.)

Among the fundamental reference works in the visual arts are these: *Illustrated Dictionary of Art Terms* edited by Kimberley Reynolds with Richard Seddon; *A Dictionary of Art Terms and Techniques* edited by Ralph Mayer; and *Oxford Companion to Art* and *Oxford Companion to Twentieth-Century Art,* both edited by Harold Osborne and both with excellent bibliographies. Valuable English translations from outstanding French works include: the *Larousse Encyclopedia of Prehistoric and Ancient Art,* the *Larousse Encyclopedia of Byzantine and Medieval Art,* the *Larousse Encyclopedia of Renaissance and Baroque Art,* and the *Larousse Encyclopedia of Modern Art,* all under the general editorship of René Huyghe and all setting the art of each era in its social, economic, cultural, and political context.

The fifteen-volume McGraw-Hill *Encyclopedia of World Art* embraces all of the visual arts, including the so-called useful (practical or decorative) arts with painting, drawing, sculpture, and architecture. Its authoritative long essays and first-rate bibliographies are made more useful by an outstanding index occupying one volume. Excellent illustrations in color and black-and-white appear at the back of each volume.

The *Praeger Encyclopedia of Art* in five volumes has outstanding concise articles on the visual arts and artists, covering painting, architecture, sculpture, *et al.,* and periods, schools, media, and movements in the world of painting. Small color and black-and-white illustrations of good quality accompany most articles. Also, there is *Gardner's Art Through the Ages* by Helen Gardner, a single-volume illustrated survey of art from ancient to modern. Another one-volume art history written with great authority but simply and easy to read is E. H. Gombrich's standard text for art appreciation courses, *The Story of Art* (original edition, 1952). Other broad-gauge resources are Grolier's *Encyclopedia of Visual Art,* Sir Lawrence Gowing, general editor (ten volumes), and *Dictionary of American Art* by Matthew Baigell.

Periodical literature about the visual arts is indexed since 1933 in Wilson's *Art Index,* a quarterly publication that is cumulated like its semimonthly sister publication, *Readers' Guide to Periodical Literature.*

PAINTING AND SCULPTURE

Art books featuring reproductions of great paintings are almost without number. There are two valuable indexes that locate particular paintings in books and in catalogs of museum exhibitions also telling in most cases where the original work can be found. Both were compiled by Isabel S. Monro and Kate M. Monro: *Index to Reproductions of American Paintings* and *Index to Reproductions of European Paintings*. Also see *Encyclopedia of Themes and Subjects in Painting: Mythological, Biblical, Historical, Literary, Allegorical and Topical* by Daniel Howard. From time to time UNESCO issues another volume in its encyclopedic series *Reproductions of World Art*.

Contemporary art gets its due; see such books as *Phaidon Dictionary of Twentieth-Century Art*, *Dictionary of 20th Century Art* edited by Bernard S. Myers and Shirley D. Myers, and *Dictionary of Contemporary American Artists* by Paul Cummings. Various special aspects of the visual arts are addressed also, from the market to feminism: *Encyclopedia of Modern Art Auction Prices* by Michele Berard, and *Dictionary of Women Artists: An International Dictionary of Women Artists Born Before 1900* by Chris Petteys with the assistance of Hazel Gustow, Ferris Olin, and Verna Ritchie.

For further research into painting and its various schools and media, consult library catalogs, indexes, and bibliographies. Look under cultures in which painting flourished—*e.g.*, "ancient Greek painting" or "ancient Greece, painting in"; periods, *e.g.*, medieval, Renaissance, Baroque, Victorian; styles, *e.g.*, rococo, neoclassical; and movements, *e.g.*, Impressionism, Art Nouveau, Fauvism, pop art.

ARCHITECTURE

Among several other books on architecture, Talbot F. Hamlin wrote the standard history, *Architecture Through the Ages*, revised from time to time since its first appearance in 1944. Hamlin also edited the four-volume *Forms and Functions of Twentieth-Century Architecture*, covering one of the liveliest periods in the history of that art. Another major resource for architecture is contained within the massive forty-eight-volume *Pelican History of Art* edited by Nikolaus Pevsner. Pevsner also has written and compiled many individual books on architecture as well as other arts. The strength of this set in architecture is evident in the titles of several of its individual volumes, such as *The Art and Architecture of India* and *The Art and Architecture of Russia*. Good as it is on architecture, it by no means confined to that subject. Many of the volumes focus closely on other particular arts in one period and place, *e.g., Painting in Britain: The Middle Ages.*

Useful works that concentrate wholly on architecture include a collaboration of Pevsner with John Fleming and Hugh Honour, *A Dictionary of Architecture;* also the *Encyclopedia of Modern Architecture* edited by Wolfgang Pehnt, the *Dictionary of Architecture and Construction* edited by Cyril M. Harris, and *Encyclopedia of American Architecture* by William Dudley Hunt.

PHOTOGRAPHY AS ART

When photography was new it was so astonishing a technical feat that not much attention was paid by the general public to the question of whether it was art. It happens that the four men who invented the central elements of photography, at nearly the same time early in the nineteenth century, all were seeking a shortcut or a simplified way of accomplishing a specific step in one of the visual arts. Jacques Daguerre wanted to speed the process of painting scenes such as those in the Paris Diorama. Nicéphore Niepce wanted to speed the process of making lithographic prints. Thomas Wedgwood wanted an easy way to make permanent the images he had been able to produce fleetingly by letting the sun shine on treated paper. And William Henry Fox Talbot was looking for a scientific way to produce landscape drawings that he was unable to execute with pen or brush.

Most of the early photographers were artists, and some early critics accepted the new medium as equal or superior to the best the older visual arts could produce. But when late in the nineteenth century George Eastman's cheap, simple cameras and roll film made everybody a photographer, the artists began to look to the integrity of their art. The encyclopedias treat this early history and the later development of the art quite nicely.

Among individual books on the subject, the history is especially well handled by Beaumont Newhall, probably the preeminent historian of photography, and until her death his wife, Nancy Newhall, probably the greatest of the early photography critics. Their important works, jointly or singly, include among others an anthology of the observations of the pioneers, *On Photography,* the illustrated biographic collection *Masters of Photography,* and *The History of Photography from 1893 to the Present Day.* The literature is large and continuing to grow and is studded throughout with

Beaumont Newhall's name. There are, naturally, many eminently worthwhile works by others, among them *Encyclopedia of Photography* edited by Bernard E. Jones and *Encyclopedia of Practical Photography* by Herb Taylor.

THE DECORATIVE ARTS: USEFUL? ORNAMENTAL? ART?

The term "useful arts" once covered even such skilled occupations as coal mining, along with architecture, the making of clothing, and such decorative arts as jewelry, enamelwork, metalwork, and pottery. In encyclopedias you can look them up separately, and the treatment you will find is generally quite complete. Collectively addressed, as the *Britannica*'s *Macropaedia* does under the title "Decorative Arts and Furnishings," for example, the article runs to some 225,000 words and would make a separate book of more than five hundred pages. But the other encyclopedias don't agree on just what belongs under such a blanket title. And small wonder: There is no completely satisfactory overall work on this extremely diverse field, basically because there is no uniform definition of it.

There is, in the Louvre at Paris, a Decorative Arts Museum (Musée des Arts Décoratifs, before World War II known as the Bibliothèque [Library] d'Arts Décoratifs). It includes furniture and room furnishings and examples, in the fully furnished rooms that comprise it, of interior design. By some standards all these are elements of the decorative arts, along with ceramics and stained glass, silverware and glassware, metalwork and mosaic, tapestry and rugs and carpets, and quite a few others.

Should some of these elements be considered crafts instead of art? Or arts and crafts? The low estate of these decorative arts during the Industrial Revolution moved the reformer and poet William Morris to invent the Arts and Crafts Movement to restore pride of workmanship to the artisans and some sense of taste to the consuming public. The name and eventually the movement caught on. But there still is no canon to delineate conclusively just what we mean when we speak of the decorative arts. It's the expert's choice. Two of the experts have gotten together to delineate *their* canon, and it may well serve your purposes. See *Dictionary of Decorative Arts* by John Fleming and Hugh Honour.

There is a veritable potpourri of books dealing with modes of expression that are art forms by one standard or another. The following titles are representative, both of the kinds of book you can find and the spectrum of topics they range across. Of costume: *Dictionary of Costume* by Ruth Turner Wilcox; Scribner's *Encyclopedia of World Costume;* and *Esquire's Encyclopedia of 20th Century Men's Fashions* by O. E. Schoeffler and William Gale.

Of interior furnishings: *Dictionary of Interior Design* by Martin Pegler; *Dictionary of Oriental Rugs: With a Monograph on Identification of Weave* by Ivan C. Neff and Carol V. Maggs; *Dictionary of Furniture* edited by Charles Boyce; and *Encyclopedia of Furniture Making* by Ernest Joyce. Of "arts and crafts": *Encyclopedia of Crafts* edited by Laura Torbet (three volumes) and *Encyclopedia of Hand-weaving* by Stanislaw A. Zielinski. What about flower arranging (also widely studied and practiced under its Japanese name of *ikebana*)? See the *Encyclopedia of Flower Arranging and Indoor Plant Decoration* compiled by the Constance Spry School, London.

Going at it that way (looking up the genre) is easy, but when you're looking up a particular decorated object (a toleware tray? a cuckoo clock?) that you think may be under one of the decorative arts, avoid false starts: Look first under the topic's individual name. In aspects of the arts that have not been explicitly addressed here, follow the basic procedures described throughout this chapter. Drawing, for example, can be found through precisely the same procedures used for paintings. Good luck. More important: Persist.

CHAPTER 11

LOOKING UP RELIGION AND PHILOSOPHY

This chapter is divided into four parts: myth and magic, the religions of the world, religious writings, and philosophy and logic. All of these topics are covered at considerable depth by the general encyclopedias, but they are neither equally accessible nor equally comprehensive. All, including the *Britannica*'s *Micropaedia*, treat the broad topics, such as mythology, and the specific ones, such as Zeus or Olympus. The length of the longer articles is proportionate to the size of the set: In *Americana* and *Collier's* most of the long articles are significantly longer than those in *World Book* and *Academic American*, and in the *Britannica*'s *Macropaedia* (fifteenth edition) most of them are enormous.

When you go to an encyclopedia for a topic such as witchcraft, check the index first. The subject may well be tucked away under another title. In the *Britannica*, for example, while witchcraft does appear under that name in the *Micropaedia*, in the *Macropaedia* it is part of the twenty-three-thousand-word article "Occultism," where it gets a good deal longer treatment. Also, the twenty-thousand-word article "Myth and Mythology" does not deal with myths but with the nature and study of myth and mythology. To find the Greek or Roman myths themselves you have to look up "Greek religion" or "Roman religion" in the index; you will find both topics, with many others, in the thirty-seven-thousand-word article "Ancient European Religions."

Another caution about the encyclopedias in the huge area addressed by this chapter: Pay strict attention to such general cross-references in the index as this one in an index under "Religion:" *"see also* particular religions, *e.g.,* Christianity; Islam . . ." Do not make the mistake of assuming that means *only* Christianity and Islam. The indexers are merely saving space with this approach; what it really means is, "If you don't see the religion you are looking up, look under its own name."

If you are seeking Hinduism and don't find it under "religion," by all means look under "Hindu"—where you probably should have started. Or suppose you want to find out about the philosophical concepts of Thomism. You may or may not find a reference to Thomism under "philosophy," and if you do it might merely be a cross-reference to "theology," even though it is a philosophical as well as a theological topic. You will be much better off to go straight to "Thomism" unless part of your goal is to see how this particular index handles philosophical concepts and schools. If so, keep in mind that the answer to that question may be "well" or "badly" or "some of both."

THE ANCIENT RELIGIONS OF MYTH AND MAGIC

Myth, mystery, magic, the occult, the unknown and unseen—if you have a vivid imagination and like to let your mind wander idly among such notions, you know the pleasantly scary sensation of a tingling spine. If not, perhaps these pages can initiate you into that particular mystery—knowing the unknowable.

Although "myth" is neither a synonym for "religion" nor a necessary ingredient of religion, the concepts are inseparable, for both offer to explain how it all began, who runs the system, how we got here, and where we go hereafter. If the Christians' St. Paul had not coined the definition of faith as "the evidence of things not seen," it could have been borrowed for "myth." Myth explains the inexplicable and tells the history of the unhistorical. It is indeed the evidence of the unseen.

In the case of what we identify as Greek and Roman mythology, however, these bodies of myth were in fact also a virtual state religion for those ancient peoples. Because of the profound influence of their languages and cultures on our own, their mythic structure has in important ways become our own. Even in an age when few students study the classics at any depth, one can hardly get out of grammar school without at least a rudimentary knowledge of the gods and goddesses. In a sense the gods of Olympus and of the Alban Hills and Roman temples, like elves and fairies and leprechauns, are mythic creatures of our own.

For looking up the myth figures of classical times, the standard sources include three works described in Chapter 10, on the arts: the *Oxford Classical Dictionary,* the *The Oxford Companion to Classical Literature,* and *Harper's Dictionary of Classical Literature and Antiquities.* Other important ones are listed in this chapter.

Perhaps the most famous compendium of myth today is *Bulfinch's Mythology,* compiled in the mid-nineteenth century by Thomas Bulfinch, son of the distinguished New England architect Charles Bulfinch, who designed the West Front of the U.S. Capitol. Thomas, like his father a Harvard graduate, was a bank clerk who devoted his spare time to the study of classical literature and to writing. His *Mythology* is a later assemblage of three works: *The Age of Fable* (1855, mostly Greek and Roman myths, with about the last quarter of the book dealing with myths of Egypt, the Near East, the Norsemen, and the Druids), *The Age of Chivalry* (1858, the King Arthur legend and its characters), and *Legends of Charlemagne* (1863).

Another great work went beyond classical mythology to comparative religion and to relate magic to the kingly and priestly functions celebrated or depicted in myth and legend. This was the work of the Cambridge classical scholar and anthropologist Sir James George Frazer and now is universally known as *The Golden Bough.* It started out in 1890 as two volumes titled *The Magic Art and Evolution of Kings* and gradually expanded to twelve by 1915. A thirteenth volume appeared as a supplement in 1936, five years before Frazer's death, and the thirteen were known as *The Golden Bough: A Study in Magic and Religion.* The work has been abridged to a single volume several times, in 1959 by Theodore H. Gaster. The original also has been revised and enlarged, and a third edition appeared in thirteen volumes (one an index) in 1955.

Mythology of All Races is a thirteen-volume compendium of world mythology venturing a good deal further afield than Bulfinch's work and including myths of eastern and southern Asia as well as of Oceanian, African, and North and South American peoples, including the Indians. All this is in addition to the classical tales of Greece and Rome, and Slavs and Balts and the rest of northern Europe. It was compiled by Louis H. Gray, a Columbia University philologist and Orientalist, in collaboration with John Arnott MacCulloch, over sixteen years to 1932. It went out of print for a number of years but finally was reissued in 1964. This valuable resource compares the mythic explanations of various peoples for such phenomena as fire and lightning.

A more recent work is an English translation of the French *Larousse World Mythology* (1964), a single-volume, geographically organized work that identifies and describes ancient and modern myths. The range of mythologies is quite wide, and any library's catalog will point out numerous intriguing approaches.

Occult beliefs and practices, many of which have survived from ancient times, are taken up in Frazer and other standard sources in addition to the encyclopedias. Alchemy continues to have a few practitioners today, although its most conspicuous ancient objective, making gold out of baser metals, has not attracted a wide following since Hitler reportedly kept a stable of a few alchemists just in case they might have been able to help out the Third Reich's treasury. Astrology has many modern believers and practitioners, for whom Nicholas De Vore's *Encyclopedia of Astrology* (1947) or the English version of the *Larousse Encyclopedia of Astrology* (1981) may be of considerable value.

Witchcraft remains perennially popular, certainly as a subject for reading and reputedly as a system of belief. There is a host of individual titles. Among many reference works are *Encyclopedia of Witchcraft and Magic* by Venetia Newall and an illustrated encyclopedia in twenty-four slim volumes, *Man, Myth and Magic,* edited by Richard Cavendish. Russell Hope Robbins's *Encyclopedia of Witchcraft and Demonology* examines witchcraft as a Christian heresy.

A miscellany of works address various aspects of the occult: *An Encyclopedia of Fairies, Hobgoblins, Brownies, Bogies, and Other Supernatural Creatures* by Katherine Mary Briggs, *Encyclopedia of Ignorance: Everything You Ever Wanted to Know About the Unknown* edited by Ronald Duncan and Miranda Weston-Smith, and the *Encyclopedia of Occult Sciences* by Robert M. McBride.

Other religious practices with both ancient and contemporary adherents but with no uniform structure include various forms of ancestor worship, nature worship, and animism. These and still others can be looked up to advantage in encyclopedias and library catalogs, either under such headings or under the continents and countries where they are practiced (*e.g.,* African religions, South American religions), or under such headings as "religions, primitive," or, as in the case of one example, in *Dictionary of Pagan Religions* by H. E. Wedeck and Wade Baskin.

RELIGIONS OF THE WORLD

Substantial as is their coverage of mythology, it is dwarfed by the treatment of religion in the general encyclopedias. By "religion" here we exclude the occult forms and quasi-religions treated earlier in this chapter in favor of organized systems of belief that now have or formerly had large bodies of faithful, usually in many lands.

Encyclopedias of religion offer the researcher or browser the convenience of consolidating their treatment of religions in one alphabetical string, uncluttered by worldly topics. They are somewhat broader in their coverage than most general encyclopedias, and major articles in the bigger ones are considerably longer than all but the *Britannica*'s.

If your library has it, turn first to the newest of this category, the eight-thousand-page *Encyclopedia of Religion* in sixteen volumes (1986), edited by the University of Chicago historian of religions Mircea Eliade. It is comprehensive, detailed, and explicit, a major new resource.

Before the Eliade work, there were two large, standard encyclopedias of religion that still are held in many libraries despite their age and, obviously except for newer topics, are well worth consulting wherever you find them. James Hastings edited the *Encyclopaedia of Religion and Ethics* (thirteen volumes, 1908–1926; second edition in seven volumes, 1951), which has been well regarded for its broad coverage and signed, authoritative articles, many with good if necessarily dated bibliographies. Even older in its origins is the *Schaff-Herzog Encyclopedia of Religious Knowledge* in thirteen volumes (1908–12), edited by Samuel Macauley Jackson from Philip Schaff's 1884 adaptation of an earlier German work. A revision was done in 1949 and a two-volume supplement was issued in 1955. The orientation of these two encyclopedias is, respectively, liberal Protestant and conservative Protestant.

There is also a much smaller *Encyclopedia of American Religions* (two volumes, 1978) by John Gordon Melton, whose geographical focus is evident. Other concise works define religious terms and treat the general subject of comparative religion, such as *The International Dictionary of Religion: A Profusely Illustrated Guide to the Beliefs of the World* by Richard Kennedy; the *Encyclopedic Dictionary of Religion* edited by Paul Kevin Meagher, Thomas C. O'Brien, and Sister Consuelo Maria Aherne; and the *Dictionary of Comparative Religion* edited by S.G.F. Brandon.

This chapter will address religions in the following order,

reflecting the book's orientation toward the English-speaking world and North America in particular: the three world religions that evolved in the Middle East from one God through Abraham and Moses, *i.e.*, Judaism, Christianity, and Islam; the ancient Asian religions with the largest modern followings, *i.e.*, Hinduism and Buddhism; other ancient religions with contemporary followers; and modern religious sects and cults. Saints of the several faiths are treated at the end of this section.

Jew, Christian, Muslim: The People of the Book

YHWH was the unpronounceable name of the God of Abraham, Isaac, and Jacob, and unpronounceable or not, he was called Yahweh. Yahweh inspired his prophets to write the books that became the Jewish Bible, a focus and guide of their faith. They became people of the book.

The same God and the same patriarchs were claimed by the Christians when they departed from the mainstream of Judaism after the death and resurrection and ascent into Heaven of Jesus. They adopted the Jewish Bible as their Old Testament, and Yahweh inspired the Fathers of the new Church to write the books that became the New Testament. In the seventeenth century a translation of that Bible sponsored by the British King James rendered YHWH as Jehovah. The book in its Jacobean (Jamesian) English became the all-time best seller, and for four hundred years thereafter most English-speaking Christians have known Jehovah as the name of God.

But six hundred years after Jesus, the same God (Allah) called Muhammad to profess Islam, or submission to the will of god, to the Arabs, honoring the same patriarchs and accepting Jesus as a prophet (not a part) of Allah. Allah dictated the Quran to his prophet Muhammad. A new people of the book.

All three faiths, each split into several major factions or denominations, have issued a staggering number and variety of writings about their traditions, beliefs, histories, and practices, and about their martyrs and saints. The sacred documents *per se* of Judaism, Christianity, and Islam are discussed later in this chapter. Access to all the rest of these enormous literatures is the subject of this section.

As suggested earlier, all three faiths are handled excellently in the general encyclopedias—indeed particularly so in the larger sets, *Americana, Collier's,* and the fifteenth edition of *Britannica,* and especially the latter, with a very large share of its 44.5 million words devoted to all the aspects of religion. (It has more than three hundred thousand words under the titles "Judaism," "Christianity," "Protestantism," and "Roman Catholicism" alone, without counting denominations and sects and the other great religions and such general topics as religion itself.) By systematically studying the articles on religious topics in any of the three big encyclopedias one could truly become one of the country's best informed lay students of the subject.

But encyclopedic treatment of these "people of the book" and the religious systems by which they worship the same God is far from limited to the general encyclopedias. Of Judaism: The most comprehensive modern work in English is *Encyclopaedia Judaica,* published in seventeen volumes (one a supplement) in 1971–72. Yearbooks appear irregularly. The *Universal Jewish Encyclopedia* (thirteen volumes, 1939–44) and the even older *Jewish Encyclopedia* (1901–6, thirteen volumes) are still to be found here and there, although of course they are badly outdated (visualize a Jewish encyclopedia without treatment of the Holocaust from a postwar perspective and published before the creation of Israel). However, they are excellent sources for biographic and other historical material that has not found its way into the newer work, and the older work especially is still highly respected for the quality of its scholarship. See also Gale's *Encyclopedia of Jewish History: Events and Eras of the Jewish People* edited by Joseph Alpher.

Of Christianity: There is no encyclopedia of Christianity free of either Catholic or Protestant orientation, although there are excellent historical works written from both Protestant and Roman Catholic perspectives that scholars from both camps consider essentially unbiased.

The primary general reference for Catholicism is the *New Catholic Encyclopedia.* It appeared (in 1967) in fifteen volumes, augmented by a latter supplement volume, supplanting an older work that revealed the biases of an earlier time in a number of categories. The former, still valuable for many of its biographic and early historic treatments, was the *Catholic Encyclopedia* (fifteen volumes, 1907–14, with two supplements to 1922 and 1954). There is also a *Catholic Periodical and Literature Index,* a quarterly publication of the Catholic Library Association that is cumulated biennially; in 1968 it succeeded the *Catholic Periodicals Index,* established in 1930.

Karl Rahner's *Sacramentum Mundi: An Encyclopedia of* [Catholic] *Theology* is noted for its outstanding treatment of Catholic theology and doctrine. *American Catholicism* is the subject and title of John Tracy Ellis's highly readable book for lay readers. Greek and other Eastern Orthodox churches independent of Rome are addressed by a substantial body of literature, including the general encyclopedias. For further reading, check your library catalog under Eastern Orthodoxy or particular communions, *e.g.*, Russian Orthodox Church.

Reflecting the divisions within Protestantism that a long epoch of ecumenical cooperation has yet to bridge fully, there is no English-language Protestant encyclopedia *per se*. There are, however, some encyclopedias of Christianity that are edited from a clearly Protestant perspective, albeit for the most part not a polemical one. Examples, discussed earlier in this chapter are the *Encyclopedia of Religion and Ethics* and the *Schaff-Herzog Encyclopedia of Religious Knowledge*.

There are also several excellent histories of the multifarious Protestant community. Noted church historians Winthrop Hudson and Martin Marty are authors, respectively, of *American Protestantism* and *Righteous Empire. A History of Protestantism* (three volumes) has been translated from the French of E. G. Leonard's *Histoire générale du protestantisme*. Kenneth S. Latourett's *A History of the Expansion of Christianity* (seven volumes, 1937–45) addresses the spread of Christianity around the world from the beginnings through World War II. Some great older works have been reprinted, among them Philip Schaff's eight-volume *History of the Christian Church*, reissued in three fat volumes. Though its author's viewpoint is conservative Protestant, it is impeccable on that three quarters of Christian history predating the Reformation. A useful companion to any work of Church history is a reliable general-purpose work such as the *Dictionary of Church History* edited by Jerald C. Brauer (1971).

Similarly, when you are reading up on the Bible itself, consider a good Bible dictionary, of which there are many, *e.g.*, Scribner's *Dictionary of the Bible* edited by James Hastings (1909, revised by F. C. Grant and H. H. Rowley, 1963), or *Dictionary of the New Testament* by Xavier Léon-Dufour, translated from the second revised French edition by Terrence Prendergast (1977). If you're interested, pick your own from those available at your library because they vary all over the lot in depth and complexity; find one you are comfortable with.

Getting some sort of handle on Christian theology is a tricky business, because there is no single work of theology that all sects and branches accept completely. Every book of theology is, in a sense, an argument for the views put forward by the author. A dictionary of theology such as the *Dictionary of Christian Theology* by Alan Richardson may be as good a route as any, but for Heaven's sake, don't take this as a divine revelation!

Islam

A new *Encyclopaedia of Islam* was begun in 1960, a fascicle or pamphlet at a time, and completed through Volume 5 in the late 1980s. It largely supplants the *Encyclopaedia of Islam* issued in 1953, itself superseding the 1940 translation of a French-language *Encyclopaedia of Islam* put out in 1899. A well-regarded *Shorter Encyclopaedia of Islam* appeared in 1953 pulling together articles on Islamic religion and law from the then-current *Encyclopaedia of Islam*. This is still available in many larger libraries. Finally, the *Cambridge History of Islam* (1970, partly reissued in 1977) is an excellent source.

In an era when Islamic fundamentalism often dominates morning headlines and the evening news, readers wanting further background on Islam's various sects can find plenty of help in the encyclopedias and public libraries. The origins and history of the often militant minority branch of Shiah, for instance, is covered thoroughly in any general history of Islam, along with the majority Sunni branch and Muslim offshoots such as the Druse. Major Islamic sects such as the Ismaili branch of Shiah pose little difficulty, but smaller sects—*e.g.*, the Alawi sect of Syria's ruler, Hafiz al-Assad—may take a bit more searching.

A nuisance you will encounter in any such research is the modern U.S. journalistic convention of coining U.S. journalese names for foreign religious bodies. "Shiite" is the way the press (and broadcast media) insist on identifying the Shii Muslims of the sect of Shiah. Serious reference works and encyclopedias use the original form (Shii or Shiah). Often some Arabic diacritical marks will be used to indicate pronunciation, *e.g.*, the hamzah (') indicating a glottal stop, as in Shi'ah or Shi'i. This is especially true in scholarly writings. Encyclopedias will usually, but not always, supply the necessary cross-references from the newspaper forms. Valuable background on the Shi'i sect is supplied in *An Introduction to Shi'i*

Islam: The History and Doctrines of Twelver Shiism by Moojan Momen (1985).

Hinduism and Buddhism

After consulting your favorite general encyclopedia, where both of these ancient religions will receive relatively lengthy and outstanding treatment, rummage through your library's catalog to see what may be there. There is a new *Dictionary of Hinduism*. An encyclopedic history that includes much excellent material on Hinduism is *The History and Culture of the Indian People* (ten volumes) edited by R. C. Majumdar. If you come across it, look into *Encyclopedia of Indian Philosophies: Advaita Vedanta up to Samkara and His Pupils* edited by Karl H. Potter (1961).

The English-language *Encyclopedia of Buddhism* was begun in 1961, with four volumes "and counting" in the late 1980s, under the editorship of George P. Malalasekera. Numerous individual works address the life of Gautama Buddha and the history and practice of Buddhism in Asian countries and elsewhere, including the United States. There is an annotated bibliography to English-language books: Yushin Yoo's *Books on Buddhism: An Annotated Subject Guide*.

OTHER ANCIENT RELIGIONS

The other ancient religions that command substantial followings in the modern world arose in Asia. For the amateur wanting to find out something about these faiths three levels of detail are open: the general encyclopedias, encyclopedias (and dictionaries) of religion, and individual works on the particular religions. In the first category, don't overlook concise encyclopedias such as the *Columbia* and the *Century Cyclopedia of Names*, which give excellent brief treatments. In the second group are such works as the new *Encyclopedia of Religion*, the *Encyclopedia of Religion and Ethics*, and the venerable *Schaff-Herzog Encyclopaedia of Religious Knowledge*.

When it comes to the third level, writings about individual faiths, you will not easily find "encyclopedia" or "dictionary" among titles on these less famous and widespread religions. In the faiths mentioned here, a few individual titles will be cited to give you an idea of what kind of thing to look for in the library catalog. There are enough readable books in English to satisfy your curiosity, but bibliographies on the individual religions are not numerous. For Confucianism and Tao see Charles O. Hucker's *China: A Critical Bibliography* or Wing-tsit Chan's *An Outline and Annotated Bibliography of Chinese Philosophy.*

Like Buddhism and at about the same time (sixth century B.C.), Jainism came into being in reaction to the practices of the dominant Hindu cult of the day. The Jaina religion is a minor presence among the world religions today, with its adherents mostly in western India and numbering fewer than four million (vis-à-vis more than six hundred million Hindus). *Outlines of Jainism* and *Jaina culture* are representative individual titles.

Sikhism is a much later phenomenon, evolving late in the fifteenth century A.D. from among the followers of the Hindu god Vishnu. It is centered in northwestern India, especially in the almost wholly Sikh state of Punjab, where it has perhaps fourteen million communicants. There are small but visible Sikh communities in many other countries. An early twentieth-century work in six volumes, reissued in the 1960s, is *The Sikh Religion.*

The religion of Zoroaster (or Zarathustra) originated in Iran before the fourth century B.C., thus predating Islam by more than a millennium. Zoroastrianism put down Manichaeism in Iran (Persia), but after the triumph of Islam many of its followers migrated east to India, where they became known as Parsis (Persians). By the tenth century they were a persecuted minority in Iran, where the Islamic revolutionary regime seeks to extirpate their remnants today. *A History of Zoroastrianism* appeared in two volumes in 1975–1982.

Confucianism started out as a way of life and a philosophical school and evolved into a religion. It originated in the teachings of K'ung-fu-tzu, or Master K'ung, in about 500 B.C., greatly advanced by his posthumous disciple Meng-tzu (Mencius to the West). The spread of Confucian influence—and it was profound—across East Asia was accomplished by its own appeal to students; it never had a missionary presence. Glowing reports of the philosophical writings and teachings of Confucianism sent back by seventeenth-century Roman Catholic missionaries stirred wide admiration among European intellectuals for its intellectual and humanistic teachings. *The Analects of Confucius* is still in print in a famous 1938 translation under that title by Arthur Waley.

Taoism grew out of the teachings of a contemporary of Confucius, Lao-tzu, whose classic work, *Tao-te Ching* (Pinyin *Dao-de Jing*), was intended to teach "The Way to Power" to an enlightened ruler.

Like Confucianism, it was not exactly a religion but a philosophical way to a virtuous and sagacious life. And like Confucianism it has exerted prodigious influence upon Oriental thought and governance. However, during the second century A.D. a Lao-tzu cult proclaimed the sage as a god, and the Taoism that survives today is indeed a religion. It thrives today on Taiwan, with scattered adherents elsewhere. Taoism's influence as a philosophical system continues. Arthur Waley's *The Way and Its Power* (1934, reissued in 1968) supplies extensive background as well as translating the *Tao-te Ching*.

Shinto is the longtime state religion of Japan but now is more a reflection of Japanese culture and values than practiced as a religion. Shinto shrines abound in the country and are visited often by what probably is a large majority of the populace—but at their own convenience and not on any regular schedule. Shinto shrines are islands of quiet in bustling cities and are highly conducive to meditation, prayer, and silent worship. Joseph Kitagawa supplies extended treatment of Shinto in his *Religion in Japanese History* (1966).

THE HOLY ONES: SAINTS AND SAINTHOOD

One aspect of religion gets relatively short shrift from most of the general encyclopedias. This is hagiology (from Greek *hagios*, "holy"), the lives of saints. Christian saints and sainthood are treated quite well, but only two of the major encyclopedias even imply that there are non-Christian saints: *World Book* and *Britannica*.

The scanty treatment elsewhere reflects not so much chauvinism as a kind of innocent ignorance that is so general as to be scandalous. When Roman persecutions started killing stubborn Christians in conspicuous and brutal ways, that faith spontaneously began to adopt the idea of sainthood for its martyrs around the second century A.D.. At that time, several Eastern religions had been honoring saints for most of a millennium.

Hindu saints are *avataras* (human manifestations of God, some of them from other, *i.e.*, non-Hindu, religions) and *sadhus* (good ones or holy men). Jainism venerates a line of saints of earlier religious orientations culminating in its founder. In various branches of Buddhism *arhats* and *boddhisatvas* are, effectively, saints. So are the

Immortals of Confucianism and Taoism, and one of the oldest hagiographies is the Taoist *Lieh-hsien chuan* (*Lives of the Immortals*) of the early second century A.D..

Sainthood also exists in Shinto. In Islam the saint is called the *wali* of Allah, his favorite or constant obeyer. Though there is no foundation for the practice in the Quran, in much of the Muslim world the *awliya* are venerated and prayed to and special blessings sought at their tombs, which are often ornately decorated. This tendency is especially strong in the mystical Sufi movement.

World Book (under "saint") lucidly explains the concept of saint-hood in Christianity, Judaism, Islam, Buddhism, Hinduism, and Confucianism in a substantial article. *Britannica* scratches the same surface in a *Micropaedia* article, and the index cites fairly major treatments at a dozen places in the *Macropaedia*. From *Academic American*, *Americana*, and *Collier's*, nothing—beyond Christian saints. General religious reference works, notably including the *Encyclopedia of Religion*, excel here, and many useful individual books focus on saints of particular religions, such as John A. Subhan's *Sufism: Its Saints and Shrines*.

Standard Christian hagiographies include Sabine Baring-Gould's *Lives of the Saints* (sixteen volumes, revised edition, 1914) and *Butler's Lives of the Saints* edited by Herbert Thurston, S. J., and Donald Attwater (1956, revised and condensed to four volumes from the original twelve of 1756). There also is the *Dictionary of Saints* by John J. Delaney (1980).

MODERN RELIGIOUS SECTS AND CULTS

Popular interest in cults has grown substantially since the 1960s saw the emergence of many new ones and the adoption of older ones by various elements of the protest movements of the time. Public concern that some cults engaged in mind control over their adherents has fanned this interest from time to time, and scholars have paid careful attention to cults and their beliefs, practices, leaders, and followers. As a result there is a large analytical and comparative literature, and in addition many or most of the new religions have turned out a considerable body of literature defining their own practices and beliefs and narrating the lives and teachings of their founders. An indispensable resource for locating these writings is Diane Choquette's *New Religious Movements in the United*

States and Canada—A Critical Assessment and Annotated Bibliography (1985).

The best reference works for accurate and objective information about cults include both the general encyclopedias and encyclopedias of religion already identified. However, there are several outstanding works that either focus entirely on or give exceptional coverage to the newer religions, and whichever of them are available in your library may well be the place to begin your search. There are some gaps in each of them, but together they cover all the most significant cults up to a year or so before the date of publication.

The most comprehensive of these specialized reference sources is the *Abingdon Dictionary of Living Religions* (1981), Keith Crim, general editor. An outstanding descriptive review of important contemporary cults is Robert S. Ellwood's *Alternative Altars: Unconventional and Eastern Spirituality in America* (1979). John Gordon Melton, author of *Encyclopedia of American Religions,* also produced the *Encyclopedic Handbook of Cults in America* (1986).

In addition to religious cults and sects, movements that are non- or anti-religious also receive encyclopedic treatment, such as secular humanism, agnosticism, and atheism, as witness the two-volume *Encyclopedia of Unbelief* (1985), edited by Gordon Stein.

The Bahai faith has supplanted Zoroastrianism as the primary object of Iranian persecution. This offshoot of Shii Islam was established in the mid-nineteenth century by a Persian Muslim who became known as Baha Ullah (Arabic: Glory of God) after he proclaimed himself a manifestation of God along with Zoroaster, the Buddha, Jesus, and Muhammad. Bahai teachings are syncretic, emphasizing that all religions are part of a single whole. Its treatment in the *Encyclopedia of Religion* is particularly good.

The Black Muslim movement, also known as the Nation of Islam and later as the American Muslim Mission, grew out of several strains of Islamic thought and of protest among American blacks that came together under the charismatic leadership of Elijah Muhammad and later Malcolm X, who was assassinated in 1965. The movement dissolved itself in 1985 so its members could immerse themselves in orthodox Islam. A faction persisted under the controversial leadership of its minister, Louis Farrakhan. See the *Abingdon Dictionary of Living Religions,* the *Encyclopedia of Religion* on "Afro-American Religions," and the *Encyclopedia of American Religions.*

The Hare Krishna cult sees itself as heir to the teachings of spiritual descendants of a joint incarnation of the Hindu gods Krishna and Vishnu. It was established in the 1960s by A. C. Bakhtivedanta, also called the Swami Prabhupada. It encourages selflessness, piety, abstemiousness, and absolute submission to the authority of the movement. The *Encyclopedia of American Religions* is quite good here, and an excellent study of the movement is J. Stillson Judah's *Hare Krishna and the Counter-Culture* (1974).

Rastafarians take their name from Ras (prince) Tafari, who reigned, 1930–74, as Emperor Haile Selassie of Ethiopia and whom they worship as the Messiah. They believe that they as blacks are the only authentic Jews. The cult exists mainly in Jamaica. It is well treated in the *Encyclopedia of American Religions* and under "Afro-Caribbean Religions" in the *Encyclopedia of Religion.*

The Rosicrucians attract modern adherents to an occult order known to have originated in or before the early seventeenth century. Its founder is said to be Christian Rosenkreuz (1378–1484), who gained secret knowledge that he shared with disciples. Both the *Encyclopedia of Religion* and the *Encyclopedia of American Religions* excel in their handling of the topic.

Satanism, or the worship of the Judaeo-Christian Devil, has been around America since Colonial times and attacking Christianity since the days of the Gnostics and other heretical sects of the second century A.D. Its central rite is a Black Mass that deliberately profanes the Christian Holy Communion or Eucharist. Some "Devil-worshipers" are said to see Satan as supremely evil and wish to emulate him, while others feel he has gotten a bum rap from Christians and lend him their defiant moral support. The *Encyclopedia of American Religions* is quite good here.

Scientology is a religious movement developed by an American travel writer, L. Ron Hubbard, out of a psychotherapeutic approach he called Dianetics, intended to clear the mind of destructive memories. The founder and his Church of Scientology later became embroiled in controversy with former associates who sued over financial irregularities. The *Encyclopedia of American Religions* covers this sect most capably.

Transcendental Meditation (TM) grew out of an approach to meditation developed by a Hindu monk who was called the Maharishi Mahesh Yogi. He brought his method to the United States in the 1960s and enjoyed an enormous vogue, supplying each proselyte a special mantra (to each of the Beatles, for instance, in exchange for a week's earnings). After about a decade he returned to India, leaving a huge body of publicity clippings and a bemused body of followers, many of whom he had persuaded to shun drugs. The general encyclopedias do well here, as does the *Abingdon Dictionary of Living Religions.*

Followers of the Unification Church are often referred to as "Moonies," after its founder, the Korean holy man known as the Reverend Sun Myung Moon. Moon is a Presbyterian minister who was unfrocked after he revealed that God had picked him to complete the work of Jesus Christ. Moon established a church of his own, formally the Holy Spirit Association for the Unification of World Christianity. When he brought his movement to the United States he won hordes of idealistic, youthful followers and the enmity and dread of many of their parents. He was jailed for income-tax evasion, but the movement appeared to hold its own during his absence. The coverage of this group is outstanding in both the *Abingdon Dictionary of Living Religions* and the *Encyclopedia of Religion.*

Devotees of Meher Baba comprise an international cult based on the teachings of an Indian holy man of Iranian extraction who bore that name. Though it does not proselytize, it drew many adherent in the 1960s when Baba, who died in 1969, taught his followers to eschew the drug use then pandemic among the young. They accept all religions and deem their founder a manifestation of God like Vishnu, Jesus, Muhammad, and others. The general encyclopedias are very good on the Baba movement, as is the *Encyclopedia of American Religions.*

The foregoing thumbnail sketches are only samples of the deluge of cults experienced by the United States and the rest of the world in recent decades, and the comments on coverage by the various reference works reflects the kind of rummaging around you may have to do to satisfy your curiosity. Other cults, like the ill-fated People's Temple of San Francisco and Guyana, are out of existence one way or another, but one or another of the sources named in this section will supply information about them or help you locate another work that can.

The general encyclopedias usually are adequate on these subjects. Some of the newer cults, and new developments affecting the older ones, inevitably are impossible for encyclopedias to stay up-to-date on. But as the foregoing illustrations demonstrate, there are excellent specialized works you can turn to if you are not satisfied the first time around.

HOLY WRIT; BUT WHICH
TRANSLATION?

Although adherents of Judaism, Christianity, and Islam are usually characterized as "people of the book," nearly all religions have a substantial body of sacred writings. It is just that in most cases the scriptures are not as central as they are to the three faiths that emanated from the Middle East. In the other religions, controversies over translations from the original tongue of the prophet or founder have not arisen. Moreover, in the scriptures of most other faiths, either there is only one English translation, or differences between or among versions are not sharp enough to stir major doctrinal disputes.

These latter arguments apply to the case of the Quran also. Practically speaking, it is only in the Judaeo-Christian tradition that major disputes have arisen over translations of the word of God. And between the Jews and the Christians in this respect, nearly all the fighting goes on among the Christians.

Ever since Martin Luther began translating the Bible from Latin into the common language, in his case German, Protestants have placed heavy emphasis on the lay Christian's need to read and understand the Bible. It is only since the Second Vatican Council (1962–65) that Catholics have begun to promote Bible-reading by the laity. And it is mainly to Protestants that the Bible has been presented as the infallible word of God and thus essential to the understanding of every true believer.

Biblical translation is no new thing. It began when the Persian Empire controlled the Mediterranean basin and Aramaic was the common tongue. The Jews had to translate their Bible into Aramaic to educate their own children. Then Greek became the *lingua franca* and it was necessary for Jews to retranslate into Greek. The early Christians simply adopted the Jewish Bible. The books that became the New Testament were written in Greek and Aramaic, and as the Christian Church moved toward Rome and Latin became the universal language, both the Old and New Testaments had to be translated into Latin.

At the time of the Protestant Reformation, Luther and Tyndale began translating the Bible into German and English, respectively. Within a hundred years James I had rounded up fifty-four scholars whom he charged with putting the great work into modern English, *i.e.*, the educated speech of London in 1611, the year it was published. The remarkable success of the King James Version has persuaded the Protestants of every succeeding English-speaking generation that only the KJV was authentic and that God spoke in Shakespearian accents. This overwhelming success produced widespread, intransigent hostility that has greeted subsequent retranslation efforts to this day.

In the nineteenth century came another burst of scholarly activity centering on the development in Germany of a new method of "higher criticism," comparing traditional versions with surviving fragments of scripture in original languages. As these methods became more sophisticated, a new wave of analysis and criticism was introduced in the next century with the discovery and study of the "Dead Sea Scrolls" in upper Egypt in 1947–60. This was accomplished with unprecedented international, interdenominational, and interfaith cooperation, with Catholic, Jewish, Protestant, and Eastern Orthodox scholars working side by side.

Each of these periods of scholarly ferment led to new translations, which in turn set off explosions of discontent or outrage at the defilement of old versions long taken to be the original word of God. One mid-nineteenth century editor of the *Britannica,* a professor and a divine of the Free Church of Scotland, was excommunicated over an article he had written espousing and explicating the new scholarship and the new system of biblical criticism.

The mid-twentieth-century activity issued in a stream of translations under various denominational sponsorships. Among the most important were the interdenominational Protestant *Revised Standard Version* (New Testament, 1946; Old Testament, 1957), the *New English Bible* (1961–70), the French Catholic *Jerusalem Bible* (1956; English translation, 1966), the American Catholic *New American Bible* (1970), the undenominational Protestant *Good News Bible* or *Today's English Version* (1966–76), and the undenominational Protestant *New International Version* (1973–78). The Jewish Publication Society, meanwhile, had undertaken a massive new translation of the *Jewish Bible,* applying the new scholarship to the carefully restored Masoretic text, which had been the standard since the tenth century. This great project began in 1955 and was completed in 1980.

As a result of all this, amateur students of the Bible have access to incredible variety for purposes of comparing one version with another. Dabbling in this vast literature, one soon discovers that whatever God says, his recorders hear it with their own ears. For example, here are four translations of the proverb of the ant

(Proverbs 6:6–11). None contradicts the others, but the different nuances of interpretation offer fascinating insights into the ways in which the passage of time and the choices among alternative meanings affect translation.

King James Version	Jewish Publication Society
Go to the ant, thou sluggard; consider her ways, and be wise:	Lazybones, go to the ant; Study its ways and learn.
Which having no guide, overseer, or ruler, Provideth her meat in the summer and gathereth her food in the harvest.	Without leaders, officers, or rulers It lays up its stores during the summer, gathers in its food at the harvest.
How long wilt thou sleep, O sluggard? When wilt thou arise out of thy sleep?	How long will you lie there, Lazybones; when will you awake from your sleep?
Yet a little sleep, a little slumber, a little folding of the hands to sleep;	A bit more sleep, a bit more slumber, a bit more hugging yourself in bed,
So shall thy poverty come as one that travelleth, and thy want as an armed man.	And poverty will come calling upon you, and want, like a man with a shield.

Jerusalem Bible	Good News Bible
Idler, go to the ant; ponder her ways and grow wise:	Lazy people should learn a lesson from the way ants live.
No one gives her orders, no overseer, no master, Yet all through the summer she makes sure of her food, gathers her supplies at harvest time.	They have no leader, chief, or ruler, But they store up their food during the summer, getting ready for winter.
How long do you intend to lie there, idler? When are you going to rise from your sleep?	How long is the lazy man going to lie around? When is he ever going to get up?
A little sleep, a little drowsiness, a little folding of the arms to take life easier.	"I'll just take a short nap," he says; "I'll fold my hands and rest a while."
And like a vagrant, poverty is at your elbow and, like a beggar, want.	But while he sleeps, poverty will attack him like an armed robber.

The Bible translations named here, and in some cases many others, are available in most good libraries. In addition, a comparative version of the King James and Revised Standard versions called *The Interpreter's Bible* can be found in every substantial library and in the libraries of many churches. This twelve-volume work, done by Protestant scholars of several denominations between 1952 and 1957, places the two versions side by side on successive two-page spreads, each passage accompanied by extensive commentary to supply historical background and discuss translation problems and theological implications.

In addition to Bible texts, sizable libraries also will have texts of various books that have been excluded from the canon, or accepted order, of the Old Testament or New Testament. There are two kinds of such literature. The Apocrypha are books that the Church has excluded from the regular canon but that still offer valuable interpretative insights or background. The apocryphal books are included in many versions of the Bible as a sort of appendix. Roman Catholics and Protestants disagree as to several books the former accept and the latter do not.

Other non- or extra-canonical books are called the pseudoepigrapha, ancient works written in biblical style but that have not been accepted as apocryphal. Often these scrolls are the work of heretical sects. But they cast interesting light on both the Bible and the controversies that have stormed through the Church in all its ages, and if your mind runs that way they make fascinating browsing. The texts of the Dead Sea Scrolls are included in this body of published literature, which is fully described in the encyclopedias and clearly identified in the bibliographies. If your library doesn't have them you can get them through interlibrary loan, but do your homework first and know (from available bibliographic sources) what you really want.

For readers wishing to locate a particular Bible passage that is half remembered, or whose wording is known but whose location is unknown, there are two approaches. If a Bible concordance is at hand, that will be the safest bet, with one proviso. Since, as noted in Chapter 3 a concordance lists the location of every substantive word in the book, no one concordance can be really adequate for two distinctly different translations.

A Good News Bible concordance, for instance, will be of little help in finding many passages in the King James Version. In the case of the ant proverb, if you remember "thou sluggard," as many do, and look up the key word, "sluggard," you won't find it. But there is a way around that obstacle. Try "ant." Curiously enough, you will find only one entry, and it will take you right to the proverb. Of course, there are many, many concordance entries with scores and hundreds of references—"lord," for example. These are arranged in the order of their appearance, Bible book by book and verse by verse, with each entry supplying enough surrounding text to let you know when you've found the right one. Here is an example from the concordance to the New American Bible, from the word LORD in the section covering the [New Testament] Book of Acts [of the Apostles]:

1:24	O L, you read the hearts of men.
2:20	of the great and glorious day of the L.
2:21	be saved who calls on the name of the L.
2:25	I have set the L. ever before me,

If you do not have access to a concordance, a workable substitute is a dictionary of quotations. The problem is that such a work is most likely to use only the language of either the King James or the Revised Standard Version. And that is not much help for any of the newer translations in many cases, unless, of course, you are a real whiz at inventing paraphrases with which you can experiment.

There is an extremely large body of Bible scholarship, and a good deal of it is fairly readily comprehensible to the lay reader. Note that some of this material questions or attacks the authenticity of the Bible or its divine inspiration or provenance; sources can be found to support every viewpoint. Bibliographies covering all this material are extensive, explicit in identifying the thrust of each work, and available in virtually every library. The general encyclopedias are outstanding in their coverage of the Bible, biblical literature and criticism, translations, etc. *Britannica*'s "Biblical Literature" article alone runs to some 110,000 words—approximately the length of this entire book—in the *Macropaedia*.

Other general reference works worth consulting include the *Interpreter's Dictionary of the Bible* (four volumes, 1962), and the *Cambridge History of the Bible* (three volumes, 1963–70). There also are numerous other Bible dictionaries, atlases, semipopular periodicals such as *Biblical Archaeology*, and other study aids.

PHILOSOPHY AND LOGIC

Much is made these days of "secular humanism" as a new religion, but have you heard of the Church of Humanity, founded in nineteenth-century London by disciples of the French philosopher

Auguste Comte? What stirred the Greeks to the murderous suppression of the Pythagoreans? (Not a good ad for Zeno and the Stoics' argument that a good man was protected by his virtue.) Why was justice the biggest philosophical problem for Utilitarian philosopher John Stuart Mill? If this sort of question intrigues or perplexes you, read on. It's easy stuff to find out.

Chinese and Indian sages were already at it, but practically speaking and for the Western world, the Greeks gave us philosophy and logic, as well as the names of those pursuits (from *philosophos,* "love of wisdom," and *logos,* "reason" or "word"). Philosophy and logic are now treated as separate disciplines, but the latter still is the indispensable tool of the former. Thales of Miletus, who preceded Socrates by about a hundred years, is generally regarded as the first of the Greek philosophers. A couple of centuries later—for the West, anyway—Aristotle invented logic in his *Organon.* That philosopher's work, incidentally, has been given a popular key in Mortimer Adler's *Aristotle for Everybody.*

There are several major resources for look-it-up-type inquiries into questions on philosophy and logic. Important among them are the general encyclopedias, which address the subject seriously and generally quite well. The *Britannica* has far more than a quarter of a million words on the two topics. Incidentally, the relation of what was called inductive logic to mathematics is addressed in the discipline of foundations of mathematics, which is touched on in Chapter 12.

Unless you know exactly what you are looking for by name, your best bet for a starting point is likely to be one of the encyclopedias. Each has an article describing the principal schools of philosophy and identifying the great philosophers and the major works associated with each school, varying in breadth and depth, of course, with the character of the encyclopedia. These sources are conscientious in systematically listing all the important aspects of each school. On the contrary, a general, introductory-level book about philosophy may deal with only the most important handful of the twenty or so schools of Western philosophy from Atomism to Utilitarianism.

Philosophy bulks large in the ancient religions of Asia, especially so in Confucianism and Taoism. For resources in Asian philosophies, see the sections "Hinduism and Buddhism" and especially "Other Ancient Religions" earlier in this chapter. Additional sources include S. N. Dasgupta's *A History of Indian Philosophy* (five volumes, 1922–55), and the various volumes treating Asian philosophies in the *Harvard Oriental Series* (forty-seven volumes, 1890–1968).

The beginnings—indeed, the whole basis—of Western philosophy and logic are a massive element in classical literature, and major reference sources are discussed under that subject in the section "Literature" in Chapter 10, dealing with the arts. They are included in this list for your convenience: *Encyclopedia of Religion and Ethics, Great Books of the Western World, Harper's Dictionary of Classical Literature and Antiquities, Harvard Classics, Oxford Classical Dictionary,* and *The Oxford Companion to Classical Literature.*

Among other useful and generally accessible works are the *Encyclopedia of Philosophy* (eight volumes), the *Dictionary of the History of Ideas,* Philip P. Wiener, editor in chief (five volumes), the four-volume *History of Ideas,* and the *Encyclopedia of Ethics.* An old work that is beautifully comprehensible to the lay reader is Will Durant's *The Story of Philosophy* (1926). And that indefatigable distiller of ideas Frank N. Magill published *Masterpieces of World Philosophy in Summary Form* (1961).

CHAPTER 12

Looking Up the Physical Sciences and Mathematics

The nonscientist in today's world is hard put to understand what the headlines are talking about when they reel off "atom-smashing" and "gene-splicing" and "black holes" and "electromagnetic resonance scanning" and "polychlorinated" this and that. The trouble is that we have to be able to comprehend some of that stuff to reach intelligent judgments and choices in careers, community affairs, politics, and investing, to name a few.

You can put the blame quite properly on school systems that no longer insist on making us competent to understand modern sciences before letting us out of high school. However, we are out, and we still have to cope. Fortunately, there are ways.

This chapter concentrates on looking up the physical sciences: astronomy, physics, and chemistry; and mathematics. The life sciences (biology, botany, zoology) and the Earth sciences (geology, paleontology, hydrology, meteorology, etc.) are addressed in Chapter 9, and the social sciences (psychology, sociology, political science, economics, and that lot) appear in Chapter 13.

THE PHYSICAL SCIENCES IN GENERAL

There are some excellent resources. Be guided in your choices by your own level of understanding of the particular scientific field you are looking up. If you know nothing at all about the subject, by all means start with one of the encyclopedias written to be understood by junior-high-school students, specifically *World Book, Academic American, Compton's, International,* and *Merit Students.* They are accurate, explicit, and illustrated where appropriate with drawings or photographs that help explain. Most of all, they are written in simple, direct English, and where it is essential to use scientific jargon, they explain it.

If you have a rudimentary knowledge of a scientific subject but are not up on the newest developments or don't know anything about some special aspect of it, or if you want to go beyond the five encyclopedias cited in the preceding paragraph, then consult the rest of the flock: *Americana; Collier's;* and *Britannica,* especially in the *Micropaedia.* The *Macropaedia* in most of the "hard sciences" will start out comprehensibly enough but before you get very far into an article—say, for example, "Physical Principles and Concepts," or "Analysis and Measurement [Physical and Chemical]"—you are going to find the going a bit heavy unless you are at home with inevitably difficult concepts, physical formulas expressed in Greek letters, etc. If you can handle that sort of thing comfortably, of course, you will be delighted with the scope and precision of the article.

On the other hand, the *Macropaedia's* general survey articles, such as "Physical Sciences," are quite accessible to the intelligent lay reader with only a general knowledge of chemistry and physics. Best of all, if you have the time, next time you visit your library to look up something in the physical sciences, shop around in all three of the more advanced encyclopedias on the same topic and find your own level of comfort.

There are several additional resources for fully accurate research on scientific subjects. All are revised frequently. The biggest and best of these is the *McGraw-Hill Encyclopedia of Science and Technology,* which also publishes an excellent yearbook. This fifteen-volume work is about at the *Britannica Macropaedia's* level of difficulty, but it goes into significantly greater detail on most subjects because it is about half as big and concentrated wholly on science and technology. It does not carry biographies. *Van Nostrand's Scientific Encyclopedia* is a huge single-volume work with relatively concise articles on every aspect of all the sciences.

Other general scientific works well worth looking into and notable for their readability are the one-volume *Harper Encyclopedia of Science* and Isaac Asimov's *New Intelligent Man's Guide to Science.*

Various scientific dictionaries are available, and almost anything of this sort with a fairly recent copyright date that you can find in your library will be useful. An example is *Dictionary of the History of Science,* edited by W. F. Bynum, E. J. Browne, and Roy Porter. For access to the scientific periodical press, there are two from Wilson: the *Applied Science and Technology Index,* which indexes some three hundred individual publications and dates back to 1958; and the *General Science Index,* started in 1978 and covering about ninety broader-gauge science periodicals. For science history going back to the earliest times—*i.e.,* ancient Greece—look for George Sarton's *History of Science* (two volumes, 1959, 1970).

The books that will be discussed in the following sections illustrate what's available. New popular and semipopular treatments are being written constantly. There are hundreds of others. Look around in your library and dip into any volume that looks interesting to you. Discuss your particular interests with the reference librarian. He or she may well know of something new that just came in.

ASTRONOMY

Astronomy's origin in prehistory is evident from prehistoric observatories that have survived in various parts of the world. Astronomy, through the good offices of Nicolaus Copernicus, launched the Scientific Revolution. These days new discoveries from the space age outdate every new book in the field almost before its ink is dry.

However, take heart. Only infrequently in the history of human study of the heavens do new discoveries invalidate previous knowledge. Usually they simply add new knowledge, often helping to make something previously known easier to understand and explain.

Both the general and scientific encyclopedias cover the space age, astronomy, astrophysics, cosmology (the nature and origin of the universe), and the solar system exceptionally well. Their treatments are readable and general, beautifully illustrated, and almost entirely free of mathematical formulas.

The number of popular works in these fields is increasing steadily, and almost every library has a collection of special encyclopedias and dictionaries of astronomy for the nonscientist. Important among these are the *Cambridge Encyclopedia of Astronomy* (1977), editor-in-chief Simon Mitton; McGraw-Hill's *Encyclopedia of*

Astronomy (1983); another *Encyclopedia of Astronomy* (1971) by Gilbert E. Satterthwaite; the *Concise Encyclopedia of Astronomy* by Alfred Weigert and Helmut Zimmerman (second English edition 1976, translated from the German); and the *Macmillan Dictionary of Astronomy* (1979), edited by Valerie Illingworth (also available as the *Facts on File Dictionary of Astronomy* and the *Anchor Dictionary of Astronomy.*

An annotated bibliography designed for readers unfamiliar with the subject is Robert A. Seal's *A Guide to the Literature of Astronomy* (1979), and it is widely held by better libraries. Verging closer to the technical but aimed at students and amateur astronomers are a couple of important works. *Norton's Star Atlas and Reference Handbook* is a 1910 classic by A. P. Norton that is regularly updated, decade after decade. Newer and also found in many libraries is the *Concise Atlas of the Universe* by Patrick Moore.

Individual books for the lay reader are proliferating too, among them, *The Collapsing Universe* and a large handful of other titles by Isaac Asimov, *Planets* by Jonathan Leonard and Carl Sagan, *New World: Discoveries from Our Solar System* by Wernher von Braun and Frederick L. Ordway III, *Between the Planets,* a popular treatment of asteroids by F. G. Watson, and *Meteors, Comets, and Meteorites* by G. S. Hawkins.

PHYSICS

Physics deals with matter and energy; it is the fundamental physical science. Classical physics treats mechanics—that is to say, how gaseous, fluid, and solid things move and are moved and how other things move in them. Physics addresses the atom and subatomic particles, and electromagnetic radiation in its various guises—electric current, magnetism, light, X rays. It includes wave motion slower than the speed of light as well, from ocean waves to sound waves.

If you are doing your looking up in a public or school library, find the section (get the classification number out of the subject catalog) and browse around. Despite the old saw, you often can tell at least something about a book by its cover; a sprightly jacket design is meant to entice the reader. The real heavyweight stuff often looks forbidding just sitting on the shelf. Find a title—perhaps encyclopedia or dictionary—and rummage through the book to try it out. And remember too to check both the reference and the circulating stacks in this fashion.

Here are some of the titles you may find: *A Dictionary of Physical Science* and *Facts on File Dictionary of Physics*, edited by John Daintith, *The Penguin Book of the Physical World*, edited by S. Larkin and L. Bernbaum, *Physics for the Liberal Arts Student* by David S. Saxon and William B. Fretter, and *Elementary Modern Physics* by R. T. Weidner and R. L. Sells. Also see *Sciences Restated: Physics and Chemistry for the Non-Scientist* by H. G. Cassidy.

Some of the most difficult concepts are presented in most engaging ways, *e.g.,* atomic physics in *Mr. Tompkins in Paperback,* a kind of entertaining, highly exaggerated parable about atoms, by George Gamow; and *The Strange Story of the Quantum,* another entertaining explanation, this one of quantum physics, by Banesh Hoffman. Be on the lookout for other whimsical or engaging titles, such as *Tracking Down Particles* by R. D. Hill or *What Is the World Made Of?: Atoms, Leptons, Quarks, and Other Tantalizing Particles* by G. Feinberg. They can turn a worrisome quest into fun. Finally, where you encounter "elementary" in a title in the world of physics, keep in mind that such books can answer your questions, but they demand your careful attention.

CHEMISTRY

Chemistry was a part of "natural philosophy" until the seventeenth century, when the Scientific Revolution led to the establishment of physics. At about the same time, what had been alchemy and a few other strains of primitive scientific inquiry came together into a new discipline concerned with identifying the substances of nature and observing how they interacted with one another.

Today that science has a number of subdisciplines, including organic and inorganic chemistry; physical and analytical chemistry; and biochemistry, which is a kind of joint discipline with biology. Those terms are logical topics to search under in card catalog or bibliography. (They may be listed under their own names or as subordinate topics under chemistry.) Bibliographic sources in chemistry (as also in physics) are generally for the professional and the serious student rather than the lay reader. Naturally, some of what you can find may be helpful, depending on the particular subtopic you are looking up and on how comfortable you are with chemistry in general. There is one annotated bibliography aimed at high school and college students not specializing in chemistry: *Selected Titles in Chemistry*. It is published at intervals of several years by the American Chemical Society.

Most encyclopedias in the field address the needs of the chemist or advanced chemistry student, but one of the more readily accessible ones is the *Encyclopedia of Chemistry*, edited by Clifford A. Hampel and Gessner G. Hawley. Well-written introductory texts often prove to be excellent sources for the nonchemist. Among these is *A Short History of Chemistry* by J. R. Partington, a compact encyclopedic approach to the field. Other accessible works are *Chemistry: A Cultural Approach* by W. F. Kieffer and *Sciences Restated: Physics and Chemistry for the Non-Scientist* by H. G. Cassidy (1970). Also see *Discovery of the Elements* by M. E. Weeks and H. J. Leicester and *Why Do Chemical Reactions Occur?* by J. A. Campbell.

MATHEMATICS

Perhaps no other academic or intellectual discipline has seen its subdisciplines proliferate so rapidly as mathematics.

When the first encyclopedists undertook to assemble in one place the sum of human knowledge, they aimed to make it accessible to the enlightened ones who were constantly advancing the sum of knowledge—stretching, as it were, the circle of knowledge. After many centuries and the adoption of such notions as public education for all, the goal of the encyclopedists changed, to become making the knowledge of various fields available to the lay reader, and no longer just to the specialist in his or her area of specialization.

But math, with its ability to construct abstract models of reality and to test them without risking destruction of the materials that would go into them in "real life," grew faster than anyone could count, adding branches and subdisciplines with blinding speed. Topology is a branch of mathematics, a kind of off-beat geometry. It deals with the properties of distorted surfaces, *e.g.*, that of a Möbius strip, which can be made from a strip of paper given a half-twist and glued into a loop so that its inner surface is a continuation of the outer. When the Dutch mathematician Brouwer, probably the most influential name in topology, was born in 1881, that subdiscipline of geometry did not exist. There are many, many other similar illustrations in other aspects of mathematics. Today many a mathematician looks to the advanced general encyclopedia for information and understanding about other, new subdisciplines of mathematics. Thus in effect mathematicians are changing the encyclopedists' rules once again. In fact, "changing the rules" is an apt epithet for much of what mathematics does.

Since the beginnings of the Scientific Revolution it has become increasingly evident that mathematics was in one way or another the very handmaiden of science. Mathematical formulas are indispensable to the physicist and astronomer, to the chemist and biologist, to the social scientist. Without math airplanes would not fly, oil would not be found or pumped, computers would not compute, the modern world would not exist. Yet this set of scholarly topics that is so essential to modern human existence daunts most of us and leaves us behind, rubbing our eyes and wondering what those people are talking about.

The bad news is, we're not alone. Sometimes the topologist wonders what the AI (artificial intelligence) hotshot is talking about. The good news is that if we are careful and persistent, the rest of us can find out, too.

But only if we are careful and persistent; for mathematics is a language using a different set of symbols from those with which we write literate sentences. Mathematicians do not need to be literate to communicate with one another—at least not very literate. They need to be numerate. Public education in America today does not make most of us numerate (and not enough of us literate, either, to be sure).

It is, then, a rare mathematician that can write about his or her piece of the mathematical turf in ways that enable the rest of us to understand. Because most expert mathematicians are long since resigned or otherwise conditioned to try to communicate only with one another, it's very hard to find one able and willing to put his or her ideas in ordinary English instead of in the formulas of mathematical abstractions.

Because general encyclopedias naturally turn to the top authorities to write about any field, and because mathematicians tend to write for one another, a general encyclopedia rarely is a good place to turn for comprehensible knowledge about any math concepts trickier than addition, subtraction, multiplication, division, and perhaps plane geometry.

There are exceptions to this bleak assessment, on one topic here and another there, in this encyclopedia or that, but unless you are pretty numerate yourself, don't get your hopes up.

As noted, there are dozens of subdisciplines in mathematics, but probably all of them may be reached from one dozen basic elements. These are the history of mathematics, the foundations of mathematics, algebra, analysis, arithmetic, combinatorics, geometry, matrix theory, number theory, probability theory, set theory, and trigonometry. These terms embrace various other concepts that many of the nonmathematicians among us have heard about. Calculus, for instance, is the central ingredient of analysis, logarithms part of arithmetic, and topology of trigonometry; but still, the twelve listed in the previous sentence are the words to look up when you want the titles of the basic mathematical topics.

Where to look becomes the question. When you (nonmathematical you, obviously) check the library catalog or any bibliography, do it with some skepticism, and look carefully for indications that the work is elementary, introductory, accessible to the reader without a background in science or math, etc. The following works are not guaranteed to be easy going, but they are good examples of the simplest and clearest writing about their topics.

For fun with math, try mathematical puzzles and number games. There are numerous titles by Martin Gardner. Arithmetic is treated lightly and comprehensibly in *Arithmetic Can Be Fun* by Munro Leaf and the *Realm of Numbers* by Isaac Asimov.

Of mathematical history and mathematics generally, unless you have a particular affinity for the field, start out with something like *It Figures* by P. Kaner and N. Langdon or *Mathematics Made Simple* by A. Sperling and M. Stuart. Then look into the classic *Study of the History of Mathematics* by George Sarton, *A Concise History of Mathematics* by Dirk J. Struik (two volumes), and *The World of Mathematics* edited by James R. Newman (four volumes). For reference there are the *Universal Encyclopedia of Mathematics* (with a foreword by Newman) and the *VNR Concise Encyclopedia of Mathematics*, edited by W. Gellert. *Mathematics: The Loss of Certainty* is one of several valuable and lucid works by Morris Kline. Others are *Mathematics in a Western Culture*, *Mathematics for Liberal Arts*, and *Mathematical Thought from Ancient to Modern Times*.

If you want to pursue math further by dipping into various of its numerous subdisciplines, see what you can find. There are lots of introductory texts around. How deeply your library may go into these fields (listed earlier) remains for you to discover. Good luck.

A final world on mathematics: The subject is filled with paradoxes that have not yet been resolved and indeed may never be. Some of them are fun, so don't let the assumed impossibility of mathematics fake you out without digging around a bit looking for the good stuff. Consider, for example, Betrand Russell's barber paradox: The barber shaves every man in town except those that shave themselves. Does he shave himself? If he does, he is one of those whom he does not shave. Does he not shave, *i.e.*, does he wear a beard? Aha! In that case, since does not shave himself, he is one of the class of men in town that he does shave.

You could look it up.

CHAPTER 13

LOOKING UP EDUCATION
AND THE SOCIAL SCIENCES

Although Prussia was requiring children to attend school early in the eighteenth century, the idea of common schools and mandatory attendance was slow to work its way across Europe. In New England it was making considerable headway by the first quarter of the nineteenth century. Elsewhere in the United States, the situation was as spotty as in Europe. But by the time the British Parliament finally passed the Elementary Education Act in 1870, America had publicly supported high schools in most states and even provided for the higher education of women at several coeducational colleges. There was one college expressly for women, Vassar, in 1861.

Ever since it came to be generally accepted that the taxpayer must provide educational facilities and teachers and that the children must attend school, Americans have been hotly concerned about the quality and costs of the public school. This concern extended early to higher education, which began in the Massachusetts Bay Colony with Harvard College in 1636, nearly a century and a half before the Declaration of Independence. By the nineteenth century, universities began spreading west across the continent, supported by federal land grants that were enabled even before the U.S. Constitution by the Articles of Confederation.

The early development of local school boards and districts as bodies that could levy taxes and hire teachers obviously reflected but also helped intensify American concern about education, and various popularly supported efforts to reform it are nearly as old as education itself. All this has helped develop a large literature on the subject. How to find what you want in that welter of fact, lore, and judgment soon became a problem, and so it remains.

EDUCATION

The general encyclopedias do well in the field of education. Start there, and if you want to press on, the following suggestions will take you to good sample resources pretty much across the whole range of education. Most of them can be found in a well-appointed public library. Those listed here are not uniformly easy reading, but nearly all of them are quite accessible to the nonspecialist. When you want to go further, bibliographies will extend your range as desired.

Worthy of note among general works on education are two encyclopedias. One is very old but still found in many libraries and excellent for its historical treatments, *viz.*, the *Cyclopedia of Education* edited by Paul Monroe (five volumes, 1911–13, reprinted 1968). An *Encyclopedia of Education* edited by Lee C. Deighton appeared in ten volumes in 1971, and a ten-volume *International Encyclopedia of Education* was issued in 1985 with Torsten Husen and T. Neville Postlethwaite as editors in chief. There also is an *International Encyclopedia of Higher Education* (ten volumes, 1977), with Asa S. Knowles as editor in chief.

A thorough and well-annotated general bibliography is essential to any study of the field beyond the encyclopedias general and special. One such is Michael Sedlak's *American Educational History: A Guide to Information Sources* (1981). For periodicals, see *Education Index,* which covers more than three hundred of them in addition to educational journals and the proceedings of various educational organizations in Canada and the United Kingdom as well as the United States. The *World Year Book of Education* reviews international developments in education annually and has statistical and other records about the entire field.

There are dozens of works on every imaginable aspect of education. Only in the largest public libraries and at universities and teachers colleges will you find much of a choice on most of the special subtopics, but the books are out there and accessible through interlibrary loan if you want to pursue them. A major resource for looking up educational topics is the Educational Resources Information Center, known to librarians and educators as ERIC. This is a national clearinghouse for information about everything educational. It operates under the auspices of the U.S. Department of Education. The subfields of education that you might want to inquire into have titles such as educational philosophy, educational theory, comparative education (among countries and societies), educational economics, educational problems, and, of course, education history.

Some of the fields are subjects of wide popular interest: special education for the physically handicapped, the mentally impaired, the gifted. Others generate impassioned controversy but are basic to the entire profession; *vide* educational testing. Books objective and books polemical state their cases. Yes, and a flood of books annual, *e.g.*, in the last instance, the *Mental Measurement Yearbook.*

Books of the sort discussed earlier in this chapter look at education from a theoretical or philosophical or historical viewpoint. The body of explicit and pragmatic literature is as large. Witness the range reflected in these examples: the annual *Trade and Technical Careers and Training: Handbook of Accredited Private Trade and Technical Schools;* the National University Extension Association's *On Campus/Off Campus Degree Programs for Part-Time Students; Continuing Education: A Guide to Career Development Programs;* and Mortimer Adler's *A Guidebook to Learning for the Lifelong Pursuit of Wisdom.*

Your library can help you locate particular schools or teachers: It is possible to find out the faculty departments and often virtually the whole faculty of colleges and universities in North America and in most major countries of the world. In the developing countries you can identify the higher-education institutions and get an assessment of the education situation in each country in the American Council on Education's *International Directory for Educational Liaison.*

There may be any number of reasons for looking up a particular school. The resource materials for finding out general information sometimes but not always overlap with those you will use if you are looking for a school to attend. This chapter will address the question both ways. For general information, then: UNESCO's *Directory of National Institutions of Higher Education in Asia and the Pacific* lists departments and faculty members for each school; the *Commonwealth Universities Yearbook* of the Association of Commonwealth Universities lists universities and their schools, departments, officers, and department heads throughout the [British] Commonwealth; outside the Commonwealth there is the *International Handbook of Universities and Other Institutions of Higher Education.* Europa's

World of Learning lists the world's higher educational institutions along with libraries, museums, research institutions, and learned societies. In the United States you can look up any college or university faculty member and find out where he or she teaches in *The National Faculty Directory* (a four-volume annual).

Identifying colleges and universities as possible places to study has been much simplified by the rapid development of publications listing and describing both American and foreign institutions. In addition, some libraries have, usually in the form of microfiche, substantial collections of college catalogs. A sampling of the kinds of publication you can consult for information about colleges and universities follows. All are either annual or frequently revised.

In the United States:

Accredited Institutions of Post-Secondary Education

American Junior Colleges

American Universities and Colleges

College Blue Book (five volumes)

The College Handbook

Comparative Guide to Science and Engineering Programs

Directory of American Medical Colleges

Education Directory: Colleges and Universities

Guide to Alternative Colleges and Universities

The HEP Higher Education Directory

Index of Majors

New American Guide to Colleges

Peterson's Guide to Graduate Study

Peterson's Guide to Undergraduate Study

Outside the United States:

Commonwealth Universities Yearbook

International Handbook of Universities and Other Institutions of Higher Education

Directory of National Institutions of Higher Education in Asia and the Pacific

Global Guide to International Education

Guide to Study in Europe

Schools Abroad of Interest to Americans

Work, Study, and Travel Abroad

World Guide to Higher Education

There also are publications for those seeking scholarship and tuition aid:

The College Money Handbook: The Complete Guide to Expenses, Scholarships, Loans, Jobs, and Special Aid Programs at Four-Year Colleges

Annual Register of Grant Support

Scholarships, Fellowships and Loans

THE SOCIAL SCIENCES

The social sciences, often called the behavioral sciences, can be seen as the response of the nineteenth century to three earlier strains of influence. Those were the effects of the Enlightenment and the Renaissance among scholars of the rationalist outlook of the Greek philosophers, the flowering of science in the Scientific Revolution of the seventeenth and eighteenth centuries, and the political and social upheavals of the French Revolution and the Industrial Revolution.

Some hard-bitten critics still contend that "science" is an improper term for these new disciplines, and there is not even total agreement on which disciplines are included: Sometimes education and sometimes not; psychology yes, but to what extent? Psychiatry, for instance, clearly belongs with medicine in the healing arts. And history? One of the humanities? What about geography? And so it goes.

This chapter will discuss what can be thought of as a hard core of social sciences, *i.e.*, economics, political science, sociology, and psychology. It will also treat public opinion or survey research, which is important to all of them. Related disciplines will be discussed as appropriate, *e.g.*, cultural or social anthropology, which is addressed with sociology.

General encyclopedia treatment is as usual good, although none of the major ones is kept constantly up-to-date in all the fields, and from year to year with the passage of time and revisions one or two will be quite current on this aspect or that. Unceasing research and occasional major breakthroughs bedevil them all. In a yearly reprinting, an encyclopedia can afford to change only a specific number of pages, almost never as many as 10 percent of the total. If in a particular encyclopedia developments in a field such as, say, animal psychology are not cited after 1970, you can be fairly sure that article hasn't been updated since 1972 or 1973. If the matter is important to you, and it may not be, check the competition or go into the general literature of the field. The luck of the draw suggests that at least one of the major encyclopedias will be more recent, and certainly a good bibliography will send you to many fresh books in the field.

Beyond the general encyclopedias are several reference works on the social sciences as a whole. The *International Encyclopedia of the Social Sciences* edited by David L. Sills (nineteen volumes including a biographical supplement) is an enlarged successor of broader scope to a work begun in 1930 under the sponsorship of the American Association of Learned Societies. It has excellent bibliographic material. The earlier work, still valuable for its historical insights and still held by many libraries, is the *Encyclopedia of the Social Sciences* (fifteen volumes, 1930–35). Another book of similar vintage and still useful for the same reason is *A History of Modern Culture* by Preserved Smith (two volumes, 1930–34; reprinted, 1962).

There is an immense body of periodical literature in the social sciences, and most of it, coming from more than 250 journals, is indexed in Wilson's *Social Sciences Index*. This work originated in 1907 in a general periodical index that had particularly strong coverage of the field, the *International Index to Periodicals*, which Wilson set up as a supplement to its *Readers' Guide*. In 1955 the service was reorganized, dropping foreign listings and increasing coverage in the social sciences and humanities. A decade later the list was refined again and its name became the *Social Sciences and Humanities Index*. In 1974 that work was split apart to treat each field separately as the *Social Sciences Index* and the *Humanities Index*.

This field is also well covered, and at even greater depth, by a service described in Chapter 7, the *Bulletin* of the Public Affairs Information Service, or PAIS, a semimonthly guide to periodicals and much more in government and politics, public administration, economics, and sociology. It reaches down far enough to embrace mimeographed bulletins, government documents, congressional committee reports, and assorted pamphlets, and up far enough to overlap with some of the periodicals covered in other sources such as *Readers' Guide.*

Current bibliography in the social sciences is hard to come by because the branches of the several disciplines are so numerous and its practitioners so prolific. All the professional journals review dozens of new texts and other scholarly works with every issue. In any search for information here, before you start riffling through the card catalog at the library, remember to check the *International Encyclopedia of the Social Sciences,* where you will find decent coverage and suggested readings, excluding, of course, any works of more recent date than the encyclopedia itself.

Economics

The discipline of economics grew directly out of Adam Smith's famous treatise, published in 1776, *An Inquiry into the Nature and Causes of the Wealth of Nations,* a work still in print. It was advanced as a discipline by the writings of David Ricardo, John Stuart Mill, and Karl Marx, and by scores, then hundreds, of others.

There is a large one-volume *Encyclopedia of Economics* (1982), editor-in-chief Douglas Greenwald. The *American Dictionary of Economics* (1983) is edited by Douglas Auld, *et al.*

A lot of the literature in economics is extremely heavy going. The standard introductory-level text is still *Economics: An Introductory Analysis,* a much-revised work first published in 1948 by the Nobel laureate Paul A. Samuelson. An invaluable resource is Robert L. Heilbroner's aptly titled 1967 book, *The Worldly Philosophers: The Lives, Times, and Ideas of the Great Economic Thinkers.* The writings of a few economists, from Peter F. Drucker on the common-sense right to John Kenneth Galbraith on the literate left, are almost always readable as well as lucid.

The field can be searched through the following principal subdisciplines: economic history, economic philosophy, economic theory, and economic growth and planning. Macroeconomics, the study of the whole economy, and microeconomics, the study of individual personal or corporate economies, represent another way to divide the subject; both terms are frequent in book titles.

Political Science

This field, once "political œconomy," grew out of a joint work by the Utilitarian Socialist Henri de Saint-Simon and the Positivist philosopher Auguste Comte in 1822, *Plan of the Scientific Operations Necessary for the Reorganization of Society,* no less. They saw politics as a sort of physics of society, the mechanics by which the social order would be restructured. Later scholars brought more objective approaches to political science, but it was recognized early as one of the social sciences. In modern political science considerable effort has been expended to make the discipline itself wholly objective, studying politics dispassionately and free of advocating values.

Major writings of political philosophy, many of which predate the discipline itself, can be found in such collections as *Great Books of the Western World* and the *Harvard Classics.* Two leading political scientists, writing nearly a half century apart, have supplied excellent surveys of the discipline itself. These are Anna Haddow in *Political Science in American Colleges and Universities, 1636–1900* (1939, reprinted in 1969) and Ada W. Finifter (editor) in *Political Science: The State of the Discipline* (1984).

The principal divisions of political science are political theory, political economy (a title little used for decades that of recent years is again current); American politics, comparative politics, and international relations. Walter Z. Laqueur edited *A Dictionary of Politics* (1974). A related discipline is public administration.

Because of American citizens' direct responsibility for making explicit political choices as well as the related ubiquity of political news in the modern media, there is overlap between academic political science and the public's personal political interest. A good deal of writing from the political science community is instructive and sometimes entertaining to nonscholars.

One basic work is *The Book of America,* a political portrait of each of the fifty states by Neal R. Peirce and Jerry Hagstrom (1983). The perennial American concern about the cost of politics is addressed by the dean of that field of study in *Financing Politics* by Herbert E. Alexander, centerpiece in a long series of similar studies. The somewhat less urgent concern over smear and distortion tactics in election campaigns is examined, along with history and lore (through 1964), in the present author's *Dirty Politics.*

If your interests direct you toward election statistics—*i.e.,* who won, how big, when, and where—an invaluable resource was established in 1956 under the editorship of America's premier authority on the subject, Richard M. Scammon, in the biennial series *America Votes*. It covers elections for president, governor, and U.S. senator and representative, and it gives the totals for every candidate in every county in every state. Scammon and Ben J. Wattenberg collaborated on *The Real Majority: An Extraordinary Examination of the American Electorate*.

The rise and fall of America's political parties is the subject of a constant flood of texts; browse in what your library has. Popular works with scholarly authority by such political journalists as David Broder and pungent and readable writing by major scholars such as Aaron Wildavsky penetrate the hype and flimflam in this arena every few years.

The related field of public administration is much less volatile than political science. There is a good bibliography: *Public Administration in American Society: A Guide to Information Sources* by John E. Rouse.

Sociology

Sociology really started out as part of cultural anthropology as that discipline was emerging from the field of physical anthropology. European cultural (or social) anthropologists saw in the simpler societies of Africa samples of their own cultures in prehistoric times and climes. If political science grew out of the work of Comte (see the previous section), it was he who coined the very name sociology, which he saw as the queen of all the sciences. Important in the evolution of the modern discipline were such scholars as Ferdinand Tönnies, Max Weber, Emile Durkheim, and others, and by the early twentieth century, sociology was recognized if not as queen at least as a distinct discipline.

The subdisciplines of sociology include theory, social structures, behavior, and comparative sociology. You can get arguments over whether social psychology, social anthropology, and criminology are subdisciplines or subjects of their own; in any case, they are elements you should not leave out if you have an interest in dipping into the literature that takes a scholarly look at society and its ingredients, processes, and problems. An excellent place to start any such search in the *International Encyclopedia of the Social Sciences* (1984) edited by Michael Mann. The *Encyclopedia of Sociology* appeared in 1981.

Something of the diversity of sociological scholarship is reflected in the titles of a few of the old standard works in the field: *The Social System* by Talcott Parsons (1951), *The Power Elite* by C. Wright Mills (1956), *Male and Female* by Margaret Mead (1949), *The Authoritarian Personality* by Theodor W. Adorno (1950), *The Lonely Crowd* by David Riesman, Nathan Glazer, and Reuel Denney (1950), *Political Man* by Seymour Martin Lipset (1960, revised 1981), and *Handbook of Modern Sociology* edited by R.E.L. Faris (1964).

Social service agencies, which are partly a creation and partly a subject of study by sociologists, are considered, with ways to locate them, in Chapter 7.

Public Opinion and Survey Research

Public opinion, or, more precisely put, opinion sampling, probability sampling, or the techniques of survey research, is not one of the social sciences. It is addressed here because its contribution is an essential ingredient of most of the social sciences as well as of the practice of politics, modern marketing, and other aspects of contemporary civilization.

When these techniques are used scrupulously, the response of a properly selected sample will reflect with great accuracy the response of the whole body (or universe) of people that the sample represents (people, or laboratory animals, nine-year-old orphaned boys, widowed high-school graduates with annual incomes between fifteen thousand and twenty-five thousand dollars in your ZIP code zone). The perfection of these techniques has changed modern life and is changing it further.

A standard text that is easily readable as an introduction to the field is *Public Opinion* by Bernard C. Hennessy.

Psychology

There is ancient disagreement among scholars as to whether psychology is or is not one of the social sciences. If survey research techniques are an indispensable tool of the sociologist (as they are), the insights and basic understandings of psychology are its virtual foundation. However, there seems little dispute about psychology as one of the behavioral sciences, and since that term is increasingly used to embrace sociology, and for the additional pragmatic reason of convenience, you find psychology here.

Psychology grew out of the philosophy of ancient Greece, but it was not until the late nineteenth century that it became a scientific discipline with a rigorous approach to experimentation, observation, reporting, and analysis. The German scholar Wilhelm Wundt probably was the man who founded modern psychology, and William James introduced it to America in his *Principles of Psychology* (1890). The field developed rapidly, subdividing into various subdisciplines, and in about 1950 the influence of Norbert Wiener's *Cybernetics* combined with the emerging phenomenon of the computer to bring a whole new kind of potential, that of survey research, to psychology and psychological evaluation and testing.

As with the rest of the behavioral sciences, psychology is generally well treated in the popular encyclopedias, with articles briefer and more simply written in the smaller sets than in the larger. A four-volume *Encyclopedia of Psychology* appeared in 1984 under the editorship of Raymond J. Corsini, Bonnie D. Ozaki, Assistant Editor. A number of smaller and older works bear similar titles. There is a highly regarded specialized encyclopedia. It is the *International Encyclopedia of Psychiatry, Psychology, Psychoanalysis, and Neurology* (twelve volumes, 1977), whose editor in chief is a psychoanalyst and professor of psychiatry, Benjamin B. Wolman. It is readily accessible to the intelligent lay reader. Wolman also edited the single-volume *Handbook of Parapsychology* (1977). A useful popular treatment of the field is *What Psychology Knows that Everyone Should* by Daniel Goleman and Jonathan Freedman (1981).

The branches of psychology and historic terms you need to identify to look through the literature intelligently include these: developmental or child psychology, behaviorism or behavioral psychology, dynamic or clinical psychology, educational psychology, medical psychology, and psychoanalysis. Also physiological or nerve (or sensory) psychology, and experimental, abnormal, and differential psychology. The foregoing are aspects of human psychology. Don't overlook animal psychology, a field in which much popular writing has been done, *e.g.*, by Desmond Morris.

Finally, there are two fields of psychology that have been the scene of much fruitful and sometimes provocative research. One of these is sleep and dreams. The other, by the nature of both reporting tendencies and varying personal attitudes, arouses more general interest and is more controversial: sex and sexuality. The seminal works include the Kinsey reports that at least heralded and to some extent implemented the opening of the field to public discussion, *Sexual Behavior in the Human Male* (1948) and *Sexual Behavior in the Human Female* (1953), both by Alfred C. Kinsey *et al.* There are three influential books by William H. Masters and Virginia Johnson: *Human Sexual Response* (1966), *Human Sexual Inadequacy* (1970), and *Homosexuality in Perspective* (1979). Other important titles dealing with homosexuality include *Sexual Inversion: The Multiple Roots of Homosexuality* edited by Judd Marmor (1965) and *Sexual Preference: Its Development in Men and Women* by Alan P. Bell *et al.* The general encyclopedias are all over the lot in their coverage. Browse. There is a useful *Handbook of Human Sexuality* by Benjamin B. Wolman for the lay reader.

Psychotherapy of various kinds, including psychoanalysis and the medical specialty of psychiatry, are considered in Chapter 14.

CHAPTER 14

LOOKING UP MEDICINE AND HEALTH (PHYSICAL AND MENTAL)

Medicine so dominates modern life, and its length, quality, expense, propagation, and retirement therefrom, that no one can afford not to know how to cope with it, and even to be able to second-guess some of its presumed demands on our resources.

At the time of the American Revolution, the best-informed physician on earth would have treated you with a kind of quackery that would get him thrown out of the AMA today. Surgeons hadn't even learned to wash their hands before operating, and back two thousand years earlier, in the days of Asclepius and Hippocrates, the fellows whom today's doctors invoke in their physicians' oath, things weren't even that good.

The point here is not to diagnose or prescribe for yourself, a genuine fool's errand, but that any patient can be forgiven for wanting to know a little more about what the M.D. just said, or at least meant, and perhaps more about the drug you've just had prescribed or the food or fluid you've been ordered off. And all this may be truer than ever in an age when medical doctors almost never volunteer explanations and often seem tongue-tied when we ask them questions like "Why?" or "Why not?"

This chapter aims to simplify your finding out about disease and its diagnosis and treatment; the history and practice of medicine, surgery, and dentistry and their various specialties; psychiatry and psychoanalysis and other kinds of psychotherapy; and about clinics, hospitals, and nursing homes. It also will show you how to look for information sources about chiropractic and modes of treatment not traditional in the West, such as acupuncture, moxibustion, and the like. And it addresses reference materials on nutrition, exercise, hygiene, and the use (including side effects) and misuse of drugs, and on what is known about disease and its causes, symptoms, effects, and treatment. It does not offer medical advice.

The general encyclopedias perform well in general, but their varied updating schemes and schedules preclude any blanket endorsement. All are strongest in the medical mainstream. The mid-1980s printings of all the major encyclopedias are up-to-date on organ transplant technology up to the remarkable impact of the immunosupressant drug cyclosporin or cyclosporine, which was not available until the late 1970s, but after that their currency is various.

In this connection, even a recent copyright date (found on the back of the title page) is not conclusive; all encyclopedias that reprint annually copyright each volume every year to protect whatever changes have been made at various places in that volume. The only way you can find out how current a given article is is to look through it for discussion of some major development you know about. For instance, if an article dealing with heart (or coronary or open-heart) surgery does not mention artificial or mechanical heart implants in humans, you know that the article has not been substantively changed since 1982, the year of the first such operation. Further, if such an event is barely mentioned, with no discussion of associated major problems, such revision as there is probably was merely cosmetic, the minimum to protect the reputation of the encyclopedia.

DISEASE: DIAGNOSIS AND TREATMENT

In their consideration of human disease and its diagnosis and treatment, the general encyclopedias excel, except as noted. The family medical dictionaries and encyclopedias that you may have in your home and can certainly find in the library do a generally good and sometimes an outstanding job. Beyond them are numerous accurate works of greater depth that few general readers will understand. The leaders in this field are revised frequently. A good illustration is *The Merck Manual of Diagnosis and Therapy*, a concise reference work for physicians that is found in most fairly large libraries and is mostly comprehensible to intelligent lay readers. It is organized with a section for each organ of the body, and it covers diseases (physical and mental), diagnostic procedures, and treatment. There are numerous generally useful works such as the *Columbia University College of Physicians and Surgeons Complete Home Medical Guide* and the *Encyclopedia of Health and the Human Body*.

There are large bodies of literature on the various kinds of disease, *e.g.*, infectious, childhood, and occupational. Your primary tools in mining it are the encyclopedia index and the library catalog.

THE PRACTICE OF MEDICINE

For background on the history and present-day practice of medicine, see the encyclopedias first. Only if you want considerably greater detail are you likely to need fairly extensive medical histories such as *Sixty Centuries of Health and Physick* by S.G.B. Stubbs and E. W. Bligh, which takes the story up to the dawn of modern medicine. An old classic, *A Short History of Medicine* by Charles Singer and E. Ashworth Underwood, is updated regularly. There are plenty of others, but don't expect any history to have anything of substance on such new frontiers as AIDS, for instance. In any new field, yearbooks, magazines, and tomorrow morning's newspapers are the best bets.

If you want to look up the various medical specialties, the key terms include diagnostics, dermatology, orthopedics or physiatry, and ophthalmology (the last two also considered part of surgery). Also immunology (where the battle against AIDS is being waged), physical medicine or rheumatology, obstetrics and gynecology (ob-gyn, also considered a surgical as well as a medical specialty), endocrinology, neurology, urology, gastroenterology, pediatrics, psychiatry, sports medicine, geriatrics, etc.

Closely associated with the medical practice of geriatrics is the personal and family experience of coping with the aging process of selves and kinfolk in the fastest-growing segment of the American population. A whole new literature has emerged, books as well as periodicals, and every public library has added significant numbers of these publications. See the catalog under aging, maturity, geriatrics. You won't find it under golden years.

There are bibliographies in every field of medicine. The periodical literature of the profession includes some excellent magazines and journals aimed at the health profession but that carry many articles of interest to the nonprofessional, articles that are written in readable, often beautiful, English. The *New England Journal of Medicine* is an outstanding example. *JAMA,* the *Journal of the American Medical Association,* much of it easily comprehensible, is carried by most good public libraries.

For fundamental background on human anatomy and physiology, you still can start with an ancient classic, in its twenty-ninth or thirtieth edition, *Gray's Anatomy.* The encyclopedias are good here, too, covering both anatomy and physiology (the latter also touched on under the life sciences in Chapter 9).

Medical education and surgical training and certification are also bibliographic entries you may want to refer to, as is medical jurisprudence or medicine and the law. Malpractice and insurance against it, and medical ethics are other topics.

Surgery

The history and general practice of surgery are treated separately in some of the general encyclopedias and together with medicine in others. Subjects to look up to explore surgical specialties include general surgery, ob-gyn, orthopedic and traumatic, neuro, chest (thoracic and cardiosurgery), ear-nose-throat (otolaryngology), ophthalmology, and transplant surgery or organ transplants. Other medical and surgical specializations, such as anesthesiology, radiology or radiation therapy, chemotherapy, pathology, and hematology can be found in newer printings of the general encyclopedias and in the general medical literature.

Nursing

There are good general histories of nursing in most libraries, in addition to the encyclopedias. These individual books, including ones that are career-oriented, describe the profession of medical or surgical nursing (R.N.) and the associated fields of the nurse-anesthesiologist (an R.N.), practical nurse (licensed practical nurse or L.P.N.), nurses' aide, paramedic, and various medical technician occupations. A substantial bibliography is Bonnie Bullough's

Nursing: A Historical Bibliography (1981). See also *Nursing Handbook* (1984). Nursing magazines often are found in libraries.

Information on nursing homes, extended-care facilities, the Visiting Nurse Association, etc., can be found under those terms in the library catalog, as can general treatments of the problems of dealing with the terminally ill and the whole matter of death and dying. Look under terminal illness, death, dying, or thanatology (the study of death and dealing with its reality, a subdiscipline of psychology deeply involved with the medical subdiscipline of medical ethics). Periodicals indexes are extremely useful here, too.

Dentistry

New materials and techniques have profoundly changed the practice of dentistry, and these fascinating developments are well told in the encyclopedias. The literature about the dental profession is dwarfed by that of medicine and surgery at large, but there are numerous works on the history and practice of the dental profession, some new and quite excellent. Dental nursing and the specializations of dental diagnostics, endodontics, orthodontics, periodontics, prosthodontics (false teeth and bridges, etc.; dentists seem to prefer to call them dentures), and oral surgery, as well as the vocation of dental technician, are covered thoroughly in the literature, but for some of the specializations beyond an elementary level you may find yourself turning to interlibrary loan. There is a recent general history, *Dentistry: An Illustrated History* by Malvin E. Ring. Dental periodical literature is covered comprehensively in *Index to Dental Literature*, which is issued quarterly and cumulated.

ANCIENT WAYS AND OTHER WAYS: NONTRADITIONAL MEDICINE

When the general encyclopedias get outside the traditional turf of Western medicine, coverage in any depth is the exception rather than the rule. Since the first visits by Western M.D.s to the People's Republic of China, acupuncture has become something of a fashionable topic in American medical circles and has found its way into the encyclopedias. Moxibustion (burning selected herbs in certain locations on the body to affect illness at other points) is treated in more gingerly fashion. In the rest of the world, including continental Europe, these medical practices have long been both familiar and fairly widely practiced. In the West, herbal medicine of the conventional variety, as in various brews and plasters, is treated as folk medicine by the established medical profession.

Chiropractic, which in some ways resembles certain aspects of ancient Asian medical practice, gets short shrift from the major American encyclopedias with the exception of the *Americana,* whose treatment is short but excellent. *Academic American* is pretty good on the subject, *Collier's* and *World Book* are poor to fair, and the *Britannica's Micropaedia* article reads like something from the AMA's Committee on Quackery.

Homeopathy, a major element in the history of Western medicine, is dismissed similarly. For substantive information about nontraditional medicine, go to the library catalog in search of titles such as Chinese or Asian or Hindu medicine, ancient or even nontraditional medicine, folk medicine, and such specific titles as acupuncture, herbal medicine, moxibustion, homeopathy, chiropractic, sports or athletic injuries, and kinesiology.

MENTAL ILLNESS AND ITS TREATMENT

The boundaries between psychology in classroom and lab, and in various kinds of therapeutic applications, and in psychiatry (a medical specialty practiced only by M.D.s), and in psychoanalysis are quite fuzzy. From time to time sharp clashes occur among the various professional associations of psychologists, psychiatrists, and psychoanalysts. Indeed, since the early 1980s a massive reexamination has been going on into Sigmund Freud's role in psychoanalysis and in the diagnosis and treatment of mental illness, and battle lines have been drawn among analysts. If you want to catch up on this internal controversy, you might be best served by the *Readers' Guide to Periodical Literature* or *The New York Times Index,* either of which will steer you to new books, authorities, and arguments.

Note also that psychology in its academic robes is discussed in Chapter 13 under the social sciences. However, the academic robes often also drape a psychotherapist of one persuasion or another, and some duplication is inevitable. One example is the basic special encyclopedia in the whole field: the *International Encyclopedia of Psychiatry, Psychology, Psychoanalysis, and Neurology,* Benjamin B. Wolman, editor in chief (twelve volumes, 1977). A basic reference is the American Psychiatric Association's third *Diagnostic and Statistical Manual of Mental Disorders* (1980, revised 1986) generally known, at least in the profession, as *DSM-III.*

An outstanding treatment of a relatively newly identified affliction is *The 36-Hour Day: A Family Guide to Caring for Persons with Alzheimer's Disease, Related Demented Illnesses, and Memory Loss in Later Life* by Nancy L. Mace and Peter V. Rabins.

Sigmund Freud's voluminous body of writings—apart from newly published letters, etc.—is collected in *The Standard Edition of the Complete Psychological Works of Sigmund Freud* translated from the German, edited by James Strachey, and filling twenty-four volumes. At last those of us who are not Freud scholars can find our way around in this enormous *oeuvre* by virtue of a new computer-generated tool: *The Concordance to the Standard Edition of the Complete Psychological Works of Sigmund Freud* edited by Samuel A. Guttman *et al.* (six volumes). Where to find either may be a tough question if you don't have access to a large public library or that of a college, university, or medical school.

A sample of the new titles about the founder and the controversy is: *Decline and Fall of the Freudian Empire* by Hans J. Eysenck. Several others take a similar tack.

DRUGS: THEIR USE AND ABUSE

The drug-abuse epidemic in the United States and Europe has been generating a very large body of literature aimed at identifying, measuring, understanding, and addressing that increasingly costly health and societal problem. Telephone directories list the names and numbers of such groups as the venerable and effective Alcoholics Anonymous and similar organizations of recovering addicts. Any of these organizations—Alanon for families of alcoholics, Cocaine Anonymous for addicts seeking to recover, Families Anonymous for family members of addicts to various drugs, and many more—gladly supply phone numbers of other groups and various crisis intervention organizations.

For accurate background and information about the drugs

themselves, there are abundant resources, including the general encyclopedias. Information about the therapeutic use of drugs, and the nature, effects, side effects, and so on of drugs employed by the health professions is equally abundant.

The general topic of drugs, their actions, their applications, and their effects is dealt with in such reference works as the excellent *Encyclopedia of Alcoholism* and in individual works such as the highly informative *Drugs from A to Z: A Dictionary,* a popular treatment by Richard R. Lingeman. There is also a *Complete Guide to Non-Prescription Drugs. The Merck Index* lists drugs alphabetically by their pharmaceutical names, cross-referenced from their various propri-etary and generic names, with explicit information on formula, preparation, sources, uses, etc.

Physicians' Desk Reference, universally known as *PDR,* is published annually, listing virtually all prescription drugs, organized by manufacturer and fully indexed from generic and brand names, describing the action, indications, contraindications, usual dosage, and side effects, and supplying much other information. Check with your reference librarian if you want to go further. Your library may have the *National Formulary* or perhaps the World Health Organization's *Pharmacopoeia Internationalis,* with informa-tion on standard dosages, the strengths of various drugs, etc. The better public libraries have conscientiously upgraded their holdings in this area as the drug epidemic has grown.

These books are representative of many that deal with the general subject of drugs and alcohol and their abuse: at a popular level, *The Drug Scene* by Madeline H. Engel; at a professional level, *The Addictions: Multidisciplinary Perspectives and Treatments* edited by Harvey B. Milkman and Howard J. Shaffer; *Alcohol Consumption and Related Problems* by the National Institute on Alcohol and Alcoholism; and *Alcohol Problems and Alcoholism* by James E. Royce. A good bibliographical work is *A Bibliography of Drug Abuse, Including Alcohol and Tobacco* by Theodora Andrews, and selections from the periodical literature are abstracted in the bimonthly journal *Drug Abuse and Alcoholism Review.*

Examples of books offering guidance and support for family members of drug addicts and the terminally ill include the follow-ing: *Alcoholics Anonymous* by Alcoholics Anonymous World Services, *Hope for the Children* by Patte Wheat and Leonard L. Lieber, *In the Company of Others* by Jory Graham, and *Make Today Count* by Orville Kelly.

HELPING YOURSELF: HEALTH, EXERCISE, AND NUTRITION

"Doctor books" of home remedies, nursing care, and suggestions on child-rearing have been dog-eared standbys in most households for generations, and that genre is alive and well. Countless worried mothers have telephoned descriptions of symptoms to their pediatricians, eliciting responses something like this: "If Dr. Spock says it's measles, it must be measles." The good doctor is still in print (since 1946) with his *Baby and Child Care* by Benjamin Spock. Far from abandoning his flock, the first of which are now grandparents, he has continued to advise them with *Dr. Spock on Vietnam* (1968) and *A Teenagers Guide to Life and Love* (1970).

Others, of course, are at it, too, including the classic trio by Arnold Gesell and Frances L. Ilg, *Infant and Child in the Culture of Today* (since 1943), *The Child from Five to Ten* (since 1946), and *Youth: The Ages Ten to Sixteen* (since 1956). Frances Ilg and Louise B. Ames are the authors of another classic, *Child Behavior* (1955), addressing behavior problems up to age ten.

For home nursing and first aid the standard works are the Red Cross manuals *Home Nursing* and *First Aid*. There are many, many more. Check your library catalog under titles such as child care, child guidance, pediatrics, and nursing.

There is an excellent yearbook in the field of health, the *Medical and Health Annual* edited by Ellen Bernstein and published by *Encyclopaedia Britannica*. It carries long feature articles on selected topics of current interest, a careful review of the year's important developments in thirty to forty fields of medicine and health, and some two dozen "Health Information Updates" on topics, different each year, such as drugs for heart failure, health-related problems like snoring, and detecting children's eye problems. *World Book* published a similar annual for a time but, unfortunately, abandoned it.

Health on the road is a concern for many prudent travelers. A valuable form of health insurance for them is *Traveling Healthy: A Complete Guide to Medical Services in 23 Countries* by Sheilah M. Hillman and Robert S. Hillman (1983).

The cult of fitness in recent times has grown enough to feed a large industry that provides facilities, foodstuffs, clothing, equipment, inspiration, and exhortation in the form of audio- and videocassettes and reading material for the faithful or would-be faithful. In addition to the works of exercise advocates, who usually are true believers with real missionary zeal, fortunately there are many sources of objective information. Use your common sense, and consult your doctor or your reference librarian in case of need. The latter will not prescribe anything more costly than a good read.

Apart from health food fads and infatuation with augmenting your vitamin and mineral intake, the nutrition terrain may not be as perilous as that of fitness. A sensible look at nutrition is taken in *Food Hygiene and Food Hazards* by Andrew B. Christie and Mary C. Christie. The literature as a whole ranges from the scholarly to the popular. Good samples are the readable *Food and Nutrition in a Changing World* by Jean Mayer, who is president of Tufts University and a world authority on nutrition, and the sensible *Jane Brody's Nutrition Book* and *Jane Brody's The New York Times Guide to Personal Health*.

A lot of bunk is promulgated by some purveyors of health foods and vitamin and mineral supplements, who would love to see you load up on their products but who, not knowing your weight, proportion of fat, blood chemistry, and such, may talk you into consuming what could prove to be toxic quantities of these various chemicals.

The works cited earlier of nutrition scholars and reputable journalists frequently discuss the RDA or Recommended Daily Allowance of various vitamins and minerals. But if you want to see for yourself, the standard work is available in most libraries. It is *Recommended Dietary Allowances* by the Food and Nutrition Board of the U.S. National Research Council.

Gesundheit!

CHAPTER 15

LOOK UP YOUR RIGHTS: FIND OUT HOW TO PROTECT THEM

In the United States citizens enjoy somewhat different rights than in most other countries, even including the United Kingdom and the Commonwealth countries, where in criminal cases they have in common with us the presumption of innocence until proven guilty. The fact of a written constitution, which enumerates individual freedoms in the very process of constructing a government, sets the American situation apart.

It would be silly to suppose the rights granted by the U.S. Constitution are not violated from time to time, but when such violations do occur they are prosecuted and punished by the courts, as almost every session of the U.S. Supreme Court reminds us.

One significant distinction between the British and American systems affects citizens engaged in fighting the system and journalists reporting such actions more than the rest of us, but it still has a high symbolic importance to U.S. citizens. That is that the British Crown is free to—and does—make it a crime to betray "official secrets." Freedom of the press granted by the U.S. First Amendment prohibits any such law in the United States.

The presumption of innocence that Americans share with the Commonwealth nations is part of our common law heritage and places us opposite the rest of Western Europe and Latin America, where the heritage of the Code Napoléon gives the benefit of doubt to the state. In the United States the state must prove the accused guilty; in France, for example, the accused must prove himself innocent.

There is one attribute of the U.S. legal system that sets it apart from all others in the world: number of lawyers. We have more lawyers in absolute numbers, more per capita, more per square inch, more by any other test, than any other nation. As one result we sue each other more frequently than any other people, and to protect ourselves against that possibility we draw contracts and other legal agreements more assiduously and more frequently than anyone else. So it becomes quite important for us to know where to turn to find a lawyer when we need one, and to be able to get some understanding of our legal rights in any potentially disputed situation.

There are several basic reference works that are useful to the lay reader. One important category is dictionaries. Legal language employs Latin for its substantive terms and phrases, a souvenir of the time when all the educated people of Europe were fluent in that language. The nonlawyer needs translations for Latin derivations like *tort* (wrongful act, from *tortus*, "twisted") and phrases summarizing essential truths about the law such as *de minimis non curat lex* (the law does not concern itself with trifles). Legal dictionaries clarify these meanings at once, although perhaps not as well as a classic law-school limerick:

> There was a young lawyer named Rex
> With minuscule organs of sex,
> Who, charged with exposure,
> Replied with composure,
> *"De minimis non curat lex."*

Black's Law Dictionary is a huge volume of legal terms and phrases defined succinctly, in which you can find out something of the significance of an existing or contemplated legal action. It has been published with frequent revisions since 1882. A smaller work of more recent origin is the *Dictionary of Legal Terms* by Steven H. Gifis (1983), and newer still is *Words and Phrases* from the West Publishing Company. *Corpus Juris Secundum* is one of several legal encyclopedias.

Another resource is valuable for both lawyers and the laity: the *Martindale-Hubbell Law Directory*. This five-volume set names every law firm in the United States and Canada and lists all the lawyers associated with each. It is indexed by firm names, individual names, and state or province and city. There is a thumbnail professional and biographic sketch of each lawyer, and a wealth of accompanying information such as court calendars. It is revised annually. Another basic reference work indexes the periodical literature in the whole field of law in the United States and the rest of the English-speaking world. It is the *Index to Legal Periodicals,* produced by Wilson for the American Association of Law Libraries. It covers nearly four hundred journals, appears monthly, and is cumulated annually and triennially.

But *Martindale-Hubbell* and a world of legal journals won't do you much good if you are in trouble and can't afford a lawyer. If you are an indigent defendant in a criminal case you may be better off than in a civil matter. Most major U.S. jurisdictions now have public defenders to protect the legal and constitutional rights of criminal defendants.

This has been the case ever since the U.S. Supreme Court reversed the convictions of some defendants who had not been represented in their trials by legal counsel, and the state legislatures were quick to get the message. Where public defenders do not exist, the court appoints a private attorney to defend the accused, traditionally without compensation but with the jurisdiction defraying the lawyer's expenses. This picture is changing, however, and more and more court-appointed defense attorneys are paid a fair fee by the jurisdiction. Even without compensation, however, such appointments are not unalloyed charity, in that they give extremely valuable defense experience to usually young lawyers.

To ensure the indigent competent legal advice in civil law, the bar associations have established Legal Aid Associations that assign lawyers to clients who need representation but are unable to pay for it. Directories to these associations can be found in libraries and city telephone directories under such headings as Legal Aid Bureau, Legal Aid Society, and Legal Assistance Foundation.

LOOKING UP THE LAW ITSELF

Several publishing houses put out the actual text of federal and state law, and the place to look in your local library is under Legislation or U.S. Code or Public Law. For state law check under New York (or wherever): Laws. Prentice-Hall and Commerce Clearing House (CCH) serve libraries and law firms with looseleaf services reporting and providing relevant commentary on new legislation. Other publishers, notably West Publishing Company, supply bound volumes of individual state laws in annual revisions. These are organized by particular fields of legislation—*e.g.,* Municipal Law, Education Law, and Criminal Law.

All substantial libraries carry a selection of such lawbooks. In them you can find the actual text of a particular current law, accompanied by background information that is quite important to the proper interpretation of the law. This includes legislative history, which reveals the intent of Congress or the state legislature in drafting the law in the first place. It also includes summaries of court decisions in cases involving similar legislation, old language removed in amendments and new language inserted, and the like.

The U.S. Government Printing Office supplies the U.S. Code containing the entire body of federal legislation. The most recent complete printing was of sixteen volumes in 1970. Supplements are issued annually. Incidentally, if you have occasion to look up a particular law, perhaps from seeing it cited in a newspaper story, it won't hurt to be able to figure out what the citation means.

When judges and lawyers refer to a federal law in writing they use a formulation such as "18 USC 2131." This means it is Title 18 of the U.S. Code, section 2131. When you get to the books themselves, you will find title numbers on the spines, several titles to a volume. Each title covers a particular body of law; Title 18, for instance, covers the U.S. Criminal Code and Criminal [court] Procedure. Each title is divided into chapters. Particular individual laws are in sections, and the "2131" in our sample means section 2131. The section numbers begin at 1 in each title and run consecutively to the end of the title; they bear no relation to the chapters in which they occur.

THE LEGAL SYSTEM AND THE PRACTICE OF LAW

So much for the letter of the law; now for how it is interpreted and applied. The basic resource here is in the form of introductory-level law-school texts. But fear not, for many of them are quite lucid. An effort has been made here to present samples that fit that description.

If you decide to go the general encyclopedia route first—almost never a bad decision—here is what you can expect to find. The legal system will be broken down into its major components, very much like the organization of the rest of this section, and descriptive essays will tell you something of the origins and development of the various aspects of the law. As always, in the shorter encyclopedias the language will be relatively simple and the articles mostly concise. That goes for *Academic American, Compton's,* and *World Book. Americana* and *Collier's* will give you increased length and depth and a bit less simple wording. *Britannica* will go on at significantly greater length and in more complex language.

Books and encyclopedia articles on comparative law will shed light on the differences among the world's legal systems: the common law of the British tradition, the civil law of the Napoleonic tradition, and the socialist law of the Marxist tradition. Some of the individual works that are not too opaque are mentioned below. In *Major Legal Systems in the World Today,* Rene David and John E. C. Brierly describe the different systems and compare Marxist law with common and civil law; this book also has an excellent bibliography. Encyclopedias handle Islamic law or Shari'ah variously, and there are several useful introductory-level books with "Islamic Law" in their titles.

The classic American work on the law of our British heritage is *The Common Law* edited by Mark DeWolfe Howe. The legal heritage of continental Europe and Latin America—*i.e.,* civil law or code law (from the Code Napoléon) is described in *The Civil Law Tradition: An Introduction to the Legal Systems of Western Europe and Latin America* by J. H. Merryman.

For an understanding of the law in America, try *An Introduction to the Legal System of the United States* by E. A. Farnsworth. If you wish to go further and get into the several branches of U.S. law, simply pursue them in encyclopedias, legal or general, bibliographies, and the library catalog.

The fundamental division in the law is that between public and private law. Public law embraces the establishment and maintenance of the state; relations between states; public safety, *i.e.,* protection against crime; the public welfare; and the judicial system. It is concerned, then, with constitutional law, criminal law, international law, and the judicial process and the administration of justice. These are the key terms to look up if you wish to read further into the elements of public law.

Private law governs property rights; the institution of the family; torts or wrongful acts, economic transactions, including business associations; and civil procedure, or the process by which private law is administered. Therefore, private law has to do with business law; family law; the laws of inheritance, or inheritance and succession, as they are often styled; property law; the law of torts; and transportation law. These titles in private law are part of substantive law. The remaining aspect governs the way cases are handled under private law; it is procedural law. These topics will take you into encyclopedia articles or individual books concerned with private law.

ASPECTS OF PUBLIC LAW

To many Americans the concept of constitutional law as an abstraction seems a rather dry and bloodless topic. Yet this is precisely the arena in which slavery was abolished, and a hundred years later blacks effectively given the civil rights of whites. In every area of public and private law, constitutional law can intrude to protect the rights of citizens from improper prosecution or legal assault. It defines what presidents and legislators and judges may and may not do. It provides every human rights organization with its own right to exist and to practice its calling.

The text of the U.S. Constitution, including its amendments, a remarkably simple and explicit document, is in most encyclopedias and is even more accessible in the *World Almanac* and its counterparts, and in countless other works. The organizations that exist variously to protect or extend or employ constitutional rights can be located in many of the encyclopedias and dictionaries of associations discussed in Chapter 7. Encyclopedia treatment of constitutional rights usually is found in articles with titles like Constitutional Law. That goes for library catalogs, too.

Crime is a popular subject in America. Indeed, crime itself is popular, particularly among the young, and among drug addicts and the malevolent and the just plain greedy of any age. Especially among those who live or work in our cities, being mugged or raped or held up is a very real prospect, as is having their homes or cars robbed. Small wonder, then, at the attention paid to crime in the news and at the tremendous popularity of the whodunit press and of police and private detective shows on TV and in the movies.

If you want some serious background on how the legal system defines and addresses crime, hit the books. The subject is criminal law. Related titles you may encounter are crime, crime and punishment, criminal justice, and criminology. There are several specialized encyclopedias, including the *Encyclopedia of Crime and Justice,* Sanford H. Kadish, editor in chief (four volumes), and the eight-hundred-page *Encyclopedia of American Crime* by Carl Sifakis (1982). (For somewhat lighter fare, try these guides to crime fiction: *Encyclopedia of Modern Murder* by Colin Wilson and Donald Seaman and *Encyclopedia of Mystery and Detection,* Chris Steinbrunner and Otto Penzler, editors in chief.)

Once the criminal has been identified, arrested, indicted, tried, and convicted, the topic turns to punishment. Look it up under penology, corrections, penal system, or punishment. There is a 530-page *Dictionary of American Penology: An Introductory Guide* by Vergil L. Williams. The literature is very large, and a great deal of it is quite readable.

Questions of international law rarely concern the general public except when a cataclysmic event focuses the headlines and the news programs on it. Not infrequently, international disputes revolve around borders, some ancient, many between newly independent nations. Where once colonial powers could settle questions of boundaries or admiralty law with a single treaty, different conceptions of territorial waters and the claims of landlocked states to marine rights have permanently changed the nature of the game. Witness the UN flap over the Law of the Sea treaty in the early 1980s. Anyone curious about what the treaty actually provided could have read up on it in any good public library in *The Law of the Sea: Official Text of the United Nations Convention on the Law of the Sea.* Most similar important UN documents bearing on past or future controversies can be found there just as easily. Consult your reference librarian.

ASPECTS OF PRIVATE LAW

Several of the main branches of private law incorporate kinds of law that are not immediately self-evident to the nonlawyer, and if you are interested in a particular topic it may be helpful to know where it fits in the legal scheme of things. For example, it may be obvious that mortgages and trusts are part of property law, but it is less obvious that bankruptcy is covered there as well.

So are copyrights and patents, and a large share of law governing the entertainment world, where copyright is of the greatest importance. If you have a significant stake in these areas, obviously you should enlist the services of a lawyer competent in the particular field. But if background information beyond the encyclopedia level is what you want, you can find it in understandable language in a number of books, of which the following are examples: *The Manual for the Handling of Applications for Patents, Designs, and Trade-marks Throughout the World* (two looseleaf volumes, with annual revision pages supplied); *The Copyright Law: Howell's Copyright Law Revised and the 1976 Act* by Alan Latman; and *Lindey on Entertainment, Publishing and the Arts* by Alexander Lindey (three volumes).

A tort is literally defined as a wrongful act, *i.e.*, an injury, derived ultimately from the Latin *torquere,* to twist, thus to injure. We get our word "torque" from the same Latin verb in its meaning of "rotate." The law of torts is liability law: finding where the liability lies for personal injuries. Negligence cases, common in the lower courts, are brought under tort law. Defamation, libel, slander, and class-action consumer-protection lawsuits all are part of this branch of private law.

It is the law of torts that puts the teeth in the consumer-protection movement. Nearly every government on Earth has some kind of liability law allowing consumers to recover monetary damages from manufacturers of faulty products. (To be sure, it is easy for the developing world; most of the manufacturers are in the developed world.) The United Nations General Assembly unanimously adopted a bible for consumer movements throughout the world, *Guidelines on Consumer Protection.* It's in your library.

The consumer movement is a lot older than you might suppose. Excesses of greed by "malefactors of great wealth" enraged Theodore Roosevelt and paved the way for the first major legislative move, the creation in 1914 of the Federal Trade Commission to protect the American consumer (who did not then bear that title) against unfair trade practices. The movement, nourished from time to time by waves of populism and new laws, grew fairly steadily until the 1960s, when Ralph Nader bought a Corvair from Chevrolet and it turned out to be a dog. When he complained he got attention from corporate gumshoes instead of mechanics, and that's when American consumerism got off the ground.

Nader didn't actually start the movement; it had strong antecedents in European as well as American socialism, and the first American consumer organization was founded more than fifty years before he was born. But Nader did bring it the messianic sense of mission and the martyr's dedication and chaste poverty it needed. The movement advanced by several orders of magnitude, and by aggressive legal actions and extremely effective lobbying efforts it permanently changed the world of product liability. Encyclopedias give it extensive attention and public libraries have extensive collections on the development and range of consumerism, including but by no means limited to Nader and his writings. Consumer law became an important subheading under "tort."

The scope of laws covering economic transactions is a good deal broader than it may seem at first glance. The law of contracts is obvious enough. Commercial law includes the sale of goods, exchange of notes and checks, issuing titles, letters of credit, etc. But it does not include corporate finance, mergers, and business associations, or business law. Labor law also falls under the general heading of law governing economic transactions, as does transportation law.

Family law is changing in America as a result of changing social attitudes, cohabitation patterns, and advances in the biological sciences. You can find sound examinations of several aspects of family law in comprehensible language under such headings as adoption, abortion, cohabitation, divorce, and marriage. Here are some representative titles: *Marriage and Cohabitation in Contemporary Societies: Areas of Legal, Social, and Ethical Change* edited by John M. Eerelaar and Sanford N. Katz; and *State, Law, and the Family: Family Law in Transition in the United States and Western Europe* and *The New Family and the Property*, both by Mary Ann Glendon. Inheritance laws throughout the United States and many other countries are digested annually in the *Martindale-Hubbell Law Directory*, cited earlier in this chapter.

CHAPTER 16

LOOKING UP ENGINEERING AND TECHNOLOGY

Engineering and technology: If they do not entirely rule our lives, they feed and dress, protect and threaten, distract and inform us, and make us run on time. When the words crept into our language, one was already ominous, the other merely esoteric.

"Engineer" was originally that crafty kind of soldier that could contrive pitfalls, explosives, or giant, hollow wooden horses. An engine was any kind of mechanical device; indeed, in the seventeenth century a pipe was an engine for smoking tobacco. But before that came the engines, and the engineers, of war. Shakespeare needed an "enginer" of that sort in the curtain scene in Act III of *Hamlet* to bring us a famous phrase. "Let it work," cries Hamlet to his mum, "For 'tis the sport to have the enginer/Hoist with his own petar." By 1900 the term was taking on its present meaning, and "civil engineer" had to be coined to distinguish the civilian builders of bridges from the military engineers who blew them up.

In Shakespeare's day, a "technic" (from the Greek *technikos*, "art") was an art, such as "musick" or making churns, and a "technologie" was a discourse on or a study of one of the arts. Not until the time of the American Civil War did "technology" come to be reserved to the various mechanical arts.

However, here we are, and since we must deal with these concepts every day, it behooves us at least to be able to find out something about them from time to time. The quality of the general encyclopedias' treatment of these subjects is excellent, based on the date of the edition and printing you are using. The

Britannica's first edition (1771) is superb on such technologies as boring out trees to make water pipes, and even counterfeiting emeralds. In the present era—in computer technology, for instance, or in aerospace engineering—last year's book isn't as good as this year's.

Of course, the same problem confronts every kind of book, and here the publishers of yearbooks oriented toward science and the technologies serve their audiences quite well. For the general reader that means the yearbook of the *McGraw-Hill Encyclopedia of Science and Technology*, *World Book*'s *Science Year*, and the *Britannica*'s *Yearbook of Science and the Future*.

Since the focus of this chapter is engineering and technology, and not science *per se*, it is worth noting that only in recent times have science and technology come to share the same turf. In all eras until society began to digest the fruits of the Scientific Revolution of the seventeenth and eighteenth centuries, science was the province of the scholarly elite, who had the time and means and learning to dabble in idle experiments. Indeed, the word *"science"* itself meant "learning." Technology (in the sense in which we use the term) was used by the poor lout who had to figure out a way to make wagon wheels last longer or how to fix a pump.

The following review of the look-up, find-out resources open to us in the various kinds of modern engineering and technology is organized by the major disciplines of engineering and then of technology, with some effort to minimize duplication where in real life there is much of it.

ENGINEERING

It has been said that science has to do with knowing, while engineering is about doing; the engineer converts the understanding of the scientist into the solving of actual problems in the physical world. There is a fairly large literature on the history of engineering and its development as a profession, and although engineers have been notoriously ponderous in their prose, some of it is decently readable. One such is *Engineering in History* by R. S. Kirby *et al.* The social responsibility of the profession is the topic of *The Revolt of the Engineers* by Edwin T. Layton.

The periodical literature in the combined fields on engineering and technology is enormous. There are a couple of major indexes, and many branches of engineering have their own. Consult your library catalog for the branches; the principal general ones are *Engineering Index* and Wilson's annual *Applied Science and Technology Index*. The former was established in 1892 and covers engineering periodicals in a number of languages back as far as 1884. It was reorganized in 1928 and indexes subjects and authors in the same alphabetical string.

The *Applied Science and Technology Index* was begun in 1913 as the *Industrial Arts Index* and embraces most aspects of engineering and technology. The original was split apart in 1957, with the other half becoming the *Business Periodicals Index*. Until 1931 this index was cumulated biennially, and annually thereafter.

The oldest branch of engineering, military, and one of the newest, nuclear, came together in the dawn of the atomic age. Although it is not generally realized, and it is hardly sprightly reading, the original documentation of that momentous encounter is available to anybody in what is known as the Smyth Report, formally *Atomic Energy for Military Purposes: The Official Report on the Development of the Atomic Bomb Under the Auspices of the United States Government, 1940–1945*. It first appeared in 1945, and it was reprinted in 1978. A stellar recounting of that process by a skilled reporter is *The Making of the Atomic Bomb* by Richard Rhodes (1987).

All the technological weapons of the military are the subject of historical review and critical evaluation from a variety of ethical and political perspectives. When you are looking for one of them, a reference book index or a library catalog will be helpful. In general, look under the name of a genus or kind of weapon rather than an individual species of weapon. For instance, it you are looking for a hand grenade, in most cases you will be better off not looking it up under that name. Instead, turn to grenade, where the original weapon, a lightweight, throwable bomb of the late sixteenth century that was shaped like a "grenade" or pomegranate, may be covered along with its modern descendants, the hand grenade and the rifle grenade and the grenade launcher.

Similarly, if your objective is information about gas warfare, or poison gas, or gas masks, you should find them all at chemical warfare, and you might not find one of them under its individual name, except here and there as a cross-reference. The foregoing caution applies to works of general reference but not to highly specific books, such as one about infantry weapons or chemical warfare. There you would indeed search the index for the particular term—*e.g.*, hand grenade or fragmentation grenade or maybe even M-1 fragmentation grenade.

The literature on military engineering and its fruits covers the new and the old. The range is suggested by a pair of titles your own public library may well hold: *War in Space* by Christopher Lee (1986), and *The Encyclopedia of the World's Warships: A Technical Directory of Major Fighting Ships from 1900 to the Present Day* by Hugh Lyon (1978). Various encyclopedic works by Jane's are in fact annual encyclopedias, though only the very largest libraries will replace them each year. Key titles are *Jane's All the World's Aircraft* and *Jane's Fighting Ships*. There are many more Jane's series, including ones on infantry weapons, fighting vehicles, weapons systems, and such largely nonmartial topics as the world's railways.

If you are inquiring into any field of engineering, it will help to know the names of its subdisciplines and the various specializations under each of those. The military persuasion has already been described. Civil engineering embraces such categories as building or construction engineering, hydraulic and maritime engineering, mining engineering, and transportation engineering. The latter includes the engineering of highways, bridges, tunnels, railways, airports, etc. Power engineering—mining, oil exploration, and the construction of plants to house power-generating equipment—and public health engineering, embracing the handling of toxic wastes and the protection of water supplies, also are aspects of civil engineering, although both power engineering and its subordinate discipline of petroleum engineering are sometimes treated as independent branches of engineering.

Mechanical engineering involves the design of engines, machines, production equipment for manufacturing and power-generating machinery, and pumps and other equipment for mine ventilation, flood control, etc. In recent times it has come to cover bioengineering, such as the design of prosthetic devices to replace human body parts lost to disease or accident. Bioengineering is often considered a separate branch.

Chemical engineering is concentrated in the processing industries, such as plastics and synthetic fibers, paper, certain aspects of food production and preservation, dyeing, the production of pharmaceuticals and agricultural fertilizers and fungicides, and special products such as rocket fuels.

Electrical and electronics engineering has been transformed by the electronics revolution from a field once concerned principally with equipment to generate and transmit electrical energy. It still does that, but it has added the whole technical end of the communications industry to its portfolio in the design of radio, television, telephone, and other communications equipment. It also designs electronic control and monitoring systems, and it addresses the engineering aspects of the computer industry.

Aerospace engineering encompasses the design and building of spacecraft with what used to be called just aeronautical engineering. The old elements, still necessary to the aviation industry and the military for flight within Earth's atmosphere, are the design of airframes, their power plants, and interdisciplinary collaboration with electronics engineers and assorted scientists in the design of "avionics" or aviation electronics systems for navigation, engine and flight control, and communications. The space end of the business lies in the realm of space vehicles: launch vehicles, satellites for any variety of missions, orbiters, engines, power-supply and life-support systems, space stations, *et al.*

Nuclear engineering involves the research and design of systems for generating power by controlled nuclear reaction, for both general public use and the propulsion of warships and other ships. It also deals with systems to produce (often as a by-product of other activities) radioisotopes for medical purposes. And it involves the design of nuclear weaponry.

Industrial engineering embraces such areas as systems engineering, operations research, and human factors engineering. It grew out of the practices of time and motion study by what were once called "efficiency experts" seeking to reduce economic waste in industrial manpower.

There are several works of encyclopedic scope in the field of engineering and its branches. One is the 787-page *Encyclopedia of Engineering Materials and Process,* H. R. Clauser, editor in chief. *Chemical Engineering Practice* edited by H. W. Cremer *et al.* (twelve volumes) is an encyclopedia of long articles by authorities in the field. Also see the *Encyclopedia of Electronics,* Stan Gibilisco, editor in chief; and the *Funk & Wagnalls Dictionary of Electronics.* Power and energy resources are treated in the *McGraw-Hill Encyclopedia of Energy,* Daniel N. Lapedes, editor in chief.

TECHNOLOGY

Any dividing line between the roles of engineer and technologist is artificial, tenuous, and inconsistent. It may be easiest to say it negatively: The work of the engineer cannot be put into effect without technology.

There is a virtually encyclopedic account of the development of Western technology from its primitive beginnings: *The History of Technology* by Charles Singer *et al.* (seven volumes). Industrial technology *per se* is dealt with in the *Encyclopedic Dictionary of Industrial Technology: Materials, Processes, and Equipment* edited by David F. Tver and Roger W. Bolz. Inventions help keep technology alive, and there are two identically titled books devoted to them, *Encyclopedia of Inventions* edited by Donald Clarke (1977) and *Encyclopedia of Inventions* edited by Peter Presence (1976).

What might be called a work of comparative technological history is Neil Longley York's *Mechanical Metamorphosis: Technological Change in Revolutionry America* (compared with Europe in the same era; 1985). An excellent overall resource is *Bibliography of the History of Technology* by Eugene S. Ferguson (1968).

The biological sciences have been affected to their core by modern technological advances, without which many of the most consequential discoveries and developments of modern times could not have occurred. This is touched on in Chapter 9 and is thoughtfully addressed in a number of new books, some descriptive but others of which address the social implications of technological progress, a concern voiced by Lewis Mumford as early as 1934 in *Technics and Civilization*. Essays on contemporary problem areas appear in *Perilous Progress: Managing the Hazards of Technology* edited by Robert W. Kates, Christopher Hohenemser, and Jeanne X. Kasperson.

The lay reader can follow a fairly simple course to find out something about a technical field in nontechnical language. Nearly every area of technology has at least one dictionary of terms used in it, as well as a bibliography of books on the subject. Many such fields have special encyclopedias, and while a lot of their content is pretty arcane stuff aimed at answering the technologist's questions, enough of it is comprehensible to nonexperts to make a search worthwhile as long as it's in your library. But don't take a cab across town to consult one of these sets without a recommendation from someone you trust. Examples of these works are the *Encyclopedia of Chemical Technology* (three volumes) and the *Encyclopedia of Microscopy and Microtechnique* edited by Peter Gray. There also are bibliographies of the very large periodical literature of technology. One of the best is a new one from the United Kingdom, *Current Technology Index.*

Inevitably, a lot of the periodicals you will encounter through a technological bibliography are highly technical, often loaded down with mathematical expressions and formulas, and frequently written in the worst jargon you can imagine. There are useful clues in the better bibliographies, but not in all of them by any means. In the descriptive material about each book cited look for words and phrases such as these: "readable," "comprehensible," "lucid," "accessible to the nonspecialist," "a layman's introduction to . . .," "introductory," "elementary," "without using mathematical formulas," "in nonmathematical language," and the like.

If you are stumped in a search for a comprehensible book, turn at once to one of the general technological dictionaries or encyclopedias. Among the best and most widely available are the following. Dictionaries: the *Dictionary of Science and Technology* (the spine reads *Chambers Dictionary of Science and Technology*) edited by T. C. Collocott; the *McGraw-Hill Dictionary of Scientific and Technical Terms*, Daniel N. Lapedes, editor in chief; and the *Dictionary of Technical Terms* by Frederic Swing Crispin. The outstanding *McGraw-Hill Encyclopedia of Science and Technology* appeared in a new edition in 1987. Among other modern encyclopedic works of general interest are the *Encyclopedia of Energy* and the *McGraw-Hill Encyclopedia of Space*.

Masstech: How-Things-Work Books

Many otherwise rational people grow livid on contemplating the huge and steadily growing literary genre of the book telling the uninitiated how things work. The head librarian of a publishing house that produces books on medicine and science (some of which explain how these things work) cries out against this genre: "I really am bored with them! I prefer the *Yellow Pages* under 'Repair.' "

Others find them easy to use and to understand. Dozens of titles in Isaac Asimov's enormous literary output, which ranges from everything scientific to ribald verse to holy scripture to literary criticism, are how-things-work books with their titles recast as a question: *How Did We Find Out About . . .?* If you want to find out how anything works, you can do it in one of three steps.

First and easiest, turn to a general encyclopedia. Depending on the depth of your curiosity, you may or may not be satisfied. Indeed, you may find nothing at all. Second, try whatever encyclopedic approach to answering the how-it-works question your library has. An example is the *Encyclopedia of How It Works: From*

Abacus to Zoom Lens edited by Donald Clarke. And if this approach leaves you still wanting more, go to the single-topic books in the how-it-works roster of books. A good one for the nonmechanic is *Engines and How They Work* by Geoffrey Boumphrey.

Don't forget interlibrary loan, by the way.

In the unlikely event that nothing works, move on to textbooks or consider a course at your local community college.

Computers and Computer Technology

At the bottom of many, perhaps most, of the advances in all the technologies that have been realized in the second half of the twentieth century are the computer and its applications. Indeed, when we speak of "the new technology" or "new technologies" we speak of technologies either spawned or at least enabled by the underlying technology of the computer. Whatever we call it—the computer, data processing, information systems, information processing, or data storage and retrieval—it has changed the way we live and work. It has redefined the way records are kept, preserved, and retrieved, and thus the way we look things up.

While it is true of any active field that a bibliography is out-of-date as soon as it is printed, this disclaimer is especially pertinent to the computer literature. As recently as 1970 the innards of a computer were a thicket of tens of thousands of little ceramic doughnuts strung on crisscrossed wires, and it took a roomful of them to have the computing power of a half handful of microchips in a modern microcomputer.

When you are looking up something in this field, unless it's a topic like "computer development in the 1940s," check the copyright date of the book before you take seriously anything it has to say about "modern" or "recent" developments. Anything older than a couple of years has to be regarded with caution. It is not necessarily mistaken or wholly invalid, but it is unlikely to be really up-to-date.

The foregoing caveat about books also is true of encyclopedias. You are safe enough turning to one of the general encyclopedias for general information—*e.g.*, background on the history and development of the whole data processing phenomenon, but you must remember that the encyclopedia's knowledge of the field ended, at the very latest, about a year before the copyright date on the back of its title page.

The field of computers and data processing abounds in dictionaries, and single-volume encyclopedias. Because they are physically smaller than general encyclopedia sets and because their interest is completely confined to their specialized field, they find it tremendously easier to be up-to-date until a very short time before publication. A 1986 encyclopedia of personal computers is likely to be as current as a 1988 or 1989 printing (copyright date) of a general encyclopedia. Even so, never look for the latest information about computers even in a specialized computer encyclopedia if it's more than two or three years old.

As in the case of the general encyclopedias, age does not invalidate coverage of events and developments in earlier years.

Sample titles of computer encyclopedias follow. Some are easy and some fairly advanced. See what your library has, and take a look, including a look at the copyright date. They are: *Encyclopedia of Computer Science and Engineering* edited by Anthony Ralston, *Encyclopedia of Information Systems and Services* edited by Anthony T. Kruzas and John Schmittroth, Jr., *The Encyclopedia of Microcomputer Technology* by Linda Gail Christie, and *Encyclopedia of Microcomputer Terminology: A Sourcebook for Business and Professional People* by Linda Gail Christie and John Christie.

Properly named computer dictionaries pose a somewhat different problem, but a lot of "dictionaries" actually are encyclopedic dictionaries in their fields. Caution about dates is important. Check these: *Computer Dictionary and Handbook* by Charles J. Sippl, *Dictionary of Information Technology* by Dennis Longley and Michael Shain, *Dictionary of Computers, Data Processing, and Telecommunications* by Jerry M. Rosenberg, *Dictionary of Computing* by Frank J. Galland, *Funk & Wagnalls Dictionary of Data Processing Terms* by Harold A. Rodgers, and *Dictionary of Microcomputing* by Philip E. Burton (1976).

Less vulnerable to going out-of-date, if not completely home free, is such a work as the *International Directory of Acronyms in Library, Information, and Computer Sciences* by Pauline M. Vaillancourt.

Material relevant to the focus of this chapter also may be found in Chapters 3 (annuals, etc.), 4 (computer access), 5 (people), 7 (organizations), 12 (physical sciences and mathematics), 13 (social sciences), 17 (industry), 18 (communication), and 21 (bibliography). All else failing, try prayer (Chapter 11).

CHAPTER 17

LOOKING UP COMMERCE AND INDUSTRY

Somewhat as Caesar did with all Gaul, economists divide the world of industrial enterprise into three parts. In this case, too, the borders are hardly impermeable, but they will do for our purposes. Primary industry embraces the supply of food and raw materials: farming, fishing, forestry, and the extractive industries of mining, oil, etc. The secondary sector is manufacturing, major and minor, heavy and light, from cottage industry to heavy industrial complex. Tertiary industry is the service sector, which is occupying more and more of the world's time, money, and energy as both of the other sectors, with a few conspicuous exceptions, have fallen on hard times. This third element includes management, labor, and perhaps even more basic, finance. It's a good place to start.

BUSINESS AND FINANCE

The world of banking, finance, and investment, and the related fields of insurance and real estate is handled pretty well by the general encyclopedias once you accustom yourself to the vagaries of their terminology and therefore of their indexing. Many public libraries treat the subject extremely well, especially in major metropolitan centers and in reasonably affluent suburban communities where a significant number of residents actively pursue investment interests. Such libraries may set apart a business and finance room well stocked with appropriate reference books and such essential periodicals as *The Wall Street Journal, Fortune, Barron's, Business Week,* and the like.

Business and financial information is available in great detail about corporations whose stock is publicly held and traded. Supplying these kinds of data for the investment community is itself a very big business. The numerous resources it has created enable a careful prospective investor—or the researcher for any other reason—to assemble a remarkably complete picture of a company's history, ownership, management, manufacturing efficiencies and shortcomings, labor relations, product line, markets, capitalization, debt, sales strengths and weaknesses, the impact on its export sales (if any) of the value of the dollar against foreign currencies, and a good deal more.

Some of the key publications for this kind of research are Standard & Poor's *Register of Corporations, Directors and Executives, U.S. and Canada,* the *Million Dollar Directory* of Dunn & Bradstreet, the *Directory of Corporate Affiliations: "Who Owns Whom,"* Standard & Poor's *Corporation Records Service,* and the series of looseleaf *Moody's Manuals* that cover a range of fields including banking and finance, industrial corporations, municipal and government bonds, and public utilities.

There are many additional services that assemble investment-oriented data. Professional investors will subscribe to most of them; regular customers of brokerage houses will have access to them or the information they contain through their brokers. But for the cautious, infrequent investor, the library is a good place to start, whether to work out a buy or sell decision or merely to taste the complexity of the process and to be able to frame the right questions for a broker.

But the business information resources of a good library go well beyond the interests of most potential investors. The directories put out by trade and industrial associations—many of these directories published annually and thus kept up-to-date—describe the individual companies in their industries. Closely allied to these are the directories produced by the dominant trade magazine in a given field. An example is the international yearbook of the magazine *Editor and Publisher,* the bible of the newspaper business. It lists ownership, management, circulation, and much more for every daily newspaper in the United States and Canada.

How to find the right source to satisfy your particular quest has spawned a small genre of how-to literature, typified by *Where to Find Business Information* and *The Handbook of Business Information*

Sources. Also, you can quickly locate the particular industry directory you need via Gale's *Encyclopedia of Associations* or the *Guide to American Directories.* A European equivalent is the *Directory of European Industrial and Trade Associations.*

In the fourteen hundred or so U.S. cities where they are published (excluding the very largest, which are simply too big to handle), the city directories of the R. L. Polk Company provide immense detail on local businesses. They also identify the occupants of every dwelling, street by street, and supply a good deal of personal information on every inhabitant over age eighteen. These directories usually are found in the public libraries of large cities and are gold mines of information.

Another way to look up companies is by the products they make. In this case the first place to turn is the *Thomas Register of American Manufacturers,* a multivolume reference work that is revised annually. It is organized so you can find the company through any of several approaches: from the kind of product, *e.g.,* surgical instruments; from a particular brand name, *e.g.,* Lucky Strike cigarettes; from an alphabetical list of manufacturers; or from a geographical list ordered by state and city. *Thomas* supplies basic data on each corporation, such as home office address, subsidiaries and branches, and an approximation of its capital.

In addition to the basic reference works cited earlier, there are several encyclopedias and dictionaries available to anyone looking for information about banking and finance. Among them are the *Encyclopedia of Banking and Finance* by Glenn C. Munn, revised by F. L. Garcia; the *Dictionary of Business, Finance, and Investment* by Norman D. Moore; the *Dictionary of Finance Terms* by John Downes and Jordan Elliot Goodman; and the *Dictionary of Stock Market Terms* by Peter Wyckoff.

Wilson's *Business Periodicals Index* is an essential ingredient of a business collection, and adequate libraries will have it. However, it may well be in the general reference section instead of with the business books. Business collections usually include manuals on writing business letters. They are a mixed bag, some merely perpetuating business English. Approach them with caution. Incidentally, if what you need is business French, for example, there is a three-volume *Encyclopedia of Business Letters in Four Languages* (English, French, Spanish, and German).

There also are special encyclopedias and dictionaries covering other elements of the service industry. Since the concept of professional management was invented by Peter Drucker in the

1940s, encyclopedias and dictionaries on management have proliferated along with the rest of management literature. Among them
are, *e.g.*, the *Dictionary of Business and Management* by Jerry Martin
Rosenberg; the *Encyclopedia of Business Information Sources*, Paul
Wasserman, managing editor; the *Encyclopedia of Management* edited by Carl Heyel; and the *Handbook for Professional Managers*
(formerly *Encyclopedia of Professional Management*) edited by Lester
Robert Bittel and Jackson Eugene Ramsey.

Two similarly titled dictionaries address accounting: *A Dictionary
for Accountants* by Eric L. Kohler and *A Dictionary of Accounting* by
Ralph Estes. In real estate, there is a *Dictionary of Real Estate Terms*
by Jack P. Friedman, Jack C. Harris, and J. Bruce Lindeman. For
advertising, see the outstanding *Dictionary of Advertising Terms*
edited by Laurence Urdang. A fine annotated bibliography is
Information Sources in Advertising History by Richard W. Pollay.

MANUFACTURING INDUSTRIES

The rise of mass production really ushered in the modern world,
whose very successes led, paradoxically enough, to the postindus-
trial state. The steel and auto industries played seminal roles in the
big-league industrialization of America in the early twentieth
century and in making Americans the first wholly mobile people.
Now that the technical edge that made U.S. industry dominant has
dulled, the lead in many industries has shifted overseas, not only in
heavy industry but also in many other fields, not least in consumer
electronics products.

This basic problem and the prospects for solving it are the
subject of a growing body of writing by economists, technologists,
futurists, and an occasional industrialist. If this topic interests you,
consult your reference librarian. Your public library surely has a
number of recent books on this extremely important subject. The
general encyclopedias won't help you much here, but their recent
yearbooks may shed most useful insight, variously in feature
articles and in annual reviews of the state of various industries.

Manufacturing industries, it has been noted earlier, can be
subdivided in several ways. One not mentioned so far is by kind of
product or product family. The auto industry is an obvious
illustration. Others include aerospace, ceramics, electronics, machinery, plastics, telecommunications, and textiles. Looked at this

way, industry subdivides pretty much along the lines of engineering and technology, as discussed in Chapter 16.

Each of these fields has one or a few prominent trade journals that cover it closely. Some of them feature continuing bibliographic material on the industry, and a number of them publish yearbooks or annual review issues. In most substantial industries there are full-scale bibliographies in book form, and the larger public libraries will carry many of these.

In addition, specialized encyclopedias and dictionaries exist in many fields. Sometimes these are intended for production executives or engineers or technicians and are not very suitable to the innocent looker-up. Others are done expressly for the lay reader, and it won't take you long to find out which is which.

The aerospace industry is well represented by the following special reference books: There is a fourteen-volume encyclopedia, *The Illustrated Encyclopedia of Aviation and Space.* Also see the *Encyclopedia of Aircraft* edited by Michael J. H. Taylor & John W. R. Taylor. Most substantial libraries carry the big, comprehensive, and authoritative *Jane's All the World's Aircraft.* This large and famous set of books carries photographs, schematic drawings, and full design, engineering, and performance data on every current airplane in the world, civil and military. It is revised annually, but only libraries where being absolutely up-to-date is essential buy it each year. For most of us, being a few years behind the cutting edge in supersonic fighter design won't hurt.

America's unending romance with the automobile is alive and well whatever the perils facing the U.S. auto industry. Special encyclopedias and other works treat it with loving care. These sources include several works edited by G. N. Georgano, including the *Encyclopedia of American Automobiles,* the definitive *Complete Encyclopedia of Motor Cars, 1885 to the Present,* and *The Complete Encyclopedia of Commercial Vehicles.*

To a considerable extent, the story of America is the story of transportation—across the sea, across the vast continent—and it is not surprising that seafaring and the railroad also receive generous attention in libraries. For that matter, the general encyclopedias are quite good across the board on transportation, and special ones abound. For instance, look at *The Rand McNally Encyclopedia of Transportation,* and, from a slightly different standpoint, the *Encyclopedia of World Travel* edited by Nelson Doubleday and C. Earl Cooley, revised by Marjorie Zelko and Diana Powell Ward.

Sea travel is the focus of *The Encyclopedia of Ships and Seafaring* edited by Peter Kemp. A pair of the perennially up-to-date annuals update the modern merchant marine. The basic one is *Jane's Merchant Ships*, and its companion is *Jane's Freight Containers;* the development of freight containers revolutionized both ocean shipping and rail and highway freight. *Jane's Fighting Ships* covers the world's warships.

Rail transport gets its due also, in *The Encyclopedia of North American Railroading: 150 Years of Railroading in the United States and Canada* by Freeman H. Hubbard. The inevitable Jane's entry is here, too: *Jane's World Railways.*

The textile industry was the first offspring, or one of the first, of the Industrial Revolution, and it profoundly affected the early growth of the U.S. economy. For the products, producers, and patois of the industry today there are several resources: the *Encyclopedia of Textiles* by the editors of *American Fabrics and Fashions* magazine, *The Modern Textile and Apparel Dictionary* edited by George E. Linton, and, from a major trade publisher of the industry, *Fairchild's Dictionary of Textiles* edited by Isabel B. Wingate.

Finally, a miscellany of other manufacturing industries: *A Short Dictionary of Furniture* by J. E. Gloag (revised and enlarged edition), the *Encyclopedia of Hardware* by Tom Philbin, and the *Dictionary of Architecture and Construction* edited by Cyril M. Harris. For all else, see the catalog and the encyclopedias.

FOOD SUPPLY AND RAW MATERIALS

Much of primary industry relies on a combination of "low tech" and "high tech." Certainly that's true of farming in the modern world, some of which is literally at a Stone Age technological level; some wholly computerized and automated; and some, especially on the family farm in Europe and America, mixed. The literature on agriculture is very large. The topic is handled well by the general encyclopedias (titled variously as farming, agriculture, or agricultural technology). It also is the subject of a specialized encyclopedia, the *McGraw-Hill Encyclopedia of Food, Agriculture & Nutrition,* Daniel N. Lapedes, editor in chief.

Agricultural periodicals are indexed in Wilson's *Biological and Agricultural Index,* whose agricultural component goes back to 1916 (as *Agricultural Index* from 1916 to 1964, when the biological element was added). An excellent worldwide bibliography, *Bibliography of*

Agriculture, is produced by the U.S. Department of Agriculture. The same department also publishes an outstanding annual, the *Yearbook of Agriculture.* Each issue bears a different title on an agricultural topic of great moment, and the entire book is focused on that subject, *e.g., Water* or *Science in Farming.* These books are so substantial that they are well worth dipping into even many years after they were issued. Look them up under the department's name and the general title, *Yearbook of Agriculture.*

Farming or otherwise harvesting the "fruit of the sea" is another primary industry, and long thought of as a more romantic one than tilling the soil. By the way, if you look up fish farming in an encyclopedia, be prepared for a cross-reference to aquaculture. Some play it straight and some on the bounce. But both fishing and fish farming are well handled in the encyclopedias. *The Encyclopedia of Marine Resources* edited by F. E. Firth covers the waterfront in describing the sea's resources and their uses. A three-volume encyclopedia of commercial fishing tackle and methods is *Modern Fishing Gear of the World* by H. Kristjonsson.

Extraction and processing industries include some of the major foundations of American (or world) industry, including iron, oil, and chemical processing. A basic work on the first-named is the *Encyclopaedia of the Iron and Steel Industry* by A. K. Osborne. *The Science of Petroleum* is a six-volume encyclopedia edited by A. E. Dunstan *et al.* It is edited for the industry and not for the lay reader. If your library has it, try it on for size if you are curious about that industry, from petroleum geology and exploration to refining. There also is the *Petroleum Production Handbook* edited by T. C. Frick (two volumes).

The chemical industry is treated in several technical works not intended for but in part accessible to the lay reader. A major multivolume work is the *Kirk-Othmer Encyclopedia of Chemical Technology.* The Kirk-Othmer set is a source of information in elaborate detail about the applications of chemical technology in the whole field of nonferrous metals, from aluminum to phosphorus and beyond. Also see *The Encyclopedia of the Chemical Elements* edited by C. A. Hampel and *The Encyclopedia of Electrochemistry.*

Aspects of many of the industries cited in this chapter also are touched on in Chapter 16, on engineering and technology.

_____CHAPTER 18_____
LOOKING UP
COMMUNICATION

The written and spoken use of language is the concern of this chapter, particularly public communication via the published printed word and picture, and over the public media of radio and television. Only cynics and fools any longer deny that other higher animals communicate, but not even in fairy tales do they send each other yesterday's newspaper or watch in New York the evening news from Tokyo or London.

No, only we, of the family *Hominidae,* can transmit, store, retrieve, and even rework our thoughts by scratching marks on paper or leaving electromagnetic tracks on other kinds of stuff.

It's only fairly recently that some of us hominids have ventured beyond old-fashioned linguistics into a deeper quest for the underlying meanings of the signs, the visual or aural symbols that we leave on paper and film or tape when we communicate. This is the substance of semantics and semiotics, and if this kind of thing intrigues you, the encyclopedias will treat you well, and so, with any luck, will the catalog at your favorite library.

A lot of what you find will be pretty far out. Once in a blue moon you will come across something astonishingly lucid, perhaps one of S. I. Hayakawa's works—say, his *Language in Action* (1941), still a sort of primer in semantics. Mostly, however, you can expect titles like *Act and Quality: A Theory of Literary Meaning and Humanistic Understanding* by Charles Altieri (1981) or *The Architecture of Experience: A Discussion of the Role of Language and Literature in the Construction of the World* by Graham D. Martin (1981). If that's your bag, enjoy. If not, but you still want to find out what they're talking about, pursue it until you find something more easily comprehensible, perhaps Stephen Ullmann's *Semantics: An Introduction to the Science of Meaning* (1962).

JOURNALISM

Modern journalists are much concerned with journalistic ethics and the integrity of their calling, which today is virtually a profession for which preparation in graduate schools of journalism is increasingly common. A far cry that from the motley origins of their trade in scandal sheets, political broadsides, commercial newsletters, and court bulletins. That press whose freedom was protected by the First Amendment was polemical and ardently political—rabidly partisan long before the evolution of political parties in America.

The *journal*—in French, literally "diary" or "daybook"—got its start in the learned societies of seventeenth-century Europe as the educated elite came together to share knowledge of the gathering Scientific Revolution. The idea spread out into the realm of public affairs and political comment, and by the mid-nineteenth century it had spread further, to cater variously to the interests of women and the lower classes.

A kind of professionalism, foreshadowed by the shared early need to fight off government censorship and licensing, began to develop among the journalists of newspapers, magazines, and the newly developed press associations, starting with the antecedent to Agence France-Press in 1835. Before the end of the century, British journalists had organized a professional organization of sorts, the Chartered Institute of Journalists, and Americans had made journalism a college course at the University of Missouri. Both events nourished the tendency toward professionalism.

Broadcast journalism began with radio announcers reading brief bulletins specially prepared by the press associations and teletyped over their "radio wires." Network news departments developed a style of radio reporting, and with the rise of the movie theater the combination of motion-picture camera and unseen announcer brought us the newsreel industry. That's where things stood when television took over from the newsreels in the 1950s.

With increasing professionalism through the nineteenth century the better journalists had evolved from their tatterdemalion origins into a rather dignified lot who addressed political leaders with respect and restraint. In broadcast journalism, the orotund voices and funereal tone affected by radio announcers exerted an austere and portentous influence. News presentation was sedate, whether audio or video, and so it remained until the emergence of the 1960s counterculture, live color coverage of the Vietnam War, and the development of adversarial journalism.

You can find fuller background on any part of this eventful story in the general encyclopedias. In every case you will have to do a bit of bobbing and weaving to chase down every aspect. The treatment of Journalism in *Americana* and *World Book* is excellent and up-to-date. The *Britannica* does a very good job, especially in its *Micropaedia* piece. *Academic American* and *Collier's* are adequate. There also is the *Encyclopedia of Twentieth Century Journalists* by William H. Taft.

"THE PRESS"

The encyclopedias are pretty good here for the major newspapers and magazines, and press associations or wire services, and the feature services. They have biographies of most of the major figures—publishing moguls, not omitting the knaves and scamps, and the great journalists and cartoonists.

In addition, there is a rich general literature about the field. Full-length biographies of important publishers also shed much light on the history of the newspaper business. Thoughtful books such as *The Foreign Press* by John C. Merrill, Carter R. Bryan, and Marvin Alisky shed much light on the business in the United States as well as abroad. Merrill, a veteran practitioner and professor of journalism, has the most substantial collection of thumbnail histories of famous papers in *The World's Great Dailies,* a vein he mined earlier in *The Elite Press: Great Newspapers of the World.* Alisky, a political scientist and student of journalism's political role, wrote *Global Journalism.*

Other thoughtful academics writing critically on the press are Ben Bagdikian, a former journalist, and Doris Graber, a sometime editor, whose recent works on this subject include, respectively, *The Media Monopoly* and *Mass Media and American Politics.* The staggering obstacles in the way of establishing the press as an institution in the newly independent countries of the developing world were examined in *The Press in Developing Countries* by E. Lloyd Sommerlad. *The Right to Know* by Francis Williams examines the efforts of the press in Europe and America to maintain that right. John Tebbel, an earlier biographer of Hearst and who also published *Compact History of the American Newspaper* and *The Media in America,* wrote *The Press and the Presidency* (1985) as well.

To this point, we have been talking essentially about newspapers, and dailies at that, at least since the earliest years when all newspapers appeared weekly, fortnightly, or irregularly. The existing literature about magazines is a lot slimmer than that on newspapers, notwithstanding the great influence that many journals have had upon politics, the arts and sciences, and culture generally.

Magazines in the Twentieth Century by the journalism educator Theodore B. Peterson reviews the history of a number of influential American magazines; *Women's Magazines, 1693–1968* by Cynthia White (1971) focuses on Britain but has a chapter on U.S. women's magazines; many libraries still hold Frank Luther Mott's *History of American Magazines* (three volumes, 1938–39), covering the subject from Colonial days to the Great Depression; and the *Oxford Companion to English Literature* and the *Oxford Companion to American Literature* have excellent short sketches of the most influential English and American magazines from the very first of them down to the present day.

The press—now including magazines—also is treated in indexes, critical reviews, and directories. Of indexes, the principal ones have been cited in Chapter 3. The preeminent newspaper indexes are those of *The New York Times, The Wall Street Journal,* and *The Times* of London. But such indexing is no longer confined to this particular Big Three. There are microfilm indexes to other major U.S. dailies, a few major specialized magazines (*e.g., American Banker*), and the most important black newspapers. The big metropolitan dailies so indexed include such giants as the *Los Angeles Times,* the *Chicago Tribune, The Washington Post,* and smaller but highly influential papers such as *The Christian Science Monitor,* the *Chicago Sun-Times,* the *Denver Post,* the *Detroit News,* and the *San Francisco Chronicle.* This is a relatively recent service of the Bell & Howell Micro Photo Division. Check with your librarian.

General magazines are indexed in *Readers' Guide to Periodical Literature* and in the various specialized periodicals in indexes within their fields. It is worth noting again that trade publications in many trades and industries are indexed in the *Applied Science and Technology Index.*

Some of the major consumer magazines, notably the big news weeklies, carry periodic, usually weekly critical commentary on the performance of the daily press and broadcast journalism. Journals of opinion of the mold of *Atlantic* or *Harper's*, for instance, occasionally carry full-length articles of press criticism. The late A. J. Liebling's sporadic articles titled "The Wayward Press" in *The New Yorker* used to fill this role trenchantly. The *Columbia Journalism Review*, published by the Graduate School of Journalism of Columbia University, is perhaps the most consistent contemporary press critic, and criticism also appears in *The Quill*, published by the journalism fraternity Sigma Delta Chi but that reaches much less outside readership.

Occasional criticism, often implicit, appears in the magazine *World Press Review*, whose main role is to extract or digest current reporting and commentary in the major papers and magazines around the world.

As to directories, one yearly reference source covers newspapers, magazines, and radio-television: *Working Press of the Nation*. It lists executives and other key personnel in all departments of newspapers, press associations, feature syndicates, etc. (Volume 1), magazines (Volume 2), radio and television stations and networks (Volume 3), feature writers and photographers (Volume 4), and international publications (Volume 5). It is annual, since 1955.

For newspapers alone, the bible of the business is the *Editor & Publisher International Yearbook*, long edited by Robert U. Brown. This is the product of the weekly trade magazine of the U.S. newspaper business, and both the weekly and the yearbook are universally referred to as *E&P*, with the context making clear which one you are talking about. The *E&P Yearbook* lists ownership, business and mechanical management personnel, news executives and editors, circulation, population of the paper's city and market area, and much more for every daily and weekly newspaper in the United States and Canada. It also covers the press associations or wire services and feature syndicates, newspaper ownership of radio and television stations—the works. It is organized alphabetically, by state and alphabetically by city within the state. *E&P* has dominated this field since 1920.

An even older standby, useful in different ways, is newly titled. It is now the *I M S Directory of Publications*, long known as *N. W. Ayer and Son's Directory of Newspapers and Periodicals*. It is a large, fat volume listing every daily and weekly newspaper and every magazine published in the United States, with circulation and other pertinent information. It was established in 1880 by the pioneering Philadelphia advertising agency of N. W. Ayer & Son.

Magazines, of course, are listed in the *Readers' Guide to Periodical Literature*, which is discussed at some length in Chapter 3. There is another major resource for the periodicals press, and that is the *Standard Periodical Directory*, a biennial reference listing nearly seventy thousand general-interest magazines, trade publications, learned and professional journals, annuals, and other periodicals issued throughout the United States and Canada. It is organized by subject, with more than two hundred categories, and well indexed by both subject and title. Listings are detailed enough to give you a good picture of the content and focus of each publication even if you've never heard of it.

A Bowker publication, *Magazine Industry Market Place* (MIMP), lists magazines alphabetically, supplying basic directory information, then indexes them separately by type (business, consumer, etc.) and subject (advertising, poetry, etc). It then supplies classified lists of services used by the magazine publishing industry, doing for that field approximately what its much older stablemate *Literary Market Place*, described later in this chapter, does for book publishing.

Ulrich's International Periodicals Directory is particularly useful for its extensive foreign coverage, especially of British and Commonwealth and Western Hemisphere (including U.S.) magazines. This two-volume annual, now published by Bowker, first appeared in 1932. It describes the character of each magazine, including the kinds of material it carries (*e.g.*, book reviews). It is organized by subject categories and is well indexed. If you have access to a library that saves these directories all the way back, you should know that various editions feature special topical treatments that make them worth browsing in. The 1947 edition listed all the underground publications then known to have come out during World War II. (Wear a dust mask if you're allergic to dusty old books from the back room.)

It should be noted that magazines are also listed and described in such special-interest publications as the annuals *Writer's Market* and *The Writer's Handbook*.

There is a final category of magazine that is competently indexed: house organs, both "internal" ones published by corporations for the information and *esprit de corps* of their employees and stockholders, and "externals" circulated widely outside the company as a public-relations device. These publications are almost as numerous as business corporations. Indeed, if all of them were put out by some dozen publishing houses they would constitute a major industry. To assure yourself of that, consult the major directory of those periodicals, the *Gebbie House Magazine Directory*, which is published biennially. It is organized alphabetically by company name. The directory is oriented toward free-lance writers and gives information about the kinds of writing, photography, etc., and editorial approach wanted. In the process it reveals a good deal about the companies and their approach to public and employee relations.

Before turning from publishing, a word about the world of the book, even though it is addressed in one or more of its facets in every chapter of this volume, not least in Chapter 21 on bibliography. The definitive history of the field in America is John Tebbel's *History of Book Publishing in the United States* (four volumes, 1981). It covers the whole span from 1630 to 1980.

Book *publishing* is also the subject of the weekly magazine *Publishers Weekly*, which can be found on the desk (or in the briefcase) of virtually every business and editorial executive of consequence in the American publishing business. It is a weekly review of every aspect of the trade right down to forecasts of forthcoming books.

Library Journal is valued by librarians and the trade for its news of books but perhaps especially for its reviews of new books, which are focused explicitly on evaluating them in terms of what their purchase would add to the library's collection. This magazine appears twice a month, but monthly in midsummer and midwinter. There are many other such publications, general (*e.g.,* the monthly *Book Review Digest* or the semimonthly *Booklist*) and special (*e.g., Reviews in Anthropology*), perhaps eighty or ninety in all, from *Black Books Bulletin* to *Word Processing News*. Look 'em up.

Dozens of other periodicals are important to various segments of the book publishing field, and the simplest way to locate these probably is in the "Magazines for the Trade" section of the annual *Literary Market Place*, known to everybody in the trade as *LMP*. Its seventy-three sections range from one listing all U.S. book publishers alphabetically to one briefly describing every news service and feature syndicate that covers some aspect of publishing. Included along the way are such categories as literary prizes, authors' agents, reviewers, printers, and binders.

THE BROADCAST MEDIA

The discussion here of radio and television (including cable) broadcasting is limited to its coverage of news and public affairs, inasmuch as the artistic and popular entertainment aspects were addressed in Chapter 10. The increasing professionalism touched on in the review of the history of journalism earlier in this chapter has been approximately as evident in the broadcast as in the print media. In part this is due to the development of college and university programs in electronic journalism, sometimes following a completely separate course from the newspaper variety.

This separation is appropriate enough, for television cannot afford even to think of covering important stories with the thoroughness and depth of a newspaper. A conspicuous exception is a truly cataclysmic event like the assassination of a president; another is an ongoing sports spectacle such as the World Series or football's Super Bowl; there the newspaper can't afford to concentrate its entire budget of editorial space to the super event.

But in the major events of an ordinary year there are hundreds of terribly important national or international stories to which a *Los Angeles Times*, a *Washington Post*, or a *New York Times* will devote two or three full columns of news and background coverage. Even a small-city newspaper with limited coverage of out-of-town events will give eight or ten paragraphs to a substantial national story. That depth of coverage translates, in television terms, to impossible lengths of time.

Two or three columns in *The New York Times,* allowing space for headlines and photographs, will work out to fifteen hundred or more words of actual text. On the air it would take a reporter or news anchor ten minutes to put out fifteen hundred words at a comprehensible rate of speed—ten minutes on a twenty-four-minute "half hour" nightly news show. No; on TV, the newspaper's story of fifteen-hundred words plus photos will be dispatched in two minutes. There is, to be sure, the old photo editors' canard about one good picture being worth a thousand words. Not on your life. It may well be worth an additional four hundred or five hundred words, but it will mean very little without the kind of background only words can supply. Unfortunately, the compression, selection, intercutting, and deletion television must use to fit available time are the very tools of distortion. Some stories are complex enough so they simply cannot be treated honestly in a minute or two.

The thoughtful broadcast journalists are not only aware of these problems, they agonize over them. They realize that in today's America the nightly TV news is the major source of information about their world for most citizens. The stars themselves, the million-dollars-a-year-plus news "anchors" on all the networks and in the top fifty or sixty major local stations around the country, read several newspapers and thousands of words of "wire service" copy every day. (There is an occasional exception in a deep-voiced, gorgeous lout left over from the "rip and read" days of yore.) Thus, ironically, the very men and women we trust to tell us the news are far better informed than they can afford to inform us.

But there is a positive side. On many major stories TV will do a full-length special that will include a carefully written and presented review and analysis with a kind of immediacy and depth that a million words in print could not convey. Moreover, on such "in depth" network shows as CBS's landmark *60 Minutes,* occasionally emulated locally, a story can be gone into at sufficient depth to illumine many a dark corner and provide invaluable insights.

However, it doesn't always work. Neither commercial nor public TV is immune to bias or propaganda.

When you turn to the popular encyclopedias for the broadcasting field, be sure to cover all the bases: broadcasting; radio; television; journalism; and various stars by name, *e.g.,* Edward R. Murrow. Biographical dictionaries (Chapter 5) will do you more good on the individuals, but the encyclopedia indexes are worth checking.

The literature on broadcast journalism is not enormous. To the extent of its address to news programming, an excellent general work, *A History of Broadcasting in the United States* by Erik Barnouw (three volumes, 1966–70) is useful. Another, though not focused wholly on broadcasting, is *Media Power* by David L. Altheide (1985), treating the implications of media influence on public morals and politics. A similar concern expressly about television informs an earlier book, *The People Machine: The Influence of Television on American Politics* by a thoughtful public television broadcaster, Robert MacNeil (1968).

Radio and television people are listed in the *Working Press of the Nation,* described earlier in this chapter. The broadcast industry's weekly bible, analogous to *Editor & Publisher* in the newspaper trade, is the magazine *Broadcasting,* which also publishes an exact counterpart to the *E&P International Yearbook* in the *Broadcasting/ Cablecasting Yearbook.*

ADVERTISING AND "PR"

Advertising is as old as the oldest profession. As, among others, Pompeian graffiti from the first century A.D. make clear, prostitutes scribed their names and addresses in walls at strategic locations. This was simply an early mode of outdoor ad campaign. The way today's print advertising is created was basically fashioned in late-nineteenth-century America. But by the 1920s a new style of advertising agency had evolved, coincidentally with the beginnings of commercial radio. This confluence of events changed forever the way consumer goods are sold. The symbiosis of these two—the advertising agent and the radio broadcaster—enabled both businesses to thrive in the very teeth of the Great Depression.

Print advertising made similar advances as new speed and versatility of the printing process, new developments in the graphic arts, four-color printing, and telephone and wireless transmission of text and photographs all flowed together in the 1930s and 1940s. When TV began to emerge in the 1950s, the advertising business was ready, and another sea change washed away old buying and selling mores and washed in the new.

The general encyclopedias are good about the development of advertising, although the *Britannica*'s major treatment in the *Macropaedia* under "Marketing and Merchandising" is a bit drab. Much zestier is *World Book*'s article, as is *Americana*'s and *Collier's*, too. This is ironic because the *Britannica*'s longtime publisher, William Benton, was an ad genius who grew wealthy in the Great Depression with his own agency, Benton & Bowles. (For another irony, Benton & Bowles, which Benton left in the mid-1930s, later handled advertising for *World Book*, the biggest-selling encyclopedia in the world.)

The *Britannica*'s *Micropaedia* articles on advertising and public relations, by the way, are excellent. As with looking up the broadcast business, when you look up advertising, don't fail to ring the changes. Be sure to check indexes and catalogs under "marketing," "merchandising," and various kinds of advertising—*e.g.*, point-of-sale (or point-of-purchase), outdoor, and direct advertising (or direct mail). Otherwise you could wind up missing just what you are looking for.

None of the better general accounts of advertising in individual books seems to have the vitality of the popular books attacking the ad business that began appearing after World War II. That was the heyday of such pop exposés as Vance Packard's *The Hidden*

Persuaders (1957; revised edition, 1981); the later and more pointed *The Permissible Lie: The Inside Truth About Advertising* by S. S. Baker (1969); and the *roman à clef* by an agency account executive, Frederic Wakeman, *The Hucksters* (1946).

As agency expertise has advanced at reading the pulse of every ZIP Code zone through sophisticated market research, political organizations and clients have been quick to harness this skill to filmmakers' dexterity at oversimplifying political issues and putting the white hats on their political clients. Critical books by outside observers such as Joe McGinniss in *The Selling of the President 1968* have leveled devastating criticisms at this advertising approach to elections.

But even more lethal have been the criticisms of agency excesses by some sensitive leaders of that industry, notably John O'Toole, a major agency head. The issue is far from resolved, but interested readers can contemplate it in the McGinniss book cited and in writings by such scholars in communications and politics as Lloyd Bitzer, Doris Graber, Larry Sabato, and many others, including the present author.

Good, dispassionate background on the industry can be located through a useful bibliography, *Information Sources in Advertising History* edited by Richard W. Pollay (1979). Standard reference sources for the industry itself begin with the *Standard Directory of Advertising Agencies,* which appears three times a year. It incorporates the former *McKittrick's Directory of Advertising* with parts of the former *Standard Advertising Register* to list in three volumes all U.S. advertisers other than local companies that place their own advertising locally.

The *Standard Directory* gives each company's roster of products and identifies the advertising agencies handling them. One of its elements replaces the agency lists of both former publications and shows all advertising agencies and their key personnel, listing the clients of each agency. In the agency business one way you know who's looking for another job is by who is furtively photocopying pages from the agency list of the *Standard Directory.*

Media people—*i.e.,* those who buy TV or radio time and space in publications—rely on another kind of periodical provided by *Standard Rate and Data Service* or *SRDS,* which publishes (and constantly updates) advertising rates and other relevant information solicited from the advertising media. Another staple is the *Market Guide* issued annually by *Editor & Publisher,* with detailed local business and economic information on every U.S. and Canadian market centered on a city with a daily newspaper. Data include population, location, transportation facilities, number of banks and their capitalization, etc., to a list of industries and one of retail stores. It is organized alphabetically by state or province and city.

The public-relations field fares about as well as advertising at the hands of the major encyclopedias. That craft's origins are in the rather seamy practice of many pre–Civil War newspapers in giving "free publicity" in their news columns to faithful advertisers. Over the intervening generations the PR trade has seen major advances in professionalism along with the news media, pushed along in PR's case by a lot of huffing and puffing in various PR associations eager to lose the label of "press agent." Basically this is because the field has had a sense of inferiority from being looked down on by reporters and academics.

That situation gradually improved for the PR folk as reporters took public-relations jobs and as colleges and universities discovered the fund-raising and image benefits of competent PR staffs. Nowadays there are graduate and undergraduate PR courses and some full-fledged schools of public relations in major universities. Back at the front, public-relations people lean more and more toward identifying themselves as public affairs counselors or consultants, and not implausibly, since so much of their modern concern is with government relations.

What the latter comes down to, often enough, is lobbying, a concept that brings hyperventilation to the breast of the reformer. However, the public-affairs folk take solace in the fact that the lobbying, "the right of the people . . . to petition the Government for a redress of grievance," is protected by the First Amendment in the same sentence with religion and speech, and reform is not. Freedom to advocate it, of course, is.

There aren't many good books that tell the fascinating story of PR objectively. There are lots and lots of them that help the PR practitioner at whatever level to locate the resources to do his or her job. A basic tool for anyone wanting to find out who's who in the PR business is a couple of reference books put out by Jack O'Dwyer, a public-relations fixture and the longtime editor and publisher of a major PR newsletter. These are *O'Dwyer's Directory of Public Relations Firms* and *O'Dwyer's Directory of Corporate Communications*. The former lists staff and clients and significant attributes of PR enterprises by their firm names. The latter supplies personnel and other relevant information about the PR departments of business corporations.

Other information sources include the *Madison Avenue Handbook* edited by Chip Brill (annual since 1985), listing ad and PR agencies, and sources for finding models, acting talent, and miscellaneous services for the industry. *Professional's Guide to Public Relations Services* by Richard Weiner (quinquennial; fifth edition, 1985) lists some one thousand basic PR services, with costs. Weiner's *Professional's Guide to Publicity* (third edition, 1982) is a basic manual for working publicists who do not shun the name.

CHAPTER 19

RECREATION: FUN AND GAMES IN BOOKS

Games are among the earliest memories of mankind, and recreational activities are part of every culture on Earth. Aristotle thought of pleasant amusement as an end that was desirable in itself, like happiness. Recreation has been defined as any activity voluntarily engaged in for satisfaction—*i.e.*, for relaxation, self-satisfaction, or fun. But throughout the ages public policy did not concern itself with recreational activities except to restrain them when they got out of hand, as when the Church condemned large-scale, armed sham battles or *mêlées* at the dawn of the thirteenth century, setting the stage for the more stylized and less lethal institution of jousting.

Only in the past century or two have play and recreation come to be considered not only personal fun but also socially useful. With the rapid growth of cities in the nineteenth century, recreation and recreational facilities were fostered to help relieve the tensions of urban life. The playground movement arose to help keep children off the streets (although the textile mills of the Industrial Revolution had done a pretty good job of that). Gymnasiums were introduced into the school, and parks insinuated into the cityscape.

These recreational advances were brought about by noncommercial interests. Commercial sponsorship introduced such entertainment media as motion pictures, radio and then television, recreational travel, and, not least, professional sports.

Prizes for winning competitions are about as old as humanity, and gambling is a way of creating a prize in the absence of an official donor or sponsor. In the epics of Homer, prizes might be a woman skilled in every useful art, a cauldron, a pregnant mare, or a quantity of gold. In combat games the prize might be freedom for a slave. In the Middle Ages some combatants wagered their own freedom on the outcome. Every competitive activity is subject to wagering, including such ostensibly solo activities as solitaire, in which you may bet the house you will win and the house bets you won't. Gambling will not be addressed further in this chapter, but if you want to look it up, remember to be prepared with alternative terms such as "gaming," "wagering," "betting," and particular forms such as "pari-mutuel," "lottery," *et al.*

This chapter will take up first those sports and games usually or originally played outdoors and usually involving physical exercise and relatively strenuous exertion. Next will come relatively nonphysical games usually played indoors, such as those played with cards or dice. This will be followed by children's games and finally by hobbies and other pastimes.

The general encyclopedias are pretty much on a par here. If you are curious about a particular game—*e.g.*, poker dice—you will do best to look it up by that name under "P" in the index, although you may not find it there. Then try dice games (under "D"). The article you are referred to may omit poker dice entirely. If so, despair not. Simply turn to one of the handbooks, rulebooks, etc., discussed later and look under the appropriate category—in the case of this example, nonphysical games. The general encyclopedias, by the way, do better in organized and especially professional sports than in games, where every one of them has gaps in its coverage.

Cave paintings assure us that athletic games and competition have been part of human activity longer than records have been kept. It is supposed that early physical contests were valuable to society for keeping the strength and dexterity of hunters in tone, and we know from Homer, Plato, and the early historians that this was the case in ancient Greece, where the Olympic Games probably originated in about 1500 B.C. Such activity was so popular that within a millennium there were three other epic competitions throughout Greece—the Isthmian, Nemean, and Pythian games—and the idea then quickly spread throughout the Mediterranean Basin.

The Romans kept the spectacle idea but fundamentally altered what went on in the arena. Mere wrestling and boxing were supplanted by armed combat between prisoners of war, and then unarmed combat between human prisoners and wild animals captured for the arena. *Sic procedit humanitas.*

Little is known of recreation in Europe between the decay of the Roman Empire and the decline of feudalism, except it is supposed that important diversions for ordinary mortals (male) included primitive forms of football and of alehouse brawling. For the upper echelons, there were the delights of the chase, with hunting reserved to nobility and poaching prohibited on pain of death, and horse racing, which was indeed the sport of kings.

Gradually license to hunt game was extended (for a fee) to the masses, and by the mid-nineteenth century the efforts, noted at the beginning of this chapter, to institutionalize other forms of recreation were under way. A little later the idea of reestablishing the Olympic Games began to take hold, and in 1896 the first modern games were held at Athens. Several contemporary works relate this story at appropriate length, among them *An Approved History of the Olympic Games* by Bill Henry and Patricia H. Yeomans (1984) and the well-told *Story of the Olympic Games, 776 B.C. to 1976* by John Kieran, A. Daley, and Pat Jordan (revised edition, 1977).

Abundant general reference works address the whole diverse field of sports. See *Encyclopedia of Sports* by Frank G. Menke (sixth revised edition, 1977, revised by Pete Palmer), with the history and background of most established sports, including rules and records; similarly broad and bearing the degree of authority we have come to know from its stablemates, *The Oxford Companion to World Sports and Games* edited by John Arlott (1975). *Sports in the Western World* by William J. Baker (1982) offers a review of competitive sports; it does not address individual and noncompetitive sporting activities.

Sports terminology, often so arcane as to baffle any noninitiate, is explained in *Sports Roots: How Nicknames, Namesakes, Trophies, Competitions, and Expressions in the World of Sports Came to Be* by Harvey Frommer (1979) and *The Language of Sport* by Tim Considine (1982). See also *The Rule Book: The Authoritative, Up-to-Date, Illustrated Guide to the Regulations, History, and Object of All Major Sports* by the Diagram Group (1981), a sort of collective Hoyle for the active sports.

Sports records are well handled by the regular encyclopedias. The *Britannica* puts all the records in one enormous section. Its "Sporting Record" tables occupy fifty-five *Micropaedia* pages, enough space for more than a hundred thousand words of text. They cover virtually every sport, each with its own compendium of records embracing all the important world and U.S. competitions. Each sport is then updated yearly in the *World Data Annual*. The other encyclopedias print a few key records with the article on each sport, updating those events in their yearbooks. This is an event the *Britannica* wins hands down, at least for sports fans.

There are, of course, many other sources of annual information on sports records. In fact, *World Book* forthrightly refers its readers to the *World Almanac* for current records. Other valuable annuals include Facts on File's *The World Sports Record Atlas* edited by David Emery. *Sports Firsts* by Patrick Clark is a book of records and origins of sporting events. An excellent comprehensive bibliography to the literature of sports is *Sports: A Reference Guide* by Robert J. Higgs. Finally, as to sports in general, many writers have addressed a variety of philosophical questions that have arisen about sports. Interesting among these are such as *Sports and Social Values* by Robert L. Simon; and *From Ritual to Record: The Nature of Modern Sports* by Allen Guttmann, an examination of amateurism and professionalism.

As the Renaissance was spreading across Europe, an English nun, it is thought, wrote the first published work on fishing whose fame is still celebrated. In the early mid-fifteenth century, Dame Juliana Berners (born in 1388) was prioress of the nunnery of Sopwell associated with the Abbey of St. Albans, by the River Ver in Hertfordshire. Years later her name (as Dam Julyans Barnes) appeared as author of a rhymed treatise on hunting published in 1486 with others on falconry and heraldry in *The Boke of St. Albans*. To the second edition (1496), the publisher, Wynken de Worde, added the *Treatyse of fysshing with an Angle,* styling her Dame Julyans Bernes. Later research identified her as Juliana Berners, and thus she passed into tradition as the author of the first book on hunting and fishing published in England, and but for *The Compleat Angler* perhaps the most famous.

The latter work, a pastoral by the Royalist biographer of John Donne and other English divines among his fishing companions, made Izaak Walton immortal. From 1653 it was published in five editions during Walton's lifetime and in more than three hundred since. To the fifth Walton's young friend Charles Cotton added a section on fly-fishing. (Walton was a bait fisherman, who counseled about the frog as bait to "Use him as though you loved him, that he may live the longer.")

As Walton's three and a half centuries in print suggest, the body of angling literature is stupendous. Arnold Gingrich published an outstanding bibliography, *The Fishing in Print: A Guided Tour Through Five Centuries of Angling Literature* (1974). Modern classics include Ray Bergman's *Trout* (revised edition, 1952), Lee Wulff's

Atlantic Salmon (1958), and the fisherman's entomological bible, *Matching the Hatch* by Ernest G. Schwiebert, Jr. (1955). The standard reference work is the *New Standard Fishing Encyclopedia and International Angling Guide* edited by A. J. McClane (1965, 1974).

As to hunting in print, the field is smaller but still very large indeed. The best general reference still is *The Hunter's Encyclopedia* edited by Ray Camp (1951), the longtime outdoor editor of *The New York Times*, and its 1966 successor, *The New Hunter's Encyclopedia* (revised 1974). Differently focused is the *Complete Guide to Hunting Across North America* by Byron W. Dalrymple (1970); see also the *Complete Book of Hunting* by Clyde Ormond (second revised edition, 1972). In both fishing and hunting categories, the books in print and available in libraries number in the hundreds.

The literature on horses and horsemanship, and their breeding and racing is old and large. See, *e.g., The Encyclopedia of the Horse* edited by C.E.G. Hope and G. N. Jackson; *A Standard Guide to Horse and Pony Breeds*, Elwyn Hartley Edwards, general editor (1980); and *Encyclopedia for Horsemen* by R. S. Summerhays (sixth edition, revised by Stella A. Walker, 1975). Of racing: *The History of Horse Racing* by Roger Longrigg (1972); *Horses and Courses* by David Hodges and Fred Mayer (1972); and *Encyclopedia of Thoroughbred Handicapping* by Tom Ainslie (1978). *The Complete Book on Harness Racing* by Philip A. Pines (fourth edition, 1982) supplies thorough background on that aspect of racing. Record books abound for this and every other sport—and in the general encyclopedias, notably *Britannica,* as suggested earlier.

Almost as soon as the world's second gasoline engine was hooked up to a set of wheels, auto racing began informally, and before 1900 organized races were being run in Europe and America. With every succeeding advance in motorized transport came a new genre of racing. The literature is ample, and it includes that for boats, planes, bicycles, and motorbikes. There are lots of encyclopedias and dictionaries. See, *e.g.,* the *Encyclopedia of Auto Racing Greats,* or the broader *Encyclopedia of Motor Sports* edited by G. M. Georgano. For non-motor boating see the *Encyclopedia of Sailing* by the editors of *One-design and Offshore Yachtsman.*

SPECTATOR SPORTS

If baseball was not invented in Cooperstown, New York, in 1839 by Abner Doubleday, he certainly changed its shape and rules from the English game of rounders and pointed it in the direction that made it not so much a national pastime as a national passion in the United States, Canada, Cuba, and Japan. We do know who invented basketball, 52 years later and 150 miles away. That was James Naismith, a YMCA gym teacher at Springfield, Massachusetts, in 1891. If it does not enthrall quite so many millions, there still is hardly a community in America where a basketball game can't be seen live on TV at least two or three nights a week all winter long.

Football's antecedents and its parallels outside the United States are a bit mixed. The game originated in the play of male children in preliterate societies, sometimes with a skull as the object being kicked around. In North America it evolved differently from its foreign cousins. Soccer, or Association Football, is as much a national craze in Europe and Latin America as baseball is in the United States. Rugby is a distinctly British variation, which also must compete for attention with soccer in the United Kingdom. Canadian football is virtually identical with the U.S. variety.

These major team sports enjoy a large body of writing. Of baseball: *The Baseball Encyclopedia* edited by Joseph L. Reichler, with official records since the National Association of Professional Base Ball Players was formed in 1971; also the *Encyclopedia of Baseball; The Bill James Historical Baseball Abstract;* and *A Thinking Man's Guide to Baseball* by Leonard Koppett. History is addressed in, among countless others, *Baseball: The Early Years* and *The Golden Age,* both by Harold Seymour.

Of basketball: *Athletic Journal's Encyclopedia of Basketball* edited by Tom Ecker and Don King; *The Modern Encyclopedia of Basketball* edited by Zander Hollander; and the *Official NBA Guide.* For history see the *Illustrated History of Basketball* by Larry Fox *et al.*

Of football: *The Official Encyclopedia of Football* by Roger Treat; and the *Pro Football Guide* and the *Football Register,* both edited by Howard Balzer and Dave Sloan. For history see *The History of American Football* and *Oh, How They Played the Game,* both by Allison Danzig. There are many others.

Ice hockey has become a major spectator sport. Part of its charm appears to lie in the mayhem its practitioners work on one another. When detected by officials, who are obliged to keep track of what goes on in the fastest nonmotorized game on Earth, the kicks and gouges send the perpetrator to the penalty box for a time while his teammates play on shorthanded, or -footed. For particulars, see *Hockey Register* from *The Sporting News; Hockey! The Story of the*

World's Fastest Sport by Dick Beddoes, Stan Fischler, and Ira Gitler is a standard work.

While Dame Juliana Berners was presumably muddying her habit on the banks of the River Ver, a couple of hundred miles to the north an anonymous Scotsman was inventing golf. By the seventeenth century that game was entrenched in London and even being played in North America. By the late twentieth century, of course, Americans would traipse in crowds numbering hundreds along the course after golf tournament stars, and millions would watch from home by television. What started as an innocent (or devilish) individual participant sport has become a major, maybe *the* major, nonteam spectator sport.

Basic resources include the *Encyclopedia of Golf* by Webster Evans, *Golf Magazine's Encyclopedia of Golf* edited by Robert Scharff and the editors of *Golf Magazine*, and the *Dictionary of Golf* edited by James Green. For history see, among numerous others, *A History of Golf Illustrated* by Henry Cotton (the U.S. edition of the British work *Golf: A Pictorial History*); or *Lords of the Links: The Story of Professional Golf* by Geoffrey Cousins.

Tennis as the mass passion it now is would have been incomprehensible to the French royals who, early in the Middle Ages, played its precursor as a form of handball, *jeu de paume* or "the palm game." Its evolution branched several ways, and by the late nineteenth century, rackets having been substituted for the hand alone, it was firmly established as lawn tennis in England and Wales and had spread across the empire and to the United States. A basic work for Americans is the *United States Tennis Association Official Encyclopedia of Tennis* edited by Bill Shannon. Others worth consulting include *The Story of Tennis* by Lord Aberdare and *Women's Tennis: A Historical Documentary on the Players and Their Game* by Angela Lumpkin.

Track and field sports, like every other athletic pursuit under the sun (or floodlights), has its day in the encyclopedias and in the record books devoted to the particular family of events. A basic resource is *Track and Field Athletics: The Records* compiled by Peter Matthews for those Stout fellows, Guinness and their *Book of Records*.

The encyclopedias and their yearbooks do well enough by the winter sports, and so does the public library. However, you'd better look them up separately—*i.e.*, as skiing, ice-skating, curling, etc. Many library resources limit winter sports to bobsledding, ice-boating, etc.

So it is with water sports (a classification you find only infrequently) or aquatic sports, which in some organizing schemes includes motorboating and lifesaving. Water polo is sometimes included, but you are best advised to pursue individual titles: swimming, diving, etc.

For every sport there is an ample body of writing. In seeking background on any of them, start out with its name in an encyclopedia or simply consult your library catalog. A search under "bowling" will immediately turn up a number of works—e.g., *The Perfect Game: The World of Bowling* by Herman Weiskopf (1978). Write your own ticket; it will take you just where you want to go.

NONPHYSICAL GAMES AND RECREATIONS

Playing cards appear to have been invented in China sometime after the seventh century A.D. and not later than the tenth. Their first appearance in Europe, so far as we know, was in Italy at the very end of the thirteenth century—interestingly enough, three or four years after Marco Polo returned to Venice from Cathay.

In the English-speaking world one name dominates talk of card games and their rules. *According to Hoyle* is in perhaps equal parts book, legend, and tradition. The book is edited by Richard L. Frey (1965; revised editions, 1970 *et seq.*). The legend surrounds the man, Edmond Hoyle (*c.* 1671–1769), a supposed English barrister whose knowledge of card and board games made his name immortal through such works as *A Short Treatise on the Game of Whist* (first edition, 1742).

Since Hoyle's death in 1769, countless other writers on games have updated his rules, borrowed his name, and played his game, thus perpetuating the tradition. Among these hitchhikers on Hoyle, each one an estimable expert in his own right, are the following: *Goren's Hoyle Encyclopedia of Games; With Official Rules and Pointers on Play, Including the Latest Laws of Contract Bridge* by Charles Henry Goren (1961; previous editions of this version, also appealing to bridge players, were known as Culbertson's Hoyle). Also *Foster's Complete Hoyle* by Robert F. Foster (1946 and revised periodically), which includes rules for such games as Old Maid and Go Fish. There are almost numberless other versions of Hoyle, one of them *The New Complete Hoyle* by Foster with Albert H. Morehead and Geoffrey Mott-Smith (1956 *et seq.*).

Others toil in the Hoyle vineyard without copping his name. One of the best of these is John Scarne, who started out as a magician and whose great dexterity at manipulating cards and dice brought him a new career at detecting card and dice cheats. His *Encyclopedia of Games* is a standard work. Also consult *Games* by Jesse H. Bancroft (revised and enlarged periodically since 1939), with indoor and outdoor games for home and playground, solitary and group, social and athletic, and indicating appropriate age groups.

Chess is a field whose literature never stops proliferating. Every championship tournament becomes another page or more in the next chess book. You can pick your favorite master, opening, or theme and find at least a handful of titles to choose among. A good reference work is the *Encyclopedia of Chess* compiled by Anne Sunnucks. There are all manner of ominous titles in this literature—*e.g., Chess Traps, Pitfalls, and Swindles*. Watch out!

CHILDREN'S GAMES AND TOYS

Play is observed in the young of all mammalian species, and "playful" as an adjective for adult human behavior has always carried at least a faint connotation of childishness or immaturity—witness "kittenish," "coltish," "child's play," and "puppy love." The literature on children's games and toys is not vast, certainly nothing like the volume of writing about children's literature. But there certainly is enough to find whatever you want, and that includes the encyclopedias. Check the library catalog (games, children's; children's games; children's sports; etc.), where you can expect to find titles such as *The Family Book of Games and Sports* by Helen Joseph, *A Guide for Games* by David Cyril Johnson, and *Encyclopedia of Toys* by Constance Eileen King.

HOBBIES AND PASTIMES

Apart from its meaning as a fairly obscure falcon, the word "hobby" in its sense of avocational pursuit is of rather recent origin. It has been, like "Bobby," a nickname for Robert. It is certain that in its present usage it split away from "hobbyhorse," but how it got there is not entirely clear. The hobbyhorse originated as part of the costume of one participant in the old English morris dance. It was a form worn around the waist and fashioned of wicker or fabric, perhaps buckram, to suggest a horse or pony. The dancer who wore it played the role of the evil sprite Hobbididance—the same Prince of Dumbness that bedeviled Poor Tom in Shakespeare's *King Lear* (Act IV, Scene 1). But how this hard-luck creature got into the shape of a stylized horse is not clear. Part of the muddle is that in those days Hobin or Hobbin was as common a nickname for an ordinary dray horse as Dobbin.

Be that as it may, the encyclopedias treat the hobby of hobbyists variously, the *Britannica* not deigning to treat it at all. Popular literature, however, handles it very well and in growing numbers of works.

For the hobby of collecting virtually anything, look into *Hobby Collections A–Z* by Roslyn W. Salny, among others, a work whose range is as broad as the title suggests, supplying intriguing background on various kinds of collectibles as well as suggestions for acquisition and organization. For philatelists (from the Greek *philos,* "loving," and *taxos,* "tax," thus the stamps signifying that a tax had been paid), *Scott's Standard Postage Stamp Catalogue* since 1867 has indeed been the standard annual catalog for the hobby of stamp collecting, with illustrations and descriptions of stamps and present-day value in U.S. currency.

And for the numismatist (from the Latin *nomisma,* "coin"), *Coins of the World* by R.A.G. Carson is a historical review of coins from the ancient world to modern times. See also, among many others, *A Catalogue of the World's Most Popular Coins* by Fred Reinfeld and Burton Hobson and based on Reinfeld's 1956 work, featuring photographs of coins and dealer prices in U.S. currency, the latter element obviously only as valuable as the time of the edition. There are several special encyclopedias and dictionaries for this hobby.

Glass collecting is treated in the *Encyclopedia of Glass* edited by Phoebe Phillips, which includes a bibliography. More detail but a narrower focus is reflected in the *Encyclopedia of Victorian Colored Pattern Glass* by William Heacock (five volumes).

There are even books on hobbies such as collecting matchbooks, beer cans, bottle tops, and hubcaps. If you invent a new one, write the book. There seems to be a market.

CHAPTER 20

HOW-TO-DO-IT AND SELF-IMPROVEMENT BOOKS

The world of how-to-do-it literature is sometimes put down as a dreary world of dull people doing dull things by themselves, and obviously anyone to whom this view is important is welcome to it. The most famous modern work of this ilk probably is Dale Carnegie's *How to Win Friends and Influence People* (1936), a book much parodied and teased and yet one that left millions of readers persuaded that it had improved their lives. It is still in print.

The genre has been spoofed in the 1962 Pulitzer Prize musical comedy *How to Succeed in Business Without Actually Trying,* and a generation earlier in *How to Sleep,* an Oscar-winning movie short by Robert Benchley (1935). The fact is, however, that the title of virtually every literally instructive text might well begin *How to Find Out About* . . . (Books on how things work, in contradistinction to how to do it, are dealt with briefly in Chapter 16 on technology.)

There are numerous literary and scholarly ornaments in the how-to genre. An early one, it is said, was a sermon by the Reverend Rector of Diss, John Skelton, who was court poet to Henry VII and tutor to Henry VIII. "How to be Happy Though Married" was the title of the sermon, an argument much explored by Henry VIII, though whether it was the sermon that set him on that track must be left to speculation. A certain poignancy is lent the story by the fact that Father Skelton was himself married, for which he was suspended from the priesthood.[1]

---

[1] The tale of the sermon title, which need not be true, was said to be so by the Rev. E. J. Hardy in his book, *c.* 1910, *How to Be Happy Though Married.* The other facts presented are matters of public record.

John Maynard Keynes's three 1939 essays, "How to Pay for the War," were extremely influential. *How to Read the Bible* (1946) was one of the most useful and respected works of the classicist and Bible scholar Edgar J. Goodspeed, one of the translators of the *Revised Standard Version.*

Even the Greek satirist and rhetorician Lucian got into the act *c.* A.D. 169 with *How to Write History,* a work that though amusing and biting, was a sharp and serious attack on the practice of disguising panegyric as history. If it did not quite have an explicitly how-to title, nevertheless John Dewey's *How We Think* (1910) added up to a how-we-ought-to manifesto that had an important part in launching progressive education (for good or ill). The title is paraphrased in *Self-Help* (1859) by Samuel Smiles, an ardent Scottish apostle of the work ethic who did so much to sell Victorian morality and helped pave the way for Horatio Alger.

Now, then: In the face of all this erudition, how come how-to books don't get no respect?

Perhaps because they are so common. Henry Wallace, a fuzzy liberal politician of the 1940s, once got off a fulsome tribute to the common man: "God must have loved the common man because he made so many of them." To this one acerbic critic rejoined, "God must have loved the common man because he made him so common." God knows the how-to genre is common, perhaps precisely because it promises to elevate us commoners to a level of knowledge or accomplishment we thirst after. There are thirty-four pages of how-to titles in *Books in Print,* and those are large pages with tiny, tiny print.

That brings us to a word of caution when you consider turning to the literature of how to do it: Don't start your search with "how to." A title search initiated there will soon have you squinting, bored stiff, and thinking about taking a nap. If, of course, you are in the library catalog and merely seeking the class number of a specific title, that's a different matter.

But if you are starting out cold to find a book that offers to teach you how to do something, by all means look it up by subject. It may take you a few moments to analyze the topic to figure out how it will be cataloged or indexed. Is it sink repair? Kitchen repair? House or household repair? Home repair? No, but that is a cross-reference to dwellings—maintenance and repair. You have to be flexible enough to adapt to the decisions of the people who picked the categories. It's not always tricky; from car care it's a simple matter to get to auto maintenance. These two items are important elements in the how-to literature.

Occasionally you find books that offer to preview the how-to literature for you. There's an old one called *How-to-Do-It Books: A Selected Guide,* which still is worthwhile; you may find it in your library. Many of the titles will be out of print, but the categories will be extremely helpful in figuring out how to formulate the categories you want to look up.

The latter book has been supplanted by one from the mid-1980s called *Self-Help: 1400 Best Books.* The problem with it—at least in its first incarnation—is that its index contains numerous blind references to articles that weren't in the book and page numbers that take you to entirely different topics. Alas, it's a not uncommon failing.

The difference between those two titles brings up an interesting point about this literature. It really is three literatures: one about how to find things out, one on how to do practical or physical things, and the third about how to attain mental or spiritual or social—or financial—goals.

The primary focus of the *Self-Help* book mentioned earlier is on the second and third categories more than the first. Carpentry and home workshop aren't there. Health and self-education are. By now it is evident that there is no unanimity of terminology here; the phrase "how to do it" is far from universal. The British use "know-how" for it, and Americans use "do-it-yourself" interchangeably with "how to do it." As for "self-help," it is interchangeable with "self-improvement," and thanks to the various human-potential movements, "self-realization" or even (mercy!) "self-actualization."

It is worth noting that none of these phrases need appear in a title to qualify for the how-to-do-it label. Titles beginning with the gerundive form of a verb often are how-to books: See such openers as *Learning, Making,* and *Becoming* in the following lists. Also, using the imperative mood of a verb as the first word signals at once the how-to intent of the word: *"Break"* and *"Write"* are examples in the lists.

In the accompanying lists there is no intent to recommend titles but only to organize fairly representative samples into categories to demonstrate that there are categories that are meaningful, as they put it in self-actualization circles. There are eight families into which these oh-so-abundant books may be divided, plus a fairly generous miscellaneous one. For purposes of convenience, they can be assigned shorthand names as follows.

1. Greed, or frugality: getting something for nothing, or how to economize by doing it yourself.

2. Self-help, self-improvement, self-realization, self-fulfillment, self-development, self-education, and all that.

3. Health and nutrition, medical self-care or family care, mental health, physical fitness, sexual health, etc.

4. Home, car, and garden: how to maintain and repair your house and car, home craftsmanship, and growing your own flowers or vegetables or both.

5. Food and drink, including the enormous field of cookbooks.

6. Business success, career advancement, be your own boss, run your own business, etc.

7. Investment, personal and family finances, etc.

8. Entertainment, hobbies, pets, etc.

9. Miscellaneous, off-the-wall, other.

It is obvious that many of these categories have been addressed to one degree or another in earlier chapters, but the point here is locating the do-it-yourself or learn-it-yourself literature that offers to make you an expert or at least an initiate in one or all of them.

The following examples are chosen to suggest something of the range of subjects you can find under the nine categories into which we have parceled off the wonderful world of how-to:

1. Greed, or frugality:
   How to Get It from the Government
   How to Win at Cards Without Actually Cheating
   How to Win Prize Contests
   How to Avoid Lawyers
   Write Your Own Will

2. Self-help, self-improvement, and all that:

How to Take Charge of Your Life
Managing Yourself: How to Control Emotion, Stress, and Time
Coping with Difficult People
How to Get Your Point Across in 30 Seconds—or Less
Instant Piano (with cassette)
Learn French in 30 Days
Encyclopedia of Careers and Vocational Guidance
How to Avoid the Retirement Trap
How to Think About God
How to Be Born Again

3. Health and nutrition, family care, physical fitness, sexual health, etc.:

How to Be Your Own Nutritionist
Dr. Nagler's Body Maintenance and Repair Book
Encyclopedia of Alternative Medicine and Self-Help
Break the Drug Habit
How to Become a Former Asthmatic
How to Beat a Bad Back
Learning to Speak Again . . . After a Stroke
Encyclopedia of Modern Bodybuilding
How to Be Wrinkle-Free
How to Discipline Without Feeling Guilty
How to Make Love to the Same Person for the Rest of Your Life and Still Love It
Becoming Orgasmic
Making Love: How to Be Your Own Sex Therapist
Encyclopedia of Baby and Child Care

4. Home, car, and garden:

How to Buy a Condominium
How to Buy a Home
How to Protect Your Home Against Burglars
How to Cope With Household Disasters
The Home Owner's Complete Guide to Remodeling
How to Clean Practically Anything

Good Housekeeping's Step-by-Step Encyclopedia of Needlecraft
Reader's Digest Book of Sewing
Erica Wilson's Embroidery Book
How to Fix Damn Near Anything
Popular Mechanics Do-It-Yourself Encyclopedia
Encyclopedia of How It's Made
Do-It-Yourself Materials Guide
The Practical Home Handyman
The Popular Mechanics Step-by-Step Home Repair Manual
Encyclopedia of Home Wiring and Electricity
Encyclopedia of Household Plumbing
How to Build a Hot Tub
How to Drive
How to Build a Two-Car Garage
How to Service and Repair Your Own Car
Motor's Auto Repair Manual
Chilton's Auto Repair Manual
Glenn's Foreign Car Repair Manual
Complete Book of Hot Rodding
The Home Mechanic's Outdoor Handbook
How to Build Bird Houses and a Bird Feeder
Encyclopedia of Gardening Techniques
Encyclopedia of Indoor Gardening
Encyclopedia of Organic Gardening

5. Food and drink:

How to Eat Better and Spend Less
How to Mix Drinks
The Art of Cooking by Apicius (first century A.D.)
The Boston Cooking-School Cookbook by Fannie Farmer (1896)
Betty Crocker's Cookbook
The Joy of Cooking
Mastering the Art of French Cooking
The Frugal Gourmet
The Heritage of Southern Cooking

White Trash Cooking
Encyclopedia of Fish Cookery
Encyclopedia of Chinese Food and Cooking
New Encyclopedia of Wines and Spirits

Cookbooks comprise the only branch of publishing that seriously threatens the Holy Bible as the all-time bestseller. Authors of long-popular cookbooks are assured of a steady parade of royalties for years on end. They must be doing something right. The field is so vast that bibliographers are hard put to embrace it. Several specialized bibliographies cover historic periods and various regions. One lists late-twentieth-century American cookbooks, Marguerite Patten's *Books for Cooks* (1975).

Cookbooks themselves rarely incorporate bibliographic material, although everyone knows that most recipes came from someone else. James Beard was a conspicuous exception; he was scrupulous about listing his sources, not only in the narrative of a particular recipe but also at the back of the book.

The following titles, more of them about food than actual cookbooks *per se,* are worth noting in their own right and are cited here because of their bibliographic sections, which range from good to outstanding: *Food in History* by Reay Tannahill, *Tea and Coffee* by Edward Bramah, *The World Atlas of Cheese* by Nancy Eekhof-Stork, *Food and Drink in Britain* by Constance Anne Wilson, the *L. L. Bean Game & Fish Cookbook,* the *Encyclopedia of Chinese Cooking* by Wonona Chang *et al.,* and *James Beard's American Cooking.*

6. Business success, career advancement, etc.:

How to Become a Doctor

How to Form Your Own Corporation Without a Lawyer for Under $50.00

How to Write Reports

How to Divide the Word

How to File and Index

Up the Organization: How to Stop Corporations from Stifling People and Strangling Profits

How to Fire an Employee

How to Use United Nations Documents

How to Become a Successful Freelance Writer

How to Get Happily Published

How to Typeset from a Word Processor
How to Secure a Copyright
Jobs After Retirement

7. Investment, personal and family finances, etc.:
   How to Read a Financial Report
   How to Invest
   How to Be Your Own Stockbroker
   How to Avoid Probate

8. Entertainment, hobbies, pets, etc.:
   How to Watch a Football Game
   How to Break 90
   How to Break 90—Consistently!
   How to Break 100
   How to Play Golf in the Low 120s
   How to Stay Alive in the Woods
   Fodor's Budget Travel: Britain
   The Radio Amateur's Handbook
   Encyclopedia of Animal Care
   Encyclopedia of Dogs
   Cathletics: Ways to Amuse and Exercise Your Cat

9. Miscellaneous, off-the-wall, other:
   How to Adopt a Child
   How to Run a Club
   How to Buy at Auction
   How to Hold a Garage Sale
   How to Read Tea Leaves
   How to Win Elections
   How to Read Hands
   The Complete Spy (espionage techniques and paraphernalia)
   How to Apply to Graduate School Without Actually Lying
   How to Become a Bishop Without Being Religious
   How to Find Your Family Roots
   Amo, Amas, Amat and More: How to Use Latin to Your Own Advantage and to the Astonishment of Others

Satis est.

CHAPTER 21

BOOKS ABOUT BOOKS: BIBLIOGRAPHY

"Bibliography," both as a term and as a concept, is awash in contradictions. Usually thought of as an aspect of literature, or perhaps of librarianship, it is actually a subdiscipline of history. Its name, which comes to us via Latin from the Greek *biblion*, "book," and *graphein*, "to write," thus means "writing books." Before Gutenberg it meant copying books—high desk, quill pen, parchment, and all. It continued to mean copying or writing books right up to the eighteenth century, when it began to take on its present connotation of writing *about* books.

Just what kind of writing about books, however, was far from settled. A new approach began to emerge: so-called critical bibliography. This did not focus on critical analysis of the content of books but rather on their physical trappings—binding, typeface, paper, gilding of their edges, etc. It was used to evaluate the actual age of a book—for instance, one claimed to be quite ancient. True or false? The kind of bibliography that involved listing books and describing their content and authority and scope became known as enumerative or descriptive bibliography.

There are many highly regarded works on the nature and proper role of bibliography that are taught and studied today. A lot of them were written a generation or two ago, and some are much older than that. But these fine old books about bibliography are studied by librarians and historians and bibliographers and other scholars, and very rarely indeed by the rest of us. Incidentally, there is an excellent fairly recent book on the subject, *Elements of Bibliography* by Robert B. Harmon.

So much for scholarly and traditional meanings. For the modest purposes of this book, enlightened by the critical standard of Humpty Dumpty,[1] the term "bibliography" will mean a list of books that also tells us something of what the books are about.

Theorists are now contemplating the possibility that present or imminent developments in microchips may enable the computer to create the ultimate bibliography, one that would list every book ever written. If that dream does come to pass, it will make great reading for bibliophilic computers, but because of the incredible proliferation of books in the twentieth century, nobody else would be able to read fast enough to get through it in an ordinary seventy- or eighty-year lifetime.

To recapitulate: Bibliographic literature tells us titles and authors and a bit about the content of books, enabling us to pursue them if we choose and to know what we will find when we get there.

Apart from your own curiosity or interest, you don't need a bibliography to guide you in the library as long as you know exactly what you are looking for, or if you don't care. If you are just seeking something to read—anything, perhaps a new mystery— you can browse along the New Mystery shelf and pick one out. Sometimes, of course, it does not turn out to be that easy. Suppose you are in search of a book with an author you don't know and a title you only half remember. In this case you do need help, and fortunately your library has plenty of bibliographic tools to provide whatever assistance you may need.

Naturally, you can turn your question over to the reference librarian. But seriously consider doing it yourself, as long as you can spare a little time. Rummaging around the library on this kind of quest could expose you to one of the quiet joys of researching in the world of books: serendipity. You never know what marvelous title or quotation, what exotic character or delightful odd discovery may simply drop into your lap while you're searching for something else.

Every adequate library has many of the bibliographic resources described later in this chapter, and most major libraries have all of them and a good many more. Together they are an arsenal that

---

[1] " 'When *I* use a word,' Humpty Dumpty said in a rather scornful tone, 'it means just what I choose it to mean—neither more nor less.' " (*Through the Looking-Glass*, Chapter 5).

should enable you to win any battle with a stubbornly invisible book.

However, there is one problem you can't always solve, even with all these resources. If that half-remembered title you're searching for is very recent, finding it may give you some trouble. Ordinarily, there is some lapse of time—perhaps a month or two—between the publication of a book review and the arrival at your library of a bibliography that indexes it or quotes from it or others like it. There are alternative ways to approach such a problem, and these are examined at the end of this chapter, following the forthcoming discussion of the book-finding tools available to you.

BIBLIOGRAPHIC IMPLEMENTS
IN YOUR LIBRARY

Yes, there are bibliographies of bibliographies, and while the idea may seem excessively reflexive, they can be extremely helpful if you have no idea where to turn to find out about books on some exotic subject. Wilson publishes *Bibliographic Index*, covering bibliographies that have appeared since 1937 either as books or sections of books and in the fifteen hundred international publications the editors review. It is cumulated semiannually and annually.

A word about "cumulation," one of the most-used terms in the language of bibliography. It is, as it seems, an exact synonym for "accumulation." Sometimes it has the jangle of jargon in nonlibrarianly ears, but both entered English at about the same time (by the early sixteenth century) and both come straight from Latin, where *accumulare* meant *cumulare* and both meant to pile up in a heap. In the reference-book trade "cumulate" is *de rigueur* for the practice of issuing bibliographic material periodically, then combining several weekly or monthly issues into a larger integrated one covering, *e.g.*, six months or a year.

Guide to Reference Books, published by the American Library Association, is the librarian's principal asset in locating reference books and finding out which one treats what subject. Let it become your own tool of choice, too. This book is universally known as Sheehy after its editor, Eugene P. Sheehy. Before that it was called Winchell after his predecessor, Constance M. Winchell. Sheehy is organized by subject and in its thousand-odd two-column pages it describes many thousands of reference books, including all the general encyclopedias, along with every other kind of general and specialized reference source. New editions appear at irregular intervals, but the book is updated by supplements every two years. It can be found in the reference section of virtually every library— or at the librarian's desk.

One of the most useful bibliographies in the library will put you on the trail of almost any book published in English. If you are looking for a title you either know or rationally suspect exists but that you can't find in your library's catalog, this may do the trick. It is in two parts, the newer being *Cumulative Book Index (CBI)*, published by H. W. Wilson Company. This work grew out of Wilson's *United States Catalogue: Books in Print, 1899.* The latter undertook to list every book published in English in the United States, and in its fourth and last edition (1928) it expanded that scope to embrace English-language books issued anywhere in the world.

The present-day value of the *United States Catalogue* is that it will steer you even to titles that have been out of print for half a century or more. But used together with *CBI,* the combination is an unparalleled resource for finding English-language books published in the United States and Canada since 1898. It does not include pamphlets or government publications. *CBI* includes most but not all books published elsewhere in English. It is invaluable because it is comprehensive, well indexed, well organized, and easy to use. And it is published monthly and cumulated quarterly and annually.

Book Review Digest is a monthly (except February and July) publication that extracts critical comment and descriptive material from book reviews published in eighty-one magazines, professional journals, etc. It is published by Wilson and is cumulated annually. *Book Review Index* does not publish extracts but indexes book reviews in more than 430 periodicals, including all the major popular magazines. It is a Gale publication and appears bimonthly. It is cumulated annually. *Booklist,* published semimonthly (except monthly in July and August) by the American Library Association (ALA) presents its own expertly done reviews of some thirty-four hundred books annually. Categories are adult, young adult, children's, and reference books, and nonprint or multimedia materials. Moreover, many of these critiques appear even before the publication date of the book discussed. If the reviews in *Booklist* or the extracts of reviews in *Book Review Digest* don't work for you, the references from *Book Review Index* should suffice.

BIP is the bellwether of Bowker's flock of reference works, mandatory in virtually every public library in the land. It and three or four of the other Bowker books described here will cost even modest libraries more than five hundred dollars a year and contribute usefully to the bottom line of Bowker's parent, Xerox. *BIP* (not pronounced "bip" but as initials, *B-I-P*) is *Books in Print,* an annual seven-volume set with well over ten thousand pages that indexes by both author and title about seven hundred thousand books in print in the United States, including those published elsewhere and available in America. It is a primary bibliographic tool. As soon as a book goes out of print, Bowker's computers transfer its entry to *Books Out of Print,* another annual that also has an annotated list of wholesalers who handle remaindered books.

Because there is no room in *BIP* for a subject index, there is a thriving market for the four-volume *Subject Guide to Books in Print,* which indexes under Library of Congress subject headings nearly six hundred thousand nonfiction books in its approximately seven thousand pages. *Forthcoming Books* is a bimonthly Bowker publication containing indexes by author, title, and subject to books scheduled for publication within the coming five months. In addition, it cumulates books described in prior issues that have now been published—*i.e.,* are in print—since the last previous edition of *Forthcoming Books.*

Children's Books in Print is another annual, of about a thousand pages, that indexes, by author, illustrator, and title, about forty-five thousand books for children or about children's literature. Bowker's *Paperbound Books in Print* appears twice a year, its three volumes containing some five thousand pages and listing by author, title, and subject all paperbacks known to be forthcoming at the time of publication. It covers text as well as trade books, for juveniles as well as adults. Then there is *British Books in Print,* a four-volume annual of some seven thousand pages listing, also by author, title, and subject nearly four hundred thousand British titles currently in print. If you need one of these works, it is indispensable, which of course is why they are everywhere. Use them; help your library get its money's worth.

Other kinds of bibliographic index abound. By no means all of them are Bowker products. There are some independents, but the field is dominated by a big three, Wilson and Gale in addition to Bowker. Wilson is one of the oldest firms in the business. Gale, much younger, created a healthy niche by identifying markets not yet addressed by others and staking its claim. It is the publisher of the *Science Fiction Book Review Index, 1923–1973* and *1974–1979,* with periodic supplements. Among Wilson's many publications is one of the indexes to works of fiction held in numerous libraries, the *Fiction Catalog*. Bowker publishes another, *Fiction, 1876–1983: A Bibliography of United States Editions.*

Two massive resources for locating books come to us from the Library of Congress. In their original form of bound volumes of heroic size, they are awkward to handle. Unfortunately, both are also extremely tricky to use. These are the *Library of Congress Catalog* of printed cards and the *National Union Catalog*, commonly called the *LC Catalog* and the *NUC*. Since 1983 these catalogs have been issued only on computer tape or in microform. If you have access to them this way, whatever apprehensions you may have about the new technology, at least you won't get tennis elbow schlepping those heavy books around.

Any amateur researcher turning for the first time to either of these catalogs is emphatically advised to ask the help of a competent reference librarian. The *LC Catalog* lists, in a number of uncumulated series, most of the holdings of the Library of Congress published since 1898. The *NUC* lists books that are held fairly widely among U.S. libraries, and it features a coded list of the libraries where a particular work may be found. It is thus a major resource for the interlibrary loan program. The main entries in the *NUC* are primarily listed by author, and it may be helpful in locating corporate or collective authors, whose identities sometimes are obscure in title-oriented catalogs.

Both of these enormous files are accessible in the flesh at the Library of Congress in Washington. Many major libraries now have them accessible by computer or in microform, but many others still have their old bound volumes. In these books—which, again, have not been issued since 1983—the actual three-by-five cards are reproduced, photographically reduced, eighteen cards to a three-column page, and bound into periodic series of bulky tomes that use up a whole wall or two in many libraries. Neither the *LC Catalog* nor the *NUC* cumulates prior editions into the present one, so if you have reason to go into either one for the first time, venture in only with a trustworthy guide: the aforementioned competent reference librarian.

The Reader's Adviser is a large, comprehensive, annotated bibliography published by Bowker that undertakes to identify the world's greatest books, its judgments supported by authoritative critical commentary. It is subtitled as follows: *Volume 1: The Best in American and British Fiction, Poetry, Essays, Literary Biography, Bibliography &*

Reference (edited by Fred Kaplan); *Volume 2: The Best in American & British Drama & World Literature in English Translation* (edited by Maurice Charney); and *Volume 3: The Best in the Reference Literature of the World* (edited by Paula T. Kaufman).

A *Publisher's Trade List Annual* (*PTLA*) is essentially the parent of *BIP* and many related products, in effect the patriarchal ram of Bowker's richly befleeced flock. It dates from 1873, and its content is the body that *BIP* and many of the others index in their various ways. *PTLA* is an immense annual compilation of the catalogs and book lists of all the book publishing houses in America, perhaps excepting the very tiniest and flakiest. It does have a section featuring the output of most smaller houses. It simply reproduces each publisher's entire annual catalog, including the various separate imprints that many of the big houses maintain. There are eighteen hundred in all and they occupy four volumes totaling some eight thousand pages. It is in a real sense the foundation stone of current bibliography for the U.S. book trade.

Readers' Guide to Periodical Literature is a major reference resource, established in 1905 and discussed in Chapter 3. It is a Wilson publication that appears monthly in January, February, May, July, August, and November, and semimonthly in March, April, June, September, October, and December. It is cumulated quarterly and annually. *Readers' Guide* first appeared in 1905, with coverage beginning in 1900. It indexes 186 general-interest periodicals, including all the popular magazines and important scholarly and professional journals. It includes book reviews, but it covers the whole content of the periodicals it indexes.

A quite different approach is taken by another extremely valuable periodical index, *Ulrich's International Periodicals Directory*. Since 1932 it has indexed the magazines themselves, instead of their contents. *Ulrich's* lists by name more than seventy thousand periodicals from all over the world, giving such information as frequency of publication, publisher, price, address and phone number, and Dewey Decimal System number along with selected other data.

Library collections instead of individual books are the focus of a special bibliography of nearly two thousand pages called *Subject Collections*. This guide lists and describes twenty thousand special collections of books, maps, etc., in nine thousand libraries throughout North America. It is updated and reissued from time to time.

A rather unusual but extremely interesting bibliographic service is provided by the *Comprehensive Dissertation Index* through an associated computer retrieval system. The index lists every doctoral dissertation ever accepted at a U.S. or Canadian university. The idea of a comprehensive index of dissertations has been around for years. Some of the efforts in this direction were sponsored by the ALA. The *Comprehensive Dissertation Index* is the work of University Microfilms International, a subsidiary of Xerox.

If the idea of indexing doctoral dissertations sounds odd, it shouldn't. Each dissertation is, by definition, a book-length work of original scholarship, carefully planned, researched, and executed over a period of at least a couple of years, by a trained scholar. The range of topics that have been explored exhaustively by more than four hundred thousand Ph.D.s over a century and a quarter is staggering.

The University Microfilms service allows the researcher to select certain key terms by which to locate several dissertations that might be up the right alley, and these can then be previewed, in effect, by reading six-hundred-word abstracts contained in the multivolume *Dissertation Abstracts International,* to which annual supplements are added. Reprints of the dissertation ultimately selected can then be bought at modest cost.

SOLVING THE PROBLEM OF FINDING OUT ABOUT RECENT BOOKS

When you are trying to locate a very recent book whose author and title you don't recall, there are several steps worth pursuing. Best of all, try your local bookstore. If for any reason (like not wanting to buy it) you don't want to take that course, there are others. If you learned about the book in last Sunday's paper or during the previous week or two, it might pay you to look through the book reviews in those several back issues. If that doesn't work, take the problem to the library and try the most recent issue of *Book Review Digest, Book Review Index, Booklist,* or perhaps even *Readers' Guide.*

Even if this doesn't work, there still is room for hope. Remember, *Forthcoming Books* covers books to be published over the coming five months. Go back three or four issues in that publication and try it that way. If that fails, you still have one more shot. The periodical bible of the book publishing industry is the trade journal *Publishers Weekly.* Most libraries carry it. In each issue it carries a lengthy section called "Forecasts," featuring thumbnail sketches of books about to be published. Go back to the appropriate date and look for your title there and in several ensuing issues.

If that doesn't do it, punt: Ask the reference librarian for help. He or she, too often unsung, is the hero of this book, the real pro at how to look things up and find things out, from whom we all can learn a lot, to our own pleasure and profit, and not infrequently to our great relief.

INDEX

AACR 2 (Anglo-American Cataloging Rules), 38
abbreviations, 27–29, 31, 78–79
Academic American Encyclopedia, 53, 55, 85, 128, 162
accounting, 237
acronyms, 79
acupuncture, 210
Adler, Mortimer J., 150
advertising, 250–252
aeronomy, 137
aerospace industry, 238
African Historical Biography (Lipschutz and Rasmussen), 98
Afro-Americans, 119
aging, 208
agriculture, 239–240
ALA Membership Directory, 117
alchemy, 165
alcoholism, 212, 213
almanacs, 67–71
Americana Annual, 65
American Film Institute Catalog of Feature Films, 155
American Guide Series, 110
American Heritage Dictionary of the English Language, 46–47, 48
American Language, The (Mencken), 77
American Library Directory, 117
American Men and Women of Science, 95
America Votes, 202
angling, 257–258

animal psychology, 204
Annual Register of Grant Support, 118
antonyms, 78
Appleton's Cyclopaedia of American Biography, 96
Applied Science and Technology Index, 227
aquaculture, 240
aquariums, 117–118
aquatic sports, 261
Arabic language, 58–59, 104–105, 170
architecture, 158–159
Area Handbooks, 122–123
Aristotle, 49, 135, 138, 139, 140–141, 183
Art Index, 157
arts and crafts, 160–161
Asimov, Isaac, 231
associations, 113–120, 133, 218
Associations' Publications in Print, 116
asterisks, 30
astrology, 165
astronomy, 187–188
atlases, 103–109
Atlas of American History, 108
Atlas of the Classical World, 108–109
atmospheric sciences, 137
Auto Guides, 110
automobile industry, 238
auto racing, 258

Baba, Meher, 177
Baby and Child Care (Spock), 214
Baedeker's guides, 109–110